How to Use Computers and Cyberspace in the Clinical Practice of Psychotherapy

Dr. Yuh-Jen Guo

How to Use
Computers
and
Cyberspace
in the
Clinical Practice
of Psychotherapy

Jeri Fink, D.S.W.

with contributions by

Dean Allman Marlene Maheu
Rob Bischoff Herbert Michelson
Yvette Colón Sheila Peck
Russell Fink Menno Pieters
Storm A. King Stephan Ted Poulos

JASON ARONSON INC.
Northvale, New Jersey
London

This book was set in 12 pt. Times New Roman and printed and bound by Book-mart Press of North Bergen, New Jersey.

Library of Congress Cataloging-in-Publication Data

Fink, Jeri.
　　How to use computers and cyberspace in the clinical practice of
　psychotherapy / Jeri Fink.
　　　　p.　cm.
　　Includes bibliographical references and index.
　　ISBN 0-7657-0173-1
　　1. Internet (Computer network) in psychotherapy. I. Title.
　RC489.I54F56 1998
　616.89'14--DC21　　　　　　　　　　　　　　　　　98-6846

Printed in the United States of America on acid-free paper. For information and catalog write to Jason Aronson Inc., 230 Livingston Street, Northvale, New Jersey 07647-1726. Or visit our website: http://www.aronson.com

To Ricky,
my lover, companion, and soul mate:
We did it!

An amber light cast a shadow of the Shiva dancing in his ring of flame. I clicked my screen back to life and watched it throw a cobalt glow onto the wall opposite. Slowly another shadow, that of the Celestial Woman, began inching its way around the room till it reached the pool of blue. Then to a rattle of thunder, and enveloped in lightning's brilliance, Yasoda, celestial handmaiden to Parvati, rejoined me after over five hundred years of forced separation.

[Nick Bantock, *The Venetian's Wife*]

Contents

PART II
QUESTIONS AND ANSWERS FOR EMERGING
TREATMENTS IN PSYCHOTECHNOLOGY

PART III
INTERNET RESOURCES FOR CLINICIANS

Acknowledgments

In a book such as this, there are so many people to thank that it seems an almost monumental task. First, I would like to thank the people at Jason Aronson Inc. who helped make this book a reality. I could not have written it without the foresight and encouragement of Michael Moskowitz, who instinctively recognized the need for mental health professionals to become involved in the electronic environment. The book came alive with Cindy Hyden, whose hard work and enthusiasm lightened some tough editing tasks. Bob Hack's and Elaine Lindenblatt's patience and refreshing sense of humor carried me through some very non-virtual edits, while Norma Pomerantz was always ready to answer questions and offer practical advice.

I would also like to thank those who made special written contributions to this book. These people are certainly the pioneers of cyberspace. History will treat their creativity and foresight with awe, recognizing their unique sense of adventure in plunging into uncharted lands. Thank you: Dean Allman, Rob Bischoff, Yvette Colón, Russell Fink, Storm King, Marlene Maheu, Herbert Michelson, Sheila Peck, Menno Pieters, and Stephan Poulos.

I want to thank my family, who put up with my electronic

tales, abbreviated visits, and frequent distractions during the time it took to complete this book. In particular, I want to acknowledge Edna and Harvey Fink, a.k.a. Grandma and Grandpa, who rolled up their sleeves and pitched in when I desperately needed an extra set of hands, and my role model, beloved "Auntie" Dora Eisenstein, a lively, active woman in her eighties who was a feminist long before anyone invented the term. The Beckers, Ryans, Woolleys, and Michelsons added humor and a lot of spice to the many times they found me lost in cyberspace.

In every book, there is a constant, abiding force that grounds a writer, enabling her to see both the forest and the trees. "Unkka"—Herbert Michelson—took on that job. In a challenging, funny, sometimes scolding, and always loving e-mail correspondence, he kept me focused on where I wanted to go. Thank you for joining me in cyberspace.

I would also like to gratefully acknowledge those very special friends and neighbors who suffered through the daily "slings and arrows of outrageous fortune" that I experienced as I ploughed my way through the Internet. They mothered me—walking, talking, feeding, faxing, and supporting—while I explored the far reaches of cyberspace. Ellen Davidoff, Shelley Frank, Janet Garfinkel, Mary Ann Hannon, Donna Paltrowitz, and Barbara Saks—thank you for being there. I couldn't have done it without you.

A special acknowledgment goes to the friends of my youth—those people who knew me when I only dreamed about writing books. Jerry and Jill, Larry and Maddy, thanks for never giving up.

Although they are not here to share this book, I want to thank my mother, my sister Judy, and my aunt Persis, who remain, in spirit, very much a part of me.

A very special thanks goes to my sons, David and Russell,

whose youth and enthusiasm carried me into territory usually reserved for Generation X-ers. David showed me a perseverance and dedication far beyond his years, meeting me frequently in cyberspace while he lived in Israel. Russell showed me soul: through his eyes I was reintroduced to possibilities that I thought I had outgrown. Without their imagination and unwavering faith, cyberspace might have been a very different place.

Last, but far from least, I thank my husband, Ricky, who gave up many days and nights to my computer screen and tales from the Web. A true patron of *my* art, he has given me a lifetime of support and unwavering faith in my work.

About the Author

Jeri Fink, D.S.W., is a psychotherapist, author, and educator. As a clinician, she treats individuals, couples, families, and groups in private practice in Merrick, New York. She is co-author (with Sondra Tuckfelt and Muriel Warren) of *The Psychotherapists' Guide to Managed Care in the 21st Century.* Also a specialist in online mental health, Dr. Fink's work has appeared in over sixty publications. Her other books include *Virtual Terror* and *From Caves to Cyberspace: The Seduction of a Virtual Reality.* Along with Sheila Peck, LCSW, and Ron Rubin, LCSW, BCD, she conducts seminars on using computers in mental health practice. She can be reached at her website, http://www.psychotechnology.com.

Contributors

Dean Allman, LCSW, practices in Aurora, Colorado. He also consults and teaches on the use of the Internet, has a growing business as a Web page designer, and is President of the Colorado chapter of CSWF as well as webmaster of CSWF.

Rob Bischoff, Ph.D., is a psychotherapist whose website *Shrink Tank* averages about 60,000 hits a year. His virtual practice is a prototype for mental health practitioners online and offline.

Yvette Colón, ACSW, is Senior Clinical Social Worker and Program Coordinator of Online Services at Cancer Care, Inc. in New York City. She has done extensive work with group psychotherapy on the Internet.

Russell Fink, the youngest contributor, is a Generation X-er who attends New York University. His essay "REAL-ITY?" attempts to unravel the nature of identity in a postmodern electronic world where anything is possible.

Storm A. King is a doctoral candidate in clinical psychology researching virtual communities. His essay "The Impersonal Nature of Interpersonal Cyberspace Relationships" questions the depth of online relationships. Resources for Researching the Psychology of Virtual Communities (http://www.best.com./~storm/) is designed for researchers who are studying virtual communities.

Marlene Maheu, Ph.D., is a clinical psychologist who is founder and editor of *Self-Help & Psychology*, an online magazine with over 40,000 readers. She is the owner of Cyber Towers Professional Center, a virtual office building that serves as an epicenter for the sharing and investigating of professional skills and technology.

Herbert Michelson, Ph.D., is a retired psychologist living in Amherst, Massachusetts. His essay "Thoughts on Cyberspace" warns about the departure from consensus reality and the spiritual morass that can result from the creation of mythical cyber "gods," a process already well underway.

Sheila Peck, LCSW, practices psychotherapy in Island Park, New York. She is the author of numerous articles, including "Computers, Clinicians, and Cyberspace," and is a director of the Private Practitioners Group, which offers seminars in both clinical and technical aspects of therapeutic practice using computers.

Menno Pieters is a student of informatics at Delft University of Technology in The Netherlands. He created The Signature Museum, a unique site on the World Wide Web that is a collection of signatures that people around the world have used.

Stephan Ted Poulos, M.A., holds degrees from Stanford University and the University of California at Berkeley. He has a keen interest in how semantics, language, and psychology relate to the Internet as a potential for therapeutic communications.

Logging On

The screen flickers into life, the electronic glow reflecting in my eyes. It is very late, the world around me long asleep. For a moment, I am alone in the silence, the only voice speaking into the dark night. And then the door opens. It is virtual. I'm logged on.

The sun streams in as I greet a friend halfway around the world. The pace quickens as I join a communal debate. My heart pounds when a flamer, entrenched deep in Australia, throws barbs at my latest comments. I flee to a place where I can be medieval princess or dashing cyborg. I change names and identities as quickly as screens, re-creating myself in countless ways, playing, experimenting, dancing with some of my most fragile fantasies. And through it all I remain unscathed, a time and space traveler sitting quietly in my office.

What is virtuality? Does it belong in my clinical office? One might flippantly define reality as everything that *isn't* cyberspace. Reality is generally defined by concrete parameters—the length of a day, the speed of a car, the nature of your work. Virtuality has none of those constraints. In fact, the only physical aspects to virtuality are the vehicles that take you into cyberspace—*things* such as the size of your screen, the feel of your keyboard, the speed of your modem. These parameters are notoriously fickle, changing with the latest sale, the newest technology, or what we can afford to pay at the moment we choose to buy. So where does that leave the individual—the self—when it ventures into a changeable, abstract environment unaffected by time, distance, or physical space?

Imagine a world where the written word dominates. There are no flowers to smell, no skin to touch, no sweets to taste. In this world, behavior is as intangible as thought, social interaction removed from its physical context. People live, work, love, and lie on screens, and the self is a multiple construct, changed at will, designed to fit environments teeming with metaphors. How do we act? What do we see? How do we change?

Today, thirty million to fifty million people around the world are living, working, playing, and making love in cyberspace. (By the next millennium, some predict that there will be as many as two hundred million people on the Internet.) They communicate in an endless variety of environments, from e-mail to virtual cafés, playing fantasy games, debating on bulletin boards, and flirting in chat rooms. Net.sex, flaming, and gendermorphing are commonplace events. Virtual communities with members spread around the world thrive as if they were next-door neighbors, chatting over backyard fences. How do human beings adapt emotionally, psychologically, and socially to function in these electronic environments?

Clearly, a new psychology is emerging. Patterns of interaction are evolving from concepts like netiquette and list protocols. Aggressive, uninhibited behavior is increasing from the anonymity and the absence of social constraints in cyberspace. The self is being split in multiple directions, adopting distinctive identities and roles. Sex is being redefined as an experience of shared fantasies and virtual caresses. The simulation of reality online has become its own, unique process. And anything can happen.

As we settle into the new millennium, humankind is facing perhaps its most dramatic adaptation. Patterns of interaction are being redefined; group process is changing; communities are restructuring. And it is only the beginning. As technology develops, improving our ability to connect in cyberspace, humans will continue to adapt to life online. We are witnessing the merging of two provocative and powerful forces: psychology and technology.

I call this merging *psychotechnology*.

When I began *How to Use Computers and Cyberspace in the Clinical Practice of Psychotherapy*, I quickly became aware of the paucity of hard research, theory, and discussion on the subject. It seemed that only a few people on- or offline were struggling to make sense of this rapid, dramatic shift in human behavior. I realized that psychotechnology was an event that was happening, rather than being designed. Like any human psychology, it was developing systems through the millions of people, young and old, who regularly entered the technological magic of cyberspace. This book came from cyberspace, from psychotherapists eager to share their experiences and their thoughts, from the virtual communities always willing to accept a new member, from the often overwhelming overload of information, good and bad, residing on the Net. Sometimes, these "voices" were loud and eager, anxious to share their clinical forays into the electronic environment. Other times, it seemed as if I were wandering in vast uncharted territories, struggling to organize an ideological shapeshifter into a coherent set of ideas. Ultimately, I had to compromise. Cyberspace is an infant technology, its inhabitants similar to the indomitable explorers of human history who circumnavigated their world in Viking boats, clipper ships, covered wagons, and space shuttles. As such, you and I are also pioneers, exploring a strange new universe with boundaries yet to be discovered. It is a trip that identifies the very new with the tools of the very old, forecasting an unpredictable future where change is the only constant.

In the following pages, you will venture into a new clinical office where psychotherapists and their patients are implementing innovative treatments based on classic theories of practice. Psychotechnology links the old and the new, using the traditional as well as cutting edge voices of theorists, from Sigmund Freud to Sherry Turkle. Psychotechnology acknowledges the social workers, psychologists, psychiatrists, and psychiatric nurses applying their skills in virtuality.

Take a deep breath. And let's surf.

PART I
THE ONLINE COUCH

1

Will the Real Illusion Please Rise?

Josh, the son of an alcoholic father and an enabling mother, had grown up in a chaotic home pierced by anger, accusations, and irrational demands. Tragedy struck when his father was driving DWI and crashed the car into a tree. He was killed. Josh had just turned fourteen.

After the accident, Josh refused to talk about his father. If his name was mentioned, Josh would remain stony silent or get up and walk away from the conversation. He would not go to the cemetery or participate in any memorial service. Josh's mother was very disturbed and constantly pleaded with him to be part of the family. Josh only withdrew further into himself.

As Josh ploughed deeper into adolescence, his grades fell, he began to act out, and eventually he found himself in serious trouble. He toyed with drugs and alcohol. One day, when the teacher's back was turned, Josh stole some computer software. He was caught. The school, exasperated, insisted on treatment or alternate placement. Josh's mother chose treatment.

The first time Josh entered Dr. Rieker's office, he stared belligerently at the psychotherapist, assuming a tough-guy pose. He and Rieker spent the next two sessions in veritable silence.

In the third session, Josh entered the office in his usual way—hands jammed into jeans pockets, eyes lowered, shoulders slouched.

"We're going to another place today," Rieker said gently. "Yeah, Josh," Rieker continued, turning on the computer. "Anywhere you want to go."

Josh's body moved subtly, shifting toward the computer. Rieker, noticing this change, used the mouse to log on to the Internet. Rieker handed the mouse to Josh, turning control over to the troubled adolescent.

Josh began to silently surf through the colors, pages, and sounds of the Internet. He checked out a music video site, an adolescent chat line, and, briefly, a gay virtual café. Eventually, he settled on a Web site that he wanted to explore—reading the text, visualizing the stories, and finding the link.

The site was called City of the Silent—one of the Web's extensive sites on death.

The story of Josh and Dr. Rieker is based on an actual clinical intervention. Using *virtual* free association, Rieker was able to communicate with his young, grieving patient. The computer became the mediator. Josh could begin to explore—and heal—himself in the safety of Dr. Rieker's office. Inadvertently, Josh had climbed onto the Online Couch.

Is the emergence of an online couch predictable in today's culture?

Postmodern culture has thoroughly embraced virtuality. There is a continuing demand for new and better virtual tools, toys, and environments that offer the illusion of actual experience. This has been part of technological evolution that includes everything from the telephone to virtual reality. Virtuality has always appealed to humans—whether it's a story about Gods and dragons told around a fire at the dawn of human civilization, an absorbing novel about a heinous, mysterious murder, or the more recent visual media of film and television. The early psychoanalytic theorists fully understood the virtual power of human metaphor and how it dramatically affects all aspects of behavior. The evolutionary shift that is occurring now is not in the power and appeal of virtuality, but in its accessibility. At no other time in human history has virtuality been able to equal or at times overpower actuality.

This book maintains that virtuality can be a potent tool in treatment. Rather than replacing psychotherapists, virtuality can be used as an adjunct in the clinical office—a means to make treatment more effective in the electronic age.

Consider how virtuality captivates a human mind. Lombard and Ditton (1997) address this issue in an article appropriately titled "At the heart of it all: The concept of telepresence." They identify the concept of *telepresence* or the "illusion that a mediated experience is not mediated" (p. 1). Simply put, human beings who experience telepresence accept the illusion that a virtual environment induced by a medium is, in fact, real. This is not dissociation or hallucination—at any given time the individual experiencing telepresence can report that it is, in fact, a virtual occurrence. The illusion of telepresence is an inborn psychological ability that temporarily removes awareness of a mediating tool such as a computer, headgear, or simulator. Imagine the therapeutic potential of such a state—the creation of a remote environment where one can experience, experiment, and explore psychological issues without the danger of actuality and *with* the illusion of being there.

PRESENCE, TELEPRESENCE, AND THE MEDIA EQUATION

To fully realize the clinical potential of telepresence, it is necessary to understand the nature and condition of presence. Presence is an essential human experience. It does not refer to the actual physical surroundings of an individual but to his or her perception of those surroundings (Steuer 1993). Presence is so basic that it is practically indistinguishable from awareness. Kim and Biocca (1997) maintain that the experience of presence involves a constantly shifting phenomenon that operates on three basic *senses of place*. "As individuals experience sensations coming from the physical environment or the virtual environment, their sense of presence or being there may oscillate. . . . Therefore, at any moment users might feel 'present' in one of three 'places' " (pp. 1, 2):

- Presence in a physical environment is the basic, conscious sense of "being there";
- Presence in a virtual environment is when sensation is mediated through a communication medium—such as books, television, or computers; and
- Presence in an imaginal environment occurs when sensations are primarily controlled by internal mental imagery as in dreams and daydreaming.

Telepresence refers to the second sense of place—an environment mediated by communications medium. Reeves and Nass (1996) discuss the illusion of telepresence through what they call the "media equation." These two media researchers propose an evolutionary explanation for the existence or persistence of telepresence. Utilizing extensive research, they contend that media engages a brain evolved in a world where only humans have the ability to maintain complex social behaviors. Consequently, the assumption that whatever *looks* human and whatever *acts* human is, in fact, human was repeatedly validated. The brain generalized this assumption to automatically presume that what appears real *is* real. This has effectively guided *homo sapiens* through two hundred thousand years of evolution. While civilization moves into a new millennium, the designs of the "old" brain for negotiating daily life remains intact. The introduction of simulated humans in media communicates with a design that has not been updated. "People can't always overcome the powerful assumption that mediated presentations are actual people and objects," write Reeves and Nass (1996). "There is no switch in the brain that can be thrown to distinguish the real and mediated worlds" (p. 12). The end result, "the media equation—*media equal real life*—applies to everyone" (p. 5). Media simulates real life so well that, automatically and unconsciously, we respond in a social and natural manner. That is why a movie can be frightening, a sitcom can be funny, and a news broadcast can be heart-wrenching. Humans can think through this response and intellectually differentiate between what seems to be real and what is actually real. However, if the intellectual effort is not made to establish the differentiation, the automatic and natural response is to assume it's real. "We have found," Reeves and Nass conclude, "that individuals' interactions with computers, television, and new media are *fundamentally social and natural*, just like interactions in real life" (p. 5).

Researchers discovered this phenomenon almost as soon as the computer was introduced and long before popular use of the Internet and virtual reality. Perhaps the earliest example was ELIZA, a popular computer program first published in 1966. Joseph Weizenbaum, a professor in the Department of Electrical Engineering and Computer Science at MIT, wrote a program to see how far the computer could go in emulating conversation. ELIZA was a "psychotherapist" who could answer "questions." Conceptually, the program was based on mirroring patient response to simulate standard English (Turkle 1995).

Technically, the program had two parts. The first part extracted information from the material typed into the program by the patient. The second part used a script that formulated an appropriate reply. Weizenbaum used Rogerian psychotherapy as a model to reflect statements back to the patient in an attempt to encourage continued communication. The program had no innate knowledge—it merely recognized strings of characters and turned them into a response. The following is an example of an exchange on ELIZA (ELIZA, no date):

Patient: I am angry.
ELIZA: How long have you been angry?
Patient: Six months.
ELIZA: Please go on.
Patient: I lost my job.
ELIZA: Do you have other reasons not come to mind?
Patient: I was fired.
ELIZA: Why do you tell me you were fired right now?

Weizenbaum was dismayed at the responses. He believed (or hoped) that ELIZA's limitations would discourage people. Instead, the program was extremely popular. Psychiatrists contacted him for its potential in therapy. People became emotionally entangled with ELIZA, personifying her, often requesting to be "alone" with the program. Without intending its effect, Weizenbaum discovered that people readily bypassed the concept of machine, responding as if the computer were expressing human understanding and compassion.

In another early study, Scheibe and Erwin (1979) used forty male and female undergraduates to investigate the tendency for subjects to personify computers. Subjects were instructed to play specific computer games while their spontaneous verbalizations were recorded. Scheibe and Erwin found that nearly two verbal comments per minute were made, with an average of nine pronoun references per subject. The most frequently used pronouns were "it," followed by "he," "you," and "they." Scheibe and Erwin classified subject verbalization into four categories: direct remarks to the computer, exclamations (including expletives), commentaries, and questions. They concluded that people easily personify the computer—casting it in a human role. "It is a mistake to regard the computer as a neutral agent in socialization," they wrote. "One can envisage, then, the emergence of a new personality type which is the human reciprocal of the computer as a component of the generalized other" (p. 108).

More recent studies have focused on technological innovations that go beyond personification into the more pervasive experience of telepresence. Kim and Biocca (1997) found that being in the virtual environment (telepresence) is very different from *not* being in the physical environment. They suggest that the sense of "not being there" in a physical environment indicates the disappearance or invisibility of the mediating device. Simply put, people "forget" they are watching a television or using a computer when telepresence occurs. While this concept seems extraordinary, consider a very ordinary "virtual" experience—the telephone. The telephone mediates the environment, plunging speakers into a virtual conversation. Although everyone *knows* that the telephone is the actual communication tool, when they are involved in conversation, speakers "forget" that it is the plastic, wires, and electronic relays that connects them. Instead, we behave as if the "other" is actually there. This is particularly apparent in the now-common occurrence of people who are walking on a street, driving a car, or sitting in a restaurant using a cellular telephone. They often appear totally removed from their surroundings, immersed in the virtual voice mediated through the telephone. This aspect of virtual conversation has become so powerful as to lead to many questions concerning the safety of cellular phones while people are driving automobiles.

Similarly, Lombard and Ditton (1997) cite numerous studies where individuals' perceptions and "the resulting psychological processes lead them to illogically overlook the mediated or even artificial nature of an entity within a medium and attempt to interact with it . . ." (p. 8). Whether it's the swashbuckling Rhett Butler on celluloid or the Tamagotchis on LEDs, telepresence is a very real and increasingly ubiquitous characteristic of human psychology.

FROM TELEPRESENCE TO AN ONLINE COUCH

If telepresence can be induced in a "safe" clinical environment, does it offer a previously unavailable tool for effective intervention?

Technology has opened the door to many new "cyber" spaces that nurture telepresence. Many of these cyberspaces are already being used to enhance human experience in simulated environments. A few researchers have already made successful attempts to utilize them in mental health. Computer use in psychotherapy is in its infancy—requiring imagination and innovation by clinicians. Part I: "The Online Couch" explores potential mental health applications that can be integrated with the present technology in any clinician's office. Chapters 2–8 examine virtual psychotherapeutic applications while Chapters 9–11 discuss the issues faced by clinicians venturing into these new modalities. Part II: "Questions and Answers for Emerging Treatments in Psychotechnology" addresses the inevitable questions that arise in a new therapeutic modality. It is presented in a twenty question-and-answer format that enables clinicians to quickly locate issues that reflect his or her interest. Part III: "Internet Resources for Clinicians" offers online addresses, glossaries, and suggested reading that will enhance a clinician's foray into the online couch.

Explorations of the field must make note of the two "realities" employed by today's technology. The human–computer interface involves many aspects of interaction. Technology has already made it possible to utilize sight and sound in a seemingly endless variety of simulations. Research and development is moving at breakneck speed, introducing new sensual experiences that heighten telepresence. Video conferencing delivered at broadcast quality will rapidly become a standard in the new millennium. Wireless connections through satellite communications have already been established. Kinesthetics and speech recognition are readily accessible even though only a short time ago they were fare for science fiction. These and other technological innovations further enhance telepresence. Inevitably, it leads to basic questions on the nature of reality and physical environs (see Part II). As discussed earlier, virtual reality has been traditionally defined in technological terms. Definitions that are based on aspects of human experience include critical components such as telepresence and psychological immersion. To clarify this, it is important to understand the two "types" of reality usually experienced in cyberspace.

AUGMENTED REALITIES

Augmented realities refer to mediated experiences or environments where the physical world is *enhanced*, not replaced. This is in sharp contrast to virtual realities where the user is immersed in a mediated environment that stimulates the telepresence response of suspending some or all awareness of physical surroundings. Augmented realities technologically lag behind virtual realities. However, there is great potential for utilization in the human computer interface. Imagine a patient terrified of a surgical procedure that "visits" the doctor and "experiences" the treatment without pain, or an agoraphobic who can manipulate a projected image of him- or herself into an actual crowd? Augmented realities are not yet adequately developed for such interventions. One of the greatest technological challenges lies in the difficulty of electronically matching the human eye in visual acuity and registration. Organic technology is so highly tuned that it is often difficult to enhance what is viewed. However, augmented realities offer many future challenges for the clinical imagination.

VIRTUAL REALITIES

Virtual realities, in contrast to augmented realities, are a far more common and diverse technology in today's electronic environment. Many find it difficult to define. U.S. Supreme Court discussions on government regulation of the Internet were complicated by a repeated question: *What is it?* There were arguments for and against calling it a broadcast medium like television, a public space like a park, or a print medium like a newspaper.

Virtual realities face the same questions. Most definitions remain narrow, focused on the technological components. Steuer (1993) maintains that defining virtual realities in technological terms excludes the human experience of telepresence. It doesn't say anything about the process or the effects of usage. Steuer (1993) devised a much broader definition describing virtual realities as *all* mediated experiences.

> Newspapers, letters, and magazines place the reader in a space in which the writer is telling a story; television places the viewer in a virtual space in which both viewer and on-screen objects are present; and video games create virtual spaces in which the game-player is an actor. [p. 5]

Broadening Steuer's definition, one might even describe psychotherapy as a mediated experience. In this context, psychotherapists have often used virtual reality tools such as written or visual material as an adjunct to treatment. The online couch is simply the next generation of clinical virtual reality tools.

2

Climbing On Board the Couch: Specific Phobias and Virtual Reality Intervention

Lydia soared above the clouds. She dove playfully in her aircraft and watched the ground alternately rise and shrink from her view. Cotton-ball clouds danced above the silvery mountains and patchwork green of farms. She passed over a city that looked like endless rows of monopoly houses with postage stamp swimming pools and streets that meandered through an urban sprawl. Lydia was no longer afraid. Instead, she was exhilarated by the experience that brought her airborne while her feet remained firmly on the gray carpet in her psychotherapist's office.

It seemed like a lifetime ago, when she had paused uncertainly in the doorway to Dr. Troy's office. It was a lovely space with grays and soft blues blending into a soothing, almost dreamy environment. Yet, Lydia had been reluctant to tackle what her boss had told her was the last obstacle in her ascent up the corporate ladder.

Lydia was terrified of flying.

On entering Dr. Troy's office, Lydia saw a bank of computers and some strange looking headgear instead of an analyst's couch.

"We're going to get you flying without leaving this room and, most importantly, without the fear," Dr. Troy said. The therapist called it virtual reality exposure. It was a computer-assisted clinical intervention in treating aerophobia.

In the early 1950s, behaviorist Joseph Wolpe observed that when an animal was fed near a feared object, the fear would slowly subside (Atwood and Chester 1987). Wolpe believed he could apply the concept to human behavior. He developed what would prove to be a highly successful therapeutic tool: systematic desensitization. Schwartz (1984) described Wolpe's system in several clearly defined clinical steps:

1. The source of the patient's fear is first identified in a clinical interview;
2. The patient and therapist construct a list of several dozen situations related to the fear;
3. The patient ranks the situations, establishing a hierarchy;
4. The patient is trained in deep relaxation; and
5. The relaxation is paired with the least frightening situation, slowly moving up the hierarchy.

Wolpe maintained that the low-level fear, when paired with the relaxation, will diminish. The conditioned response of deep relaxation would strengthen, and the conditioned response of fear would subsequently weaken. Schwartz (1984) speculates on the nature of the process:

> There is reason to believe that relaxation alone is not sufficient for counterconditioning to occur. It seems critically important that the patient have *control* over relaxation. . . . What kind of stimulus is "control," and what is its place in conditioning? [p. 136]

Although Wolpe was nearly four decades away from accessible computerized virtual realities, his work serves as a basis for a new, extremely promising modification of systematic desensitization. As Schwartz noted, the experience of control was an integral part of the intervention. Consider it in context of virtual realities as a mediated environment or experience that utilizes telepresence to nurture the illusion that there is no mediating device. Telepresence is not a form of psychological dissociation. The user retains full control of the illusion and can shift his or her awareness at any given time. If control is a critical component in the success of systematic desensitization, virtual realities have enormous potential in this treatment modality. *Control of the illusion always belongs to the user.*

This concept is apparent in understanding how virtual reality is used to affect humans in psychological interventions. In the VR Body Project (1996), for example, the aim is to juxtapose two processes involved in body experience disturbances: cognitive–behavioral and visual–motorial to alter the self-perception of one's body in the treatment of eating disorders. In contrast, virtual reality used to treat specific phobias maintains the telepresence illusion of control while exposing individuals to anxiety-producing conditions. Systematic desensitization occurs in an environment that is consciously controlled by the patient. While the perceptual experience is mediated—patients are "tricked" into the belief that a situation is real—the feet, as in Lydia's case, remain firmly on the safe and reassuring floor of the clinical office.

Can this type of illusion actually desensitize a phobic patient? Preliminary research has found very compelling results. Max North, Ph.D., Sarah North, M.S.D., and Joseph Coble, Ph.D. (North et al. 1996) have been conducting controlled studies on the use of Virtual Environmental Desensitization (VED) in their Virtual Reality Technology Laboratory at Clark Atlanta University since November 1992. Their highly publicized work on specific phobias has proven to be very successful. In their study on aerophobia (North and North 1994), the fear of flying, they used three groups to examine the effectiveness of virtual reality intervention. Subjects were male and female undergraduate students enrolled in a general psychology course who exhibited symptoms of aerophobia consistent with specific phobia.

- Group 1 was treated with imaginal systematic desensitization (ISD);
- Group 2 was treated with Virtual environment imaginal systematic desensitization (VESID) using stereoscopic head-mounted displays; and
- Group 3 was a control group and received no treatment.

They found that the intervention used for Groups 1 and 2 were equally successful in desensitizing subjects. North and North (1994) report that virtual environments created from VR technology are particularly well-suited to patients who have difficulty visualizing the hierarchical stimuli in traditional systematic desensitization. Virtual environment interventions tend to be more economical than interventions requiring patient and therapist to leave the clinical office and "adds the advantage of greater control over graded exposure stimulus parameters and the ability to isolate which virtual stimulus parameters are essential in generating a phobic response" (p. 1). Subsequent research suggests that these types of interventions can be used in treating agoraphobia and acrophobia as well as other specific phobias involving such fears as height, dark places, animals, and public speaking (North et al. 1996).

Similarly, in 1995, Hodges and Rothbaum studied the use of VRE (virtual reality exposure) with acrophobic patients at Georgia Institute of Technology's Graphics, Visualization and Usability Center. Undergraduates with clinical symptoms of acrophobia were outfitted with head-mounted displays to simulate anxiety-producing scenes from bridges, balconies, and an open-glass atrium elevator. Subjects were exposed to two months of weekly thirty-five to forty-five minute sessions. It was observed that nearly all the subjects experienced various symptoms of acrophobia during initial VR exposure, including sweaty palms, weak knees, and dizziness. At the completion of treatment, subjects were evaluated for anxiety, avoidance, attitudes, and distress when confronted with heights. They were then compared to a control group that received no treatment.

> Significant differences between the students who completed the virtual reality treatment and those on the (control) waiting list were found on all measures. The treatment group was significantly improved after eight weeks but the comparison group was unchanged (Hodges and Rothbaum 1995, p. 2).

Carlin, Hoffman, and Weghorst (1997) used a similar technique in a single subject design study. The subject was a female who had suffered from arachnophobia for nearly twenty years. She had developed spider-related obsessive-compulsive behaviors such as sealing bedroom windows with duct tape each night, putting all clothing into sealed plastic bags, and eventually becoming reluctant to leave home for fear of encountering spiders. The researchers designed a virtual "spider world" where the subject could control spiders, issue commands, put them in a variety of situations, even "touch" them. For example, spiders could be put in a cabinet with a Web, and they could be commanded to jump, climb, or ever meander across a virtual kitchen floor. After twelve weekly one-hour treatments, the subject stopped all her obsessive-compulsive spider rituals and was able to tolerate them with a "manageable" emotional reaction. Although this was only a single-subject design, it further supports North and colleagues (1996) and Hodges and Rothbaum (1995).

Perhaps the greatest limitation in VR interventions is cost and accessibility. Hodges and Rothbaum suggest that it can be done with computers and head-mounted displays for approximately $20,000 (Toon 1996). While this is too steep for the average psychotherapist, improved technology, less expensive equipment, and applications through the Internet will make this intervention more cost effective in the near future. But VR environments already on the Internet can be used right now in systematic desensitization processes with limited telepresence. For example, imaginal systematic desensitization can be achieved with the standard computer, mouse, and Internet connection as a prelude to in vivo desensitization. Consider the subject with arachnophobia described earlier. Perhaps her lower-level fears involve seeing pictures or reading about spiders. Obviously, this can be readily tackled on a computer monitor. She can then move into animated displays that increase telepresence. Online experiences can include "visits" to places like the *Arachnological Hub of the World Wide Web*, a look at *Myths, stories, poems, songs, and art about arachnids*, or a peek at an early twentieth century "good luck" postcard that featured a spider dangling from its Web. More direct experiences can include joining online chats, newsgroups, or e-mail groups with people trying to recover from arachnophobia; traveling through virtual reality environments and "meeting" spiders, or simply researching information about spiders. The hierarchy of fears, the imagination of the psychotherapist, and the willingness of the patient determine the length and nature of the online sites visited.

3

Cyberspeak!: Psychotherapy and Computer-Mediated Communication

WITH SHEILA PECK

Sheila Peck has used the computer in clinical practice in many innovative ways. Some of her most intriguing applications utilize direct computer mediated communication—e-mail—in psychotherapy. The case studies in this chapter reflect Peck's actual clinical work.

CASE 1: MARLENE AND EMILIO

Marlene, a teacher, is from the Midwestern United States. Emilio, her husband, is from Spain. He works as a translator.

They met and married in graduate school 15 years ago. Emilio was new to this country and spoke English reasonably well, but never, he says, learned to "think" in the language. Early on in their relationship, he got Marlene to promise she would learn his language so he could share more with her. She agreed that this was a good idea but somehow hasn't gotten around to it—yet. Every summer Emilio takes a "vacation," going back to his native land to visit his family for five or six weeks. Marlene stays home, though sometimes the two children accompany Emilio for part of the time.

Although it's an unusual arrangement, it seems to work reasonably well for this couple who initially built this into their relationship as a kind of "intimate distance."

For the last few years, though, the distance has grown. Marlene has great difficulty expressing feelings face-to-face, except for an intermittent rage, which seems to take over for no cause.

Emilio, on the other hand, is a quiet but open man who wants very much to share with his wife. He holds back because he is afraid to hurt Marlene.

The couple has been communicating with each other via e-mail for the past two years—each one has a separate account and they send the important news of the day and any other necessary information in a flurry of daily electronic transmissions.

I met them in January 1997, when Emilio, who was in individual therapy with another therapist, told Marlene something very important via e-mail. He thought he might be gay.

Emilio's therapist referred the couple to me. Their first session indicated to me that the couple was unable to relate directly. Neither could look at each other—they literally did not want to see each other. Even when I asked them to fantasize seeing the other, they could/would not.

We explored all the Neuro Linguistic Programming (NLP) sensing possibilities—could they experience each other by sight, by sound, by touch. None of them worked; all seemed too intimate.

I asked them to spend no more than one minute a day covertly (at home) observing each other. They were not to tell each other what they saw, but rather, to send these reports to me, via e-mail. They were also each asked to touch the other person on the shoulder once a day, briefly, and report about that as well.

I told them that although I would surely read and save *Every* communication they sent, I would rarely respond, except in session, and that I would always check with the particular sender of an e-mail for permission before I did even that.

I was making up the boundary rule as I went along as the necessity for each emerged. For instance, on occasion I would suggest that the sender of the e-mail send a copy to the partner, always keeping a copy of *my* communications for myself, much as I would a session note. And I have a whole "folder" on my hard drive of all the communications of Emilio and Marlene and my responses to them.

In addition, Emilio was printing out his e-mails and showing them to his therapist, Dr. P., who was not yet using a computer. Dr. P. and I, with permission of our clients, would talk over some of what emerged in the e-mails and try to coordinate our work accordingly.

As the e-mails grew in number, I noticed that the couple would, in session, begin to *look* at one other. Once in a while, they would be sitting so that their arms touched. This was quite a change from the beginning of therapy.

Finally, there was a small breakthrough. In one of the daily e-mails, Emilio, who had grown quite electronically expansive (as had Marlene), angrily asked, "Why the F—are we telling *You* these things instead of each other?" Click!

So I sent back one of my rare responses to each, suggesting that they send copies of their e-mails to me and to each other.

Now Emilio is planning to return to Spain for his annual estivation. The couple is aware, for the first time in years, that they might miss each other. We have arranged to do a three-way "chat" some time in July. His will not be therapy—I have deliberately attempted to avoid any resemblance to "sessions" with them—but will be a mutual checking-in, a way to stay connected.

Both Emilio and Marlene are more hopeful now and have been able to support each other in a recent family medical crisis.

It's been fascinating to work in this way, though it's also a lot of toil, at times. I've had to be careful not to inadvertently usurp the role of Emilio's individual therapist. It's so easy to send a reply without having first thought it out carefully. I also need to keep track of what I said to whom; I'm used to functioning and remembering these things aurally, not visually.

But I've welcomed the challenge that the computer has brought to me with this couple and feel that the changes that have happened would have been difficult to achieve without it.

What is computer mediated communication? Was the process described by Peck in the case of Marlene and Emilio a form of psychotherapy or a completely new treatment modality in the electronic environment?

Computer mediated communication (CMC), clearly a postmodern phenomenon, is a form identified by the mediator (the computer) as well as the communicator (the virtual ego). The machine determines existence. Without a computer, one cannot exist in an electronic environment. Simply put, the computer allows the virtual ego *to be*. This makes the definition of computer mediated communication, particularly in a clinical setting, a very slippery process constantly subject to change and the daily superficial shifts in technology.

John December (1997) attempts to capture CMC by identifying it as "a process of human communication via computers, involving people situated in particular contexts, engaging in processes to shape media for a variety of purposes" (paragraph 3). Simply put, CMC can be seen as a fluid means of human communication, unrestrained by the actual reality attributes such as time, space, geographical distance, or continuity. Perhaps it is better understood in terms of context rather than content. December (1997) suggests that there are five basic contexts for CMC:

1. individual;
2. group;
3. organization;
4. mass;
5. societal.

For example, one may have a heated public discussion via

e-mail, newsgroup, or chat with people thousands of miles away from one another, scattered in time zones around the globe. When the passionate discourse is finished, one may move on, never to speak again. Or it might develop into an ardent private affair, an ongoing e-mail relationship, or a clinically guided encounter similar to Marlene and Emilio. Using present technology, CMC tends to be fluid, cycling, and devoid of the social cues that constitute modernity. Accordingly, psychotherapy that utilizes CMC is also amorphous, shifting in response to context, technology, and the nature of patient interaction.

Obviously, a definition that is based on the inevitability of change plunges one into a dance of words, resembling the reflections in a house of mirrors where there is merely a reflection-of-a-reflection-of-a-reflection, dissolving into glassy infinity. Murray (1997) agrees, suggesting that generalized definitions of CMC are essentially meaningless. With continually developing forms of communication, new technology, increasing diversity of uses and users, and multiplicity of purposes, the *only* constant is change. The house of mirrors succumbs to its own fluidity as we swim hopelessly in a river of words. How can clinicians use these fluid concepts in practice? Murray (1997) writes:

> Many philosophers, and particularly philosophers of language, from Wittgenstein onward, suggest that words get their meaning in use; words don't have some innate immutable meaning, but their meaning is socially constructed through their use in everyday life. For CMC, this means that the meaning of definition of what CMC is arises from the forms of CMC which we use everyday . . . some forms have common features, but there is probably no feature common to all. [p. 1]

In this context, the three most common forms available today are:

- Text-based (i.e., e-mail, newsgroups, chats);
- Audio-visual applications; and
- Mixed.

In addition to context and form, Ferris (1997) observes that CMC includes both "task-related and interpersonal communication conducted by computer." This more technological approach notes that synchronous as well as asynchronous communication occurs using technology that can either store or transmit information (or both) through spaces we identify as e-mail, bulletin boards, special group networks, chats, information utilization, manipulation, and retrieval.

In Peck's Case #2, she clearly illustrates how working with technology afforded the opportunity to make a psychotherapeutic intervention utilizing CMC that would not have been possible outside of the electronic environment.

CASE 2: RENEE

Renee was to be a grandmother! She was excited and sad— sad because her son, the father of her soon-to-be grandchild, lived in Tennessee and Renee lived in New York. There was little money to travel, in addition to there being some estrangement between Renee and her daughter-in-law, Barbara.

When the baby was born, Barbara was very ill and wanted Renee to hold off coming down to visit for a few weeks until the young mother could recover from the birth. Renee felt excluded and believed that if she and Barbara got along better, she would have been invited sooner—which was probably true.

Her son, Mark, however, was very computer literate, and he set up a Web page for the new addition which included a camera that was focused on the baby and refreshed the image every few minutes. There was a place on the Web site for comments by "visitors" and a special acknowledgment of "grandma."

Renee, however, had no computer. I brought my laptop into our sessions and we would spend the first five minutes or so going online so she could see her new grandson. Besides bringing great joy to her and pleasure to me, Renee could then get past her bitterness and begin to work on what lay underneath.

When Renee finally went to Tennessee (the baby was about a month old), she had a sense of her grandson and was able to let go some of the resentment that she had originally held for Barbara.

THE VIRTUAL EGO

Sigmund Freud, in the 1923 edition of *The Ego and the Id*, clearly described the essential processes of the ego. Almost eight decades later, the same words can be used to describe a psychotechnological construct called the *virtual ego*.

> We have formed the idea that in each individual there is a coherent organization of mental processes; and we call this his *ego*. It is to this ego that consciousness is attached; the ego controls the approaches to motility—that is, to the discharge of excitations into the external world; it is the mental agency which supervises all its own constituent processes, and which goes to sleep at night, though even then it exercises the censorship on dreams. [Freud 1923, p. 7]

The digital self exists only through the mediation of a computer. In an electronic environment, one ceases to "be" when the computer is turned off. Digital existence is totally dependent on cybernetics—the merging of living organism and machine. All people in the electronic environment are, by definition, cyborgs.

Extrapolating Freud's ideas into Internet concepts, one can define the virtual ego as a coherent organization of virtual processes. It is the psychotechnological structure that mediates virtual consciousness. Freud's (1923) description of the state of consciousness as "characteristically very transitory; an idea that is conscious now is no longer so a moment later, although it can become so again under certain conditions that are easily brought about" (p. 4) accurately depicts the virtual state of being. Virtual consciousness constantly shifts, postmodern identities are recycled through the click of a mouse, digital environments are regularly reconstructed as the netizen moves through the morass of electronic geography. The metaphor is further strengthened by Freud's discussion of the ego as "the representative of the external world, of reality, reason" (p. 26). The ego exemplifies "reason and common sense" (p. 15), holding the passions of the id in abeyance. The superego balances it all, "ultimately reflect [ing] the contrast between what is real and what is psychical, between the external world and the internal world" (p. 26).

In a like manner, the virtual ego mediates between the actual reality and the virtual (electronic) reality. Clearly, the virtual ego presents an intriguing conundrum. Strangelove (1994) calls it the "uncensored self" and observes that a new type of human being is emerging from computer mediated communication. The uncensored self is characterized by its accessibility, its lack of individual or social censorship, the ability to indulge equally in synchronous or asynchronous communication, its involvement in mass participation, and its ability to be multidirectional. Consistent with these ideas, the virtual ego has often been viewed through psychodynamic constructs to understand and interpret human behavior in an electronic environment.

Essentially, the virtual ego resides on an online couch, encouraged to free associate in an environment that welcomes fantasy, dependency, removal of boundaries, and regression. In an article titled "Mom, dad, computer," Suler (1996) describes what he refers to as a transference reaction to computers. He maintains that because people see computers as human-like, they unconsciously experience it as mother, father, or sibling. "We recreate in our relationship with the computer some AS-PECT of how we related to family members," Suler writes (p. 3). He suggests that users respond to their computers in the same way they experienced their families. For example, a user might "abuse" their machine in an analogous manner to the abuse he or she suffered as a child. In contrast, a user might assume a parental, nurturing role toward the computer, keeping it clean, upgraded, adding healthy software and pretty screen savers.

> Users may rely on their computers to clarify and strengthen their sense of identity. The computer is attentive and accommodating to their needs. It mirrors them. As users customize its hardware and software, the computer becomes more and more like a responsive reflection of their needs, feelings, and ambitions. It is part of them, a reflection of who they are, a world created within themselves. By idealizing it, by participating in all the amazing, powerful things a computer can do, users strengthen their own confidence and feelings of success. [Suler 1996, p. 8]

Surely this is fertile ground for the innovative psychotherapist. It appears that the virtual ego, expressing itself through computer mediated communication, has ventured into a form that creates as well as describes behavior. E-mail, perhaps the most commonly used form of CMC, has had a powerful impact on mental health. Consider some comments from professionals who posted their ideas on Internet discussion groups:

> I never will forget when I first got my e-mail to work. I had 88 messages. I sat here and weeded my way through, mostly just reading chuckling and recognizing names of

friends. It has become a part of my early morning routine (I usually wake up around 4:30 am) to make coffee, and then enjoy that first cup of the day with all my friends on the computer. [Anonymous 1996]

[Fiona hovers over the keyboard—smiling as she remembers telling her life story—a couple of times—to anonymous e-mail friends.] I find that I disclose much more personal information to anonymous e-mail friends than I do to real-life e-mail friends. In this list there have been discussions before about transferences, which I suspect might be related to this behavior. I find that it can take months of correspondence with anonymous e-mail friends to realize that they are actually quite different from me. A picture or a telephone conversation usually brings this reality into focus. [Geiser 1996, November 7]

May I propose another research topic: IMPULSIVITY AND E-MAIL? Is there research on people answering or writing more impulsively using e-mail and then regretting it? Shouldn't e-mail have a cautioning sentence before you send it: "Are you sure you want to send this message" or "Are you sure you want to send this message to thousands of people?" I use a class listserv to teach nutrition and also physiology. I have noticed students tell their life story or their family's most intimate secrets on e-mail. I have also noticed that I reply too quickly to e-mail and have regretted this. [Caplan 1996, November 6]

Suler (1996c) believes that e-mail "may be the most important, unique method for interactive communication since the telephone" (p. 1). He suggests that there are nine essential aspects of e-mail relationships:

1. *Writing:* The ability, style, and "personality" of one's writing directly affects the nature of the communication and accordingly, the relationship.

2. *Structure:* How one actually designs and presents e-mail has a significant psychological impact. For example, the prevalence of spelling, grammar, and typographical errors suggest a personality or style. Other factors such as choice of words, greetings, signatures, use of emoticons, all present contextual cues that affect the interpersonal dynamics.

3. *History:* How a relationship develops over time offers insight into the participants as well as the intensity of the association. This emulates actuality. Some relationships develop quickly, grow intense, and then just as quickly fade. Others are slow and tentative, remaining with safe subjects and avoiding intimacy. The variations are as numerous as the participants.

4. *Content:* The content of e-mail, as in any narrative, is probably the most distinguishing psychological factor. The difference between correspondence concerning business, sex, and professional consultation clearly identifies the nature of the relationship. Naturally, themes can change and develop: a professional discourse may turn into a flamefest, an intimacy may turn into an off-line rendezvous, or a business discussion may turn into a partnership.

5. *Timing:* Obviously, e-mails exchanged on a daily basis imply a greater psychological investment in the relationship than sporadic communication.

6. *Linguistic intimacy:* Developing special jokes, words, or emoticons adds meaning and intimacy to the relationship. It can be compared to secret nicknames, special glances, and choreographed body language in actuality.

7. *Logs:* The existence of permanent records in e-mail relationships enable individuals to keep track of what has occurred, as well as to accurately recall details that might otherwise have been forgotten or overlooked.

8. *Transference:* The lack of auditory and visual cues invites transference responses that naturally affect the nature, duration, and intimacy of the relationship.
9. *Duality:* E-mail juxtaposes critical factors in human relationships: virtual vs. in-person encounters; integrated vs. dissociated identities; and conscious vs. unconscious emotional expressions.

This suggests that a narrative psychological approach can help clinicians understand the psychosocial aspects of e-mail communications and relationships. In this context, the act of knowing is socially constructed through written language. Individual narratives are significant; collective narratives carry little or no meaning. Behavior is bound and defined purely by the linguistic social matrix. Sheila Peck's patient Melanie discovered this in a psychotherapeutic e-mail intervention.

CASE 3: MELANIE

Melanie, in her late twenties, comes from a chaotic, abusive, substance-involved family where the only consistent communication rule was: "Shut up if you don't agree with me or you'll get hurt! And never, *ever* tell me about feelings!"

The tyrant/king of the family who decided on this rule was the abusive, brilliant, sometimes-charming alcoholic father, who terrorized and intimidated everyone into believing that he had the answer and that he, of course, was *right*. And this belief persists to this day, although Melanie, who was a substance abuser for more than ten years (but who has been clean for three), is working hard in her therapy to change this.

Among other things, she believed, as is typical with victims of abuse, that somehow this was all her fault. We talked about this in sessions, and she decided it would be important for her to confront her father, who lives in Texas, with events that had happened in their past and to ask for explanations.

She could not tolerate this idea. Their telephone and visiting contacts included frequent "I've been a good girl, Daddy and let's not talk about anything important" conversations which had become more and more frustrating to her. However, even when we did fantasy-talk in session about what she might like to tell him if she could, this became extra-frightening and she came close to experiencing panic.

In the course of discussing whether or not she might write to him, we came up with the idea of using e-mail, since both he and she are fascinated by this new technology. Using e-mail would keep her at a safe, not-too-emotional remove and would allow her to organize her thoughts. It would also permit quick response (as opposed to a letter), and, because both of them liked the e-mail process, would add a measure of enjoyment to the process. Finally, Melanie could bring (or e-mail) copies of her father's responses to me as a reality check.

With much trepidation and encouragement through two sessions (Melanie's managed care company had allotted her twenty), she sent an e-mail telling him that she had some things to say to him and she would like a response: Was that okay?

Surprisingly (to her), he said, "Yes," and he even promised to hang in if the process became unpleasant.

They began e-mail talk that has resulted in a very healing process for Melanie. She has realized through the e-mails that her father is probably incapable of giving her the approval and approbation for which she so longs. Nevertheless, her father has given her much more than she ever thought possible, and he has "listened" to her. She has been able to observe his denial about certain events for which she has proof and to understand that this comes from him and is *not* her fault.

In addition, every now and then, Melanie sends me an e-mail and gets a great deal of reassurance from the fact that I am "there," if only "cyberspatially."

I believe that the healing and acceptance of who she is, and who her father is, was greatly hastened by the process of e-mail. It probably would have taken much longer without e-mail. And, it may not even have been possible; in this case, the medium was a very important part of the message.

4

Shooting the Electronic Breeze: Using Virtual Communities to Treat Social Disorders

Rose, eighty years old, lives in a small apartment in the suburbs of a Northwestern U.S. city. There are very few services for senior citizens. When the long winter sets in, Rose is virtually housebound, her only contact with volunteers who come bimonthly to do her shopping. Her therapist sees her only in the warmer months, when Rose can move around more freely. Rose is depressed, isolated, and in need of social contact.

Donnie is a thirteen-year old boy who was adopted as a toddler. His parents worked with an international agency that located Donnie in a tiny rural orphanage in Colombia. After bringing Donnie home, it became apparent that he suffered from a variety of learning disabilities. His parents secured help for him at an early age, and when he entered primary school, he was put in special education classes. Donnie had many social problems that were kept under control in the special classes, however, when he entered middle school, the social gap between Donnie and his peers widened. Academically, Donnie was doing well in special education. Socially, he began to act out. The school recommended that Donnie receive outside psychotherapy.

Claire and Frank are the parents of three children, ages nine, eleven, and fourteen. Frank is a supervisor in a local print shop, and Claire works part time as a waitress. They live in the U.S.

in a small Midwestern city. Ali, their youngest daughter, suffers from a rare genetic disorder. To get treatment for her requires frequent trips to a hospital in a city three hours away from their home. Ali must be maintained on a rigid diet. As a result of Ali's disorder, her academic development is uneven and her behavior is often a problem in the family. Claire and Frank have never met another parent who has had to deal with similar problems. They feel isolated, angry, and frustrated. Their psychotherapist is very experienced in family work but has never dealt directly with anyone suffering from Ali's disorder.

Steve is thirty-two years old and is employed by a personnel agency in a major Eastern U.S. city. He has an active social life in that city. However, having a deep need for "peace and quiet," he lives in an apartment in the far suburbs and commutes to work by car. When Steve was in a serious car accident—he broke his hip and fractured several vertebrae in his back—it meant a long convalescence in a body cast. His company assured him that his job would be waiting, but he could not "commute" by computer. Friends called from the city, but few of them wanted to make the long trip to visit. Steve suddenly found himself very alone, overwhelmed by the "peace and quiet" of the suburbs. His psychotherapist, also in the city, conducts weekly telephone sessions.

Rose, Donnie, Claire and Frank, and Steve all have one issue in common: they are socially isolated, depressed, and frustrated by their present environment. Psychotherapists would generally treat them directly for these problems, possibly referring them to various private and community social groups and working on the issues as they arise. The Internet has opened a new approach to therapeutic intervention never before available to clinicians: virtual communities.

A virtual community is a network of people who connect through computer mediated communication. An actual community is defined by geographical space: buildings, streets, parks, and other public spaces. The forces that bind a community together to establish distinctive group cohesion are more difficult to identify. These forces include the voices and emotions of individuals playing, working, cooperating, arguing, supporting, competing, and residing in close proximity. If these relationships exist, it is not critical whether one enters a community by car or by computer. Socialization occurs—as well as the opportunity to overcome many social disorders.

The unique advantage in virtual communities is the opportunity for a psychotherapist to *accompany* the patient. Psychotherapists can help patients observe and practice social behaviors as they occur. One of the most intriguing aspects of the online couch is work within a virtual community. The electronic environment doesn't *change* human nature, but rather, it puts it in a new context, offering different ways to communicate and relate to others. Virtual community behavior runs the same gamut—from "good" to "bad"—as off-line community behavior.

Virtual communities that originate in cyberspace present different theoretical as well as empirical issues in research. Garton and colleagues (1997) maintain that virtual communities, along with other fairly large computer-mediated communication groups, constitute "social networks," as "when a computer connects people or organizations" (p. 2). As a social network, electronic phenomena like a virtual community is best analyzed by examining "networks of relations" (p. 2): exploring patterns, flow of information, and the effects on people and organizations. "The social network approach facilitates the study of how information flows through direct and indirect network ties, how people acquire resources, and how coalitions and cleavages operate" (p. 3).

The concept of social networks attempts to establish a framework for understanding communities that began in virtual space rather than actual space. These communities vary greatly in format and contexts, ranging from e-mail lists to virtual reality environments complete with metaphorical representations. Due to the vast numbers of people inhabiting cyberspace, virtual communities bring together special interests and needs often unavailable in real space. Simply put, Claire and Frank would have no problem finding a virtual community of parents with children suffering from the same genetic defect as their daughter, Ali.

Utilizing virtual communities in psychotherapeutic interventions requires a better understanding of patterns of relationship and flow of information that clarify social interaction on both sides of the computer and help to generalize online social experimentation to off-line daily life.

Think about the numbers of people inhabiting virtual communities. There are over 28,000 newsgroups on the Internet with over 200,000 messages posted each day. In 1986, there were only 241 groups with 946 posts a day—a growth rate of over 8,000 percent (Georgia 1996a,b). It is estimated that over 24 million people worldwide access newsgroups (Reference.Com 1996b). In addition to newsgroups, there are over 100,000 publicly accessible e-mail lists and 25,000 Web forums that are centralized bulletin boards on a single website. The number spirals when chat sites are considered. The number of channels for chats is constantly changing—every day brings a new total. To get a sense of what is happening, take into account one of the largest chat channels, The Internet Relay Chat (IRC). On any given day in cyberspace, around 10,000 chats are listed. That does not include other popular sites such as Yahoo Chat, which might have 3,000 channels, and WebChat, a relatively "new kid on the block" with over a half million registered users. That is approximately *two hundred thousand* groups, without including networks such as America Online, CompuServe, Prodigy, virtual reality formats, commercial chats, and special interest communities linked to specific websites. Naturally, all of these environments are not "communities," but rather free-floating social networks.

In *The Virtual Community: Homesteading on the Electronic Frontier*, Howard Rheingold (1993) talks about the magic of virtual communities where people "do just about everything people do in real life, but we leave our bodies behind" (p. 3). Rheingold suggests that people who are drawn into virtual communities find them richly satisfying, even addictive. He tells stories about *The Well* and the camaraderie he found with fellow users who were always available, always ready to discuss, support, and otherwise exchange experiences. "Point of view, along with identity," explains Rheingold, "is one of the great variables in cyberspace. Different people in cyberspace look at their virtual communities through differently shaped key holes" (p. 63). Virtual communities occupy a space that is ultimately a function of imagination—a mental image that concretizes digital space. The mental images vary widely—some communities create virtual constructions of physical phenomena, such as houses, streets, and cities, while others are completely text-based, such as newsgroups, with relationships based on the exchange of information, emotions, opinions, and experiences. Humans efficiently "fill in the blanks" when contextual cues are unavailable. As virtual communities spread throughout an increasingly crowded cyberspace, new communities are providing forums that let netizens use imagination and multiple identities to construct their virtual dream houses. Some of the newest, largest, and most popular online communities are so extensive that they often appear to emulate virtual *cities* rather than communities. Consider *Planet Tripod*'s opening statement to "residents":

> Jobs don't last. Careers don't last. Health is a struggle
> rather than a natural fact. Savviness lets you travel fur-

ther than money will—a lot farther. Saving money: You know you have to, but how? What's an animated graphic, and how do you put one on your homepage?

Tripod is for people trying to live well in a world of constant shift and transition. We give practical advice via real-life stories, humor, and other Tripod members who share their answers to life's hard questions. [About Tripod, No date, p. 1]

Planet Tripod, or Planet T, is the virtual home to over 300,000 Generation X-ers or "twenty to thirty-somethings." Offering "streetsmart strategies for work, life, and everything else" ("Guided Tour," p. 1), basic membership is free. Users get space for a personal Web page, with a minimal charge for premium membership. In addition, members can have chats on their Homepages and "personal conferences," as well as e-mail and e-mail forwarding. Bo Peabody, the creator of *Planet Tripod*, reports that there are over 100,000 personal Homepages, with *Tripod* growing by 1,600 to 1,700 members a day (Calem 1997).

An increasingly popular type of virtual community—perhaps the most passionately debated electronic environments—is the abstract, fanciful virtual reality community. These cyber "spaces" are identified by names such as MUDs (Multi-user Dimensions), MOOs (Multi-user Dimensions object-oriented), habitats, and virtual universes. Running the gamut from text-based to other-worldly graphics, these spaces take disembodied humans deeper into the realms of fantasy and imagination and further from the mundane confines of simulated physical parameters. Books, articles, research studies, even nonprint media have focused on these spaces that transport netizens into Gibson-like cyberworlds. Obviously, the potential psychosocial effects of virtual reality communities cannot be fully discussed here—it would take an entire book. However, it is important to consider them in a discussion of psychotherapeutic interventions utilizing virtual communities. Perhaps these virtual reality communities are the forerunners of the future—where postmodern social environments will increasingly harness human imagination and interaction and allow humans to dwell in abstract, dream-like worlds driven by conscious and unconscious fantasies of community.

James Sempsey III (1995), in his paper *The psycho-social aspects of multi-user dimensions in cyberspace*, reports that researchers have found clearly defined behavior phenomena with aspects that include the following:

- Individuals are less socially inhibited in MUDs than in real life;
- Men and women behave differently;
- Gender swapping is fairly common;
- Assuming multiple identities is common and acceptable practice;
- Many MUDders have been known to abandon their "actual" lives to spend long hours in online virtual reality; and
- People tend to be friendlier.

Perhaps one of the most powerful inducements is the draw of the narrative, which is intrinsic to virtual reality. "Everyone and every thing and every place has a story," writes Howard Rheingold (1993). "Every object in a MUD, from your character's identity to the chair your character is sitting in, has a written description that is revealed when you choose to look at the object" (p. 155). Many virtual reality communities allow users to create or build their own objects (as well as their multiple selves). The narrative becomes a shared process, a communal behavior of hundreds or thousands of minds sharing the same fantasy. Perhaps that is why some MUD-like environments are called MUSHs, or multi-user shared hallucinations. Many people seeking more "serious" applications have explored the power of collective thinking in virtual reality environments. One of the leaders in this approach is Amy Bruckman. In a presentation on the "serious" uses of MUDs, Bruckman (1994) noted that the medium:

- Brings together people from diverse geographical locations with common interests;
- Supports both synchronous and asynchronous communication;
- Promotes casual collaboration; and
- Uses physical metaphors to construct a context for social interaction.

Accordingly, Bruckman designed MediaMOO as a professional community for media researchers and MediaMOOSE for children. Others have established similar projects, including David Van Buren's *AstroVR* for astrophysicists and Pavel Curtis' *Jupiter* for researchers at Xerox PARC (Bruckman 1994).

But how can virtual communities actually be put to use in the clinician's office?

Consider Rose, the depressed and isolated senior citizen mentioned at the beginning of the chapter. Ideally, a referral to a senior citizen center would help solve many of her problems. But Rose lives in a cold climate. When the winter arrives, negotiating the ice and snow is a threat to her health. Online, many senior citizens have found community, activity, and companionship.

"One of my biggest pleasures," says 73-year-old Harvey Fink, "is taking my laptop computer—which my children gave me as birthday gift—with me during my winter trips to Florida. I use it mostly for e-mail, communicating with my children and grandchildren who are located all around the country and world—without spending a fortune in telephone bills" (personal communication, June 4, 1997).

Senior citizens are in cyberspace, surfing the Web and visiting special senior sites in increasing numbers. Although this is very different from the stereotype of older adults, the numbers clearly speak for themselves. In 1995, Intel Corporation awarded a grant to *SeniorNet* (© 1997), "the international community of computer-using seniors." The goal was to conduct a national survey of a random sample of seven hundred adults aged fifty-five years and older to determine computer usage and attitudes. Results of the survey were as follows:

- 29 percent of adults over age 55 own computers;
- 53 percent of adults over age 55, who are college graduates, own computers;
- The most popular application in senior computer owners is writing/word processing (84 percent);
- 28 percent of senior computer owners use an online service on a regular basis. More than half of them uses America Online;
- 72 percent of senior online service users exchanged e-mail or accessed news and reference information;
- Only 6 percent of senior online service users go to "live" chats; and
- 36 percent of senior online service users are online for 3 to 10 hours a week.

Where do seniors go online? *GoldenAge.Net* offers more than three hundred World Wide Web links to seniors stopping by for social, emotional, physical, and care-giving concerns (McCafferty 1996). The *Online96 Senior's File* (1996), subtitled "seniors getting a new link on life," offers twenty-eight different topics to explore ranging from travel services and senior chat room to gay seniors. There is even *OSSO*, the Online

Single Seniors Outlet, with over 160 members who hook up online.

One of the most interesting sites for seniors is the *BEV Senior Information Page*. BEV, or Blacksburg Electronic Village, is a town of 35,000 people in southwestern Virginia. BEV is a highly successful experiment to build a geographic online community. Bell Atlantic of Virginia and Virginia Tech worked together to connect all the people in the town with each other as well as with the Internet. The most interactive community on the BEV turned out to be the senior citizens. Many of them had never met before going online. With their virtual community, they were able to organize, design some of the "best" pages in town, and plan things such as group meetings two or three times a week (Chervokas and Watson 1997). On the *Seniors Information Page* (1997), they begin with:

> We are a diverse group of senior citizen from the Blacksburg area of Virginia, dedicated to the notion that "old does not mean one must retire from life." One of our primary missions is to create a simple avenue for all seniors to access the vast regions of The Internet. [p. 1]

Their page includes a Seniors Association Newsletter, a bimonthly publication of a group of "three score plus" netizens, a senior column from the *Roanoke Times*, and an assortment of information ranging from a mailing list to the nostalgia project. They have links to various sites for seniors on the Web as well as such things as local programs and government resources.

Consider the case histories mentioned earlier. Rose can work with her psychotherapist to understand the social possibilities online. Her psychotherapist can take her on a "tour" and introduce her to many of the sites. If Rose is reluctant, she can observe and discuss the possibilities online and even work, with her therapist, on learning how to conduct virtual chats and textual communication. When Rose can no longer consult with her therapist face-to-face, she can discuss everything through e-mail, further connecting her to the world outside her apartment. If she can't afford a computer, Rose can work with her therapist to explore help through the many foundations and agencies designed to work with people such as herself.

At eighty years old, with the help of her psychotherapist, Rose can be given a new window to the world.

Similarly, Donnie can also learn socialization from virtual communities. In his case, the goal is to help him develop age-appropriate social skills. "Experimenting" in a middle-school environment could be socially and emotionally disastrous. Donnie and his therapist can go online to adolescent virtual communities such as chats and "safe" Web sites to observe how other children behave. There, they can "lurk" in chatrooms, examine interests, learn about the music, sports, and celebrities that teens discuss. When ready, Donnie can begin experimenting socially by participating in chats and other adolescent discussions supervised by his therapist.

Young people are at home in an electronic environment, where physicality is suspended. Adolescents chat, flirt, argue, compete, and play online—without having to worry about the acne on their faces or whether they are too tall or too short, too fat or too thin, or simply too shy. They are far more accepting of their peers online than off-line. *Techies* are cool kids who design colorful Web pages with great music and surf the Internet as easily as they hang out at the park. There's even a new breed dubbed the "technojocks," who merge sports and technology. "It's about an information machine," writes David Diamond (1997) in *Wired*, "geared to no-tech sports-nut editors and users alike. It's about databases loaded with every stat ever kept. It's about killer execution meets dream content. And it's about having the time of your life doing it" (p. 132). Diamond is referring to the ESPNET *SportsZone*, the most popular destination site on the Web. In a reversal of the generation gap, today's kids usually know more about computers than their parents. "Indeed, there is a digital generation gap in many such families," writes Steve Lohr (1996) in *The New York Times CyberTimes*. When kids are adept at computers, "parental reaction ranges from amusement to amazement, but there is often scant comprehension" (paragraph 25).

The Internet is "in,"—witness the hanging out at various specialty sites online (Serino, no date). With thirty-eight million U.S. households having at least one personal computer, the number of young people going online is increasing rapidly. *Investor's Business Daily* reported that 55 percent of 6- to 7-year olds, 72 percent of 8- to 12-year olds, and 67 percent of teenagers spend time on the PC (Myers 1997). This does not include the college-age populations, who usually have free online access through their schools. There are many places for these young people to go. There are chats, bulletin boards, 'zines, e-mail lists, news, special Web forums—all of the different formats that are available on the other (adult) side of cyberspace. To illustrate, a young person can go to *Kidsurf Online* (1996–1997), touted as "The Internet surfboard for kids and teens." Young netizens can choose between "Kids Port" and "Teen Surf," depending on their age and interests. From that point, surfers can, among other activities, chat, read 'zines, visit their peers' Web pages, or click on to a host of other age-appropriate sites. They can visit places such as *ADOL: Adolescence directory online, Virtually React,* a 'zine, or even visit *Ask Dr. Marla,* a family practitioner who answers all questions from teenagers for free. She encourages anonymity and posts "Hot teen topics of the week" from birth control and eating disorders to depression and suicide.

Donnie and his therapist can tap into this world with the intent of generalizing the behavior learned online to actuality. Donnie will also develop a "popular" skill that will enable him to join various clubs at school. At the same time, his therapist can teach him about safe surfing—avoiding the stalkers, pedophiles, and sexually inappropriate material. Donnie can learn how to distinguish between virtuality and actuality and how to protect himself against virtual aggression. In addition, the computer can act as a tool to quickly engage Donnie to work on problems that he finds difficult or painful to address.

In like fashion, Claire and Frank can use the Internet to find a virtual community that supports their special needs. Using this type of intervention, their psychotherapist can help them focus on issues that parents in similar situations face. Various alternatives can be discussed as well as solutions used by others. In order to better educate herself on the issues, the psychotherapist can go to these highly specialized virtual communities and observe or even question other parents about issues that they are overlooking. In this case, the virtual community can better educate both patient and clinician.

Likewise, Steve can use virtual communities to ease his isolation during his convalescence. He can also communicate more frequently with his city friends and maintain an ongoing e-mail correspondence with his psychotherapist.

Rose, Donnie, Claire and Frank, and Steve are only a few examples of how virtual communities can be used to enhance, inform, and experience socialization. In this seminal approach, clinicians can work with an endless variety of environments—as observers, facilitators, instructors—the list is endless. The possibility for creating their own online therapeutic communities is also rich with potential. Presently, there are numerous professional virtual communities that offer support, information, referral, and simply companionship for mental health professionals and their patients.

5

To Be or Not To Be: Exploring the Self in a Personal Web Page

Seventeen-year old Kate is on the other side of a long and painful trial convicting her stepfather of sexually abusing her since she turned 13 years old. While he has been sent to prison, her mother is instituting divorce proceedings. Kate's two younger half-sisters, untouched by their biological father, do not quite understand why he is in jail. They only know that Kate is somehow responsible.

Kate is angry, depressed, and suffering the aftereffects of long-term sexual abuse. She will not talk to her mother, has distanced herself from her sisters, and has isolated herself from her friends in high school. She refuses to discuss anything concerning the abuse, the trial, or the present disruption in her family. Her mother is afraid that Kate will "want to kill herself."

Kate's psychotherapist has had little success in getting the adolescent to talk. Kate refuses to say anything about herself or her experiences. Her psychotherapist invites her to surf the Internet. Together they go online and browse through the electronic environment. The psychotherapist carefully guides Kate to various home pages written by adolescents. Kate reads them with great interest.

"Why don't you write your own page?" the psychotherapist suggests. "You can use your first name, another name, or no name at all. And then we can put it online through my Web hosting service."

There is a glimmer of interest in Kate's eyes. With more encouragement, Kate decides to write a home page on her favorite music. She and her therapist use a Web editor to design the page and enter information. First, Kate lists all her favorite musical groups. She links her lists to other sites all over the Internet. Then she writes descriptions about them—what they like, what they don't like, what kind of people she believes them to be. Then Kate moves closer to home—entering information about the most popular music groups in her high school. After several weeks of working together, her psychotherapist gently suggests that every home page have a section about its author. What does Kate want to write about herself? And Kate begins to tell her story.

While much of cyberspace is geared to the cycling of identities, home pages stand as a bridge to the single, stable self. Screen names, alternate personas, and multiple identities are not part of this wildly popular aspect of the Internet. On home pages, the only stories people tend to tell are about themselves. It is a replay of actuality in virtuality.

In a 1996 study conducted by The Personal Home Page Institute, it was found that approximately one in sixteen Internet users, or 600,000 people, had their own World Wide Web home pages. A year later, after the burgeoning growth of virtual communities based around free home pages such as *GeoCities* and *Planet Tripod*, the numbers are staggering. Pamela O'Connell (1997), in "Guide for Personal Web Pages" for *The Mining Company*, has evaluated 1997 research data and concluded that there are now approximately four million home pages, or 14 percent of net users. She predicts that the number will quickly grow to at least 20 percent of net users. That is a lot of people telling a lot of stories.

John Buten (1996), a graduate student at University of Pennsylvania's Annenberg School for Communications, founded The Personal Home Page Institute with a mission to investigate and promote home pages. In a small survey of randomly selected home page authors, Buten found that they tend to be young (average age is 25), male, and have been using the Internet for nine months to a year. They are relatively busy Web and e-mail users. Ninety-one percent report that they present themselves honestly and accurately. There are few or no multiple identities and experiments with personas in this virtual grassroots revolution.

Sarah Auerbach (No date), a home page author, comments on this phenomenon in her essay "*Meditations on the metaphysics of home pages.*" Auerbach's page is complete with crayon drawings and options that range from "Quotations" to "My Home Page Philosophy." Clicking on the drawing of a woman that appears to be Auerbach herself triggers violin music. "The name 'home page' suggests an easy analogy," Auerbach writes. "The home page is to the Internet world and society (one that sociologists would have a field day on and that political scientists would doubtless call anarchic) what the house is to the modern tangible society" (No date, para. 1).

Auerbach describes a virtual home. She sees it as an analogy to the physical home where the host or hostess invites outsiders in to their turf to chat; to break, to construct or initiate a relationship; or simply share "notes." Safe in your own "home," you can expose more of who you are in a polite, pleasant environment. You can serve your favorite coffee, show off your treasured collectibles, and display your cherished photographs, videos, and family heirlooms. It is a singular opportunity to create a public identity within the sanctuary of your metaphorical home. "The analogy is infinitely rich," concludes Auerbach. "Hope you've enjoyed your visit to my humble abode. Come back soon; I've just moved in and it's gonna take me awhile to get settled" (no date, para. 5).

The material that most people post on their home pages is often just *basic* data. There are photos of themselves, family, friends, lovers, and even pets. There are lists of favorite music, favorite movies, what they like, dislike, and even hate. There are special links to other websites as well as the home pages of friends. Some home pages talk comfortably, others joke, some shout, and others do nothing but *exist*. A case in point is the "Cambridge Coffee Pot" (No date), which sits in the Trojan Room of the Cambridge Computer Lab (1995) so visitors (as well as employees) can see "the state of their coffee." The content and variety is limited only by the diversity of human thought. Natalie Engel's (1966) "Chest of Lust, Longing and Obsession" is as viable as Verne's (no date) home page adage, "Drizzle, Drazzle, Druzzle, Drone . . . Be skewed, or be glued." Not surprisingly, according to The Personal Home Page Institute survey (1996), self-expression ranks as one of the most important reasons for authoring a page.

In this context, a home page is an excellent tool for psychotherapeutic intervention. It presents an opportunity to explore the self openly while maintaining a public anonymity that reduces the sense of risk-taking. In a narrative psychotherapeutic approach, the collective "Internet" becomes a nonjudgmental listener and the therapist a collaborator in the intervention.

Narrative therapy was developed and promoted by Michael White in the 1980s. In an interview with Ken Stewart (1995), published by The Dulwich Centre, White states:

> We can make it our business to work collaboratively with people in identifying those ways of speaking about their lives that contribute to a sense of personal agency, and that contribute to the experience of being an authority on one's life. And we can assist people to draw distinctions around these ways of speaking and those other ways of speaking that contribute to experiences of marginalisation, that subtract from a sense of personal agency, and that undermine an appreciation of one's authoritativeness. [p. 2]

Narrative therapy is based on the premise that people shape much of their lives and relationships through knowledge and stories that give meaning to their experience. According to The Dulwich Centre, the goal of a narrative therapy is to help patients:

1. Separate themselves from knowledge and stories that are impoverishing;
2. Challenge ways of life that are self-defeating; and
3. Encourage people to re-author their lives.

Siegal (1996) defines a narrative as the "telling" of a series of events that involve the reporting of both actual and mental experiences as well as conflicts and resolutions. Narratives help individuals make sense out of their environment, leading to choices that determine action. "Autobiographical narratives," Siegal writes, "thus historically document events, deriving meaning in an attempt to make sense out of them, and guide plans for future action. As such, narratives are simultaneously shaped by mental models and states of mind internally; externally, as a form of discourse, they are influenced by listener expectation" (p. 5).

Obviously, stories are not a recent phenomenon of the human experience. Narratives in the form of myths, films, theatre, diaries, novels, poems, and tales have been an integral part of human history. Similarly, these stories have occupied clinical offices since the first psychotherapeutic session—from play therapy to memories—shared by patient and therapist. "This verbal communication takes place within the therapeutic setting," acknowledges Siegal, "based on the primary ingredients of a secure attachment: a safe environment with contingent communication, emotional connection and repair of inevitable disruptions in the therapeutic relationship" (p. 6).

White maintains that narrative expression enables people to rewrite both story and self-image. In this process patients are empowered to reorient themselves to new knowledge or experience that may contradict damaging narratives. In this context White draws from postmodernism developments already reflected in anthropology, philosophy, and social psychology (Hart 1995).

Authoring a home page is clearly a form of narrative in the electronic environment. It exemplifies Siegal's (1996) definition, utilizing electronic text and graphics to build a virtual home that reflects the physical, mental, and virtual experiences of individuals. The identity, conflicts, and resolutions of the author emerge in the words and graphics. A home page provides what White would consider a safe environment, a nonjudgmental Internet "listener" and the illusion of an emotional connection. It is a space where the author consciously designs him- or herself, using the electronic environment to express unconscious needs, fears, and memories. The use of home pages as an intervention in a narrative psychotherapy has enormous potential in present and future practice.

Consider Kate. She is unable to tell her story—unwilling to trust any of the adults around her. However, she desperately needs to verbalize her narrative so she can work through the painful conflicts and begin to author a new narrative and self-image. There is no safe environment available for this process. Her mother is an intrinsic part of the narrative—she is unable to help her daughter in this manner. Her sisters (and home) are also part of the narrative, suspicious about Kate's role in the removal of their father from the house. Formal authority has both helped her and hurt her—the school system and legal system have resolved her physical problem but only exaggerated her conflict. She has withdrawn herself from friends and extended family. Kate is very much alone. It is simply too difficult for her to trust her new psychotherapist—that will take time and many "tests." The Internet, however, is anonymous. The nonjudgmental "listener" has no face and voice. It is virtual and it is safe. Kate believes that she cannot be hurt in the electronic environment. As a collaborator in her narrative (Kate's home page), her psychotherapist begins the difficult process of empowering Kate.

6

Digital Digging:
Group Therapy Online

WITH YVETTE COLÓN

The electronic environment is evidently fertile ground for online group therapy. Consider the classic definition of a group "as a plurality of individuals who are in contact with one another, who take one another into account, and who are aware of some signification commonality" (Olmsted and Hare 1978, p. 11). They clearly state that physical proximity or common interest make a group. Critical features include such things as a common belief, interest, or task that group members consider significant. Accordingly, Schramm (1997) suggests that there are seven basic elements in a psychotherapy group contract:

1. Regular and punctual attendance;
2. Confidentiality;
3. Participation;
4. Prohibition of physical aggression;
5. Responsibility for payment;
6. Extra-group boundaries; and
7. Completion of therapy.

All of these elements can be readily adapted to conducting group therapy online. Yvette Colón works with cancer patients and their families, facilitates an ongoing telephone support group for homebound cancer patients, facilitates online patient and family support groups, and coordinates the Internet Project. Using today's text-based technology, Colón has clearly indicated that online group psychotherapy is an extremely viable modality. New technologies that use video conferencing, higher speed, wider bandwidth and better security promise increasing clinical opportunities in this area. The following article, reprinted from *Women and Performance*, describes her creative and innovative group therapy applications in the electronic environment.

CHATT(ER)ING THROUGH THE FINGERTIPS: DOING GROUPS ONLINE
Yvette Colón

Computers are no longer remote or alien to many Americans. As new technology has led to an eruption of online communication, more and more people are taking responsibility for their own mental health care needs by using their computers to access the exponentially growing amount of information and experiences available on the Internet. Current and potential psychotherapy clients, along with psychotherapists and other mental health professionals, also have been involved in online discussion and therapy groups—shared spaces of written conversation and support—focusing on particular psychological topics. The Echo online groups have been a unique and creative approach to providing a clinical service in a direct, immediate, and non-linear way that conforms to the quickly changing paradigms of modern communication.

In 1984, I joined The Source, an early text-based commercial online service designed more for access to their information than for their purported online community. The Source offered nothing that captured my attention and my first foray into cyberspace was brief and unsuccessful. In 1993 I heard about Echo, an online community in existence for approximately three years. By this time I was a clinical psychotherapist with much experience in individual and group therapy. Echo founder Stacy Horn was looking for someone to facilitate a therapy group online, a repeat of a group that was conducted on Echo two years previously, and offered me the chance to familiarize myself with Echo before starting the group. I joined as myself and got to know the place. In early 1994, I opened a separate account and launched the experimental online therapy group. I facilitated a second group the following year. Since that time I have facilitated an online support group for cancer patients and started an online support group for partners and family members of cancer patients as part of my job as Program Coordinator of Online Services at a social service agency.

Prior to the creation of the first Echo group in 1994, I posted notices in Echo's Central and Psychology Conferences announcing the formation of Echo's experimental online therapy group. I stated that I was looking for eight people to participate in a three month experimental group therapy project. It was to be a private conference for group members only and they would be encouraged to shape and guide the group and its format. All e-mail was confidential as well.

Participants were required to respect the rules of confidentiality, commit to a three month participation, participate/post a minimum of three times per week and be willing to sign a consent form. They were asked to send e-mail to me with the following information: their real name, address, and phone number; previous group and/or individual psychotherapy experiences; topics and issues they wished to explore; and anything else they wanted me to know about them. Everyone was told that space was limited and I wouldn't be able to include all interested persons. Screenings took place solely via e-mail. By signing the consent form, participants stated that they recognized that online group therapy was an experimental process that provided them with relative safety and which might or might not help them in their face-to-face therapy. The online group would involve conferencing, interactions with the group leader and other members of the group, and some real-time conferencing, in which everyone was at their computers at the same time, "chatting" with each other much in the same way as a telephone conference call. They acknowledged the confidential relationship between therapist and patient and also attested to their realization that by using advanced technology, there was the potential that confidentiality could be broken and that their communications may be intercepted by persons other than members of the group—password protection notwithstanding. They also understood that online group therapy was an experimental process; no guarantees exist as to the therapeutic benefit which might or might not accrue as a result of participation. They were advised to consult with their present therapist, if any, about their participation in online therapy and either obtain their therapist's approval for participating in the experiment or choose to participate without the therapist's approval.

Once participants were screened and accepted, they were given access to the group on the day it was scheduled to begin. They then had access to the group 24 hours a day, seven days a week for three months. They were free to post whatever they wanted, whenever they wanted. Because anything could happen in any given 24 hour period, it was very important for me to log in every day—I did so in order to read, respond, and interpret.

The groups were primarily conducted in non real-time; that is, items were set up dealing with business and group topics and then each participant was required to open up their own item in which to discuss their issues. They were free to say as much or as little as they wanted in their own items and were encouraged to respond to others' comments and questions. In a sense, this had the effect of having multiple groups being conducted simultaneously while paradoxically maintaining order and continuity. There were real-time chats scheduled several times throughout the life of the groups.

Echo is composed of conferences. Each conference has a general name like Psychology, Culture, Health, Group. Within each conference are discussions, conversations really, about particular topics. These discussions are called items. Within each item are the responses people have posted throughout the discussion. This is what a participant would see when logging into the Group Conference for the first time:

```
**********************************************
** WELCOME TO THE GROUP CONFERENCE **

This is an experimental group experience.
Please feel free to share your feelings, thoughts, ideas &
      concerns.
**********************************************
```

The index ultimately would look something like this:

Item   1   Before We Begin
Item   2   Confidentiality
Item   3   Group Format
Item   4   Ground Rules
Item   5   Announcements Only, Please
Item   6   Introductions
Item   7   ** The Main Group **
Item   8   Group Member 1's Item
Item   9   Group Member 2's Item
Item 10   Group Member 3's Item, etc.
Item 11   Dealing With Anger
Item 12   Conflict
Item 13   Angst (Feel Free To Vent Here)
Item 14   Family Relationships
Item 15   Group Process
Item 16   Feedback

A group member could go to items 2 and 5, for example and read the openers and first responses:

Item   2   11-MAR-95 22:01 Yvette Colón, MSW
Confidentiality

Echo is a small and intimate community. For this reason, maintaining the confidentiality of this group is highly important and a requirement for participation. Please respect the confidentiality of your fellow group members, not only during the course of the group, but afterwards as well.

29 Discussion responses
2:1 Yvette Colón, MSW   07-FEB-94 22:03

FYI, your very membership in this group is confidential . . .

Item   5   11-MAR-95 22:19 Yvette Colón, MSW
Ground Rules
Here are a few ground rules. Let's discuss others you think
    are important.
Confidentiality must be maintained
Attacking others is not allowed
Please discuss everything IN the group
17 Discussion responses

5:1) Yvette Colón, MSW   10-FEB-94 19:02
    A group member just opened a new item (I happen to think it's a very important topic) and wondered whether it was okay to do that. I think it's fine, especially because the topic ties in nicely to issues in the beginning of our group.
    At the moment we'll all be making up the rules as we go along. However, if you have questions or wonder about opening an item, feel free to ask me or discuss it with the other members of the group. I'm open to any-

thing, but I want to keep things somewhat contained so that we don't lose the essence of the group.

At the beginning of the group, members go to the appropriate item to introduce themselves to the others:

Item   6   12-MAR-95 20:39 Yvette Colón, MSW
Introductions

Introduce yourselves here. Let us know who you are, how you got here, what you'd like to get out of the group and anything else you think is important.

30 Discussion responses

15:1) Yvette Colón, MSW   12-MAR-95 20:56
       I'm Yvette Colón, MSW, ACSW (e-mail: yvette). I got most of my undergraduate education in California and have a B.A. in Psychology. I have a Master's in Social Work from Smith College, class of 1990, and I'm currently enrolled in an advanced clinical social work program at NYU. Most of my social work experience has been in community mental health and hospital/health care settings. I've been an Echoid since March, 1993 and have facilitated the Group Conference before in 1994.
       I'm looking forward to seeing where this goes.
       Good luck—it's bound to be an adventure!

Compare and Contrast

In real life, therapy is time-bound. Once a week at a predetermined time, group members go to a physical office to meet with the group leader and the other members. They are appropriately discouraged from contact between sessions. The structured atmosphere of the psychotherapist's office will seem unfamiliar at first. Meeting in the psychotherapist's office precludes interruption due to phone calls, family demands, and friends' unexpected visits.

When clients sit across from me in my office, they are faced with quite a bit of information about me even without active disclosure on my part. They can see how I've decorated my office. They can make note of the pictures I've chosen to hang on the wall, diplomas and awards I've decided to display. Most can tell by looking at me that I am a bicultural/bilingual therapist; this will stir up any number of unconscious feelings, both positive and negative. They can conjecture that a significant number of my clients are Spanish-speaking only. I can see what they look like, hear what they sound like, listen to their narratives, and interpret their stories.

Assumptions are made on both sides without discussion.

Clients' physical responses, their very physical beings, are among the clues by which I gain information about their internal life. For example, a client walks into my office looking dejected, sits down with a weary sigh, and proceeds to tell me about the previous wonderful week. Another client may use loud, rapid, and pressured speech, yet claim to be calm. The clients' affects and words are not congruent. I can see clients in front of me struggle with dawning insight, try to hide barely contained rage, or make a valiant effort to put words to unknown feelings. Many men cannot openly speak about their sorrow or insecurity, but their body language might show it. Many women have difficulty showing anger or competition, but they may seem more distracted or nervous if confronted by the therapist. In real life, clients sometimes change the topic in an attempt to ward off uncomfortable feelings. The physical body gives itself away in subtle but unmistakable ways.

Unlike traditional face-to-face group therapy, the online group exists only in time and mind. It is available to participants 24 hours a day during its existence and provides instant access for members who want to post whenever they were reflective or mad or inquisitive or thoughtful. When a group member goes in and posts, there may be responses to those posts right away, in a few hours or in a few days. Most clients will go through their experiences without writing a book, appearing on the radio or television, publishing or leaving behind their stories. But on the Internet, people can leave behind a body of work, the narratives of their experiences, in a medium that is simultaneously vast and intimate. It's interactive and there is a captive audience.

The use of the computer can create an informal atmosphere for group members who are in familiar surroundings during sessions; this has both positive and negative aspects. For instance, the instant message function on Echo must be turned off when reading and posting in Group in order to avoid interruption. Group members must turn off their phones and television sets, rearrange family responsibilities, and discourage friends from making unannounced visits in order to come close to approximating the quiet, private setting of a therapist's office.

In contrast to face-to-face groups, online groups (depending on how they're designed) can sometimes offer an immediate feeling of safety that helps group members feel more comfortable. This can allow members to achieve closeness at a safe distance, resulting in their feeling less inhibited to examine aspects of themselves or issues that they might hesitate to explore in a face-to-face group. As a result, increased self-disclosure and bonding can occur earlier in the group process than in a face-to-face group.

It becomes important to differentiate between formal, structured, scheduled groups and informal, unscheduled, intermittent groups such as those held online. Continuity can be achieved more easily in an online group. Physical barriers are transcended and the traditional notion of physical community is challenged and expanded. Geographical constraints can be overcome without compromising group interactions and process. As a result, closely held assumptions about the way psychotherapy can be done are being altered. The group may also serve to diminish social isolation, anxiety, and depression. Online groups may make supportive therapy more attractive to clients who would not otherwise pursue therapy; online groups also offer privacy, informality, relative anonymity, and equality for some clients.

The ongoing themes and issues discussed in clients' virtual therapeutic communities reflect the concerns of real world communities: the emotional impact of the problems they face, changes in their relationships with others, loss, fear, isolation, and intimacy. The emotional and concrete issues discussed in these online groups are not so different from the issues that clients bring to sessions with psychotherapists: coping strategies, problem solving, loneliness, perseverance, and courage.

Transference/Countertransference

Transference and countertransference are important aspects of psychotherapeutic work. The very fact that these groups are held online can change the interactions. For example, because the group members and I do not see each other, members may idealize me or project their fantasies and wishes onto me. Because I am unseen and "mysterious," anger and frustration can be taken out on me more readily. Conversely, my idealization of and projection onto clients could be difficult as well. Because I often didn't know what group members looked like, it became easy to accept the personas they created as the group continued.

Private and public spaces intersect online in a way they don't off-line. Conducting these groups on Echo has created a unique situation in that I have been extremely active as both a user as well as a group psychotherapist. I strive to keep my two identities separate. This was a more difficult proposition in putting together the first group in 1994, especially because Echo is not an anonymous electronic bulletin board. Users may use "handles" (nicknames), but real names are a matter of public record within the community. I had met some of the group members during Echo social events and several of them knew both my personal persona and my professional persona. From the beginning it was impossible to remain a neutral therapeutic presence in the group; however, I tried to compensate for this problem by excluding anyone with whom I'd had any significant relationship, either through e-mail or posting. It did not seem to be an issue during either of the groups, the first in which several people knew of my dual identities and the second in which a few people knew.

The community-based nature of Echo highlights the dilemmas I face concerning my own position as a neutral authority in one space (on the electronic bulletin board) and not in others; I remain ambivalent regarding the coexistence of my multiple selves. In real life, there are moments when therapists and clients run into each other in professional and social arenas, but these moments can be brief and nonrevealing. I may engage in a quick conversation with or silently acknowledge a client while disclosing very little. In a text-based environment, my words as an active user are permanent unless I choose to remove them; any client can intentionally or inadvertently read old and new posts that reveal much more (personally, emotionally, intellectually) about me than clients usually know about their therapists.

On the other hand, I also have the advantage of knowing more about group members based on what they've written than therapists usually know about their clients after one or two face-to-face screenings. In the first group I "knew" many of the members because I'd seen them and read their posts for several months; in the second I had never met any of them, but still had the opportunity to read some of their posts before they joined the group.

However, I am always aware of what and where I post. I continue to post and be involved in the Echo community as my personal self and remain relatively quiet, a ghostly presence, as my professional self.

Why Bother?

The Internet has quickly become a new health and mental health care playing field. The culture of mental health care is being transformed by the emergence of Internet savvy, and by proactive, progressive, and empowered health care consumers. Online communities now exist for virtually every mental health concern. Clients and mental health professionals already share information about every aspect of mental health and illness, from finding and getting emotional support to solving practical problems. And psychotechnology has the potential to be a new way for disadvantaged communities to access mainstream resources. On the Internet, clients are redefining the traditional concept of care. One doesn't have to show demonstrable symptoms or discomfort in order to receive care. One doesn't have to post details, or post at all, to receive care. Clients can also be providers of care to others, by their words, experience, or presence.

Those seeking mental health care on the Internet have become active players in this new world. There are new technologies and new incentives for people to manage their own mental health care. What brings clients and psychotherapists together is credible information, a willingness to work together, and the belief that both client and provider input is necessary for the practice of good mental health care.

A growing body of research has demonstrated that clients who are involved with their own care have better outcomes than those who are passive. Psychotherapists must advocate—for unbiased quality—consumer mental health information with relevance to the individual client. They must share the client's perspective in order to contribute to this dimension of mental health care. Psychotherapist participation in the Internet mental health service and information world may also drive critical research issues.

Psychotherapists involved on the Internet can employ their clinical skills: They can act as a neutral authority; provide structure and information; promote cohesion; and read, respond, and interpret. They also will be challenged to develop new roles, new strategies, and new skills beyond support and psychoeducation.

Challenges

The biggest challenges I face as a therapist working online are the lack of both face-to-face contact and the non-verbal cues on which I ordinarily rely in an analogue setting. In a face-to-face group, I pay close attention to verbal and physical language, tone, inflection, and silences.

All of these things are absent in a text-based environment in which the written word can be stark and startling. In the absence of visual cues, how can I interpret silences when *everything* is silent? When I am in a room with a group, they can see that I am listening and can be encouraged to continue speaking with a mere look or a gesture on my part. In an online group, I am perceived as absent unless I post something. In group therapy, when clients are working well, the group leader's interventions are not necessary. In an online group, I must sometimes interrupt the flow of conversation by posting a response, however superfluous, in order to make my presence known.

We are all socialized in a society in which issues of race, culture, gender, and sexual orientation play an important part in the American psyche. Since the Internet appears to most as a predominantly white, male, Western, English-speaking environment, it is easy to assume that in an online group everyone is white, middle class, heterosexual, able-bodied, and American. Users are assumed to be white unless and until they announce otherwise (Asians and some Hispanics are interesting exceptions to this rule, in that they are often marked as ethnic by their names). It would be difficult to read race from the writing style of someone in an online group based on words alone. Online culture inherently demands that everyone speak/ write English and it blurs marks of difference like race, culture, and sexuality. On the Internet, geographical constraints can be overcome, but the issues of class, culture, and accessibility still loom large. I also wonder if I would experience the dilemma of neutral authority in a different way than, for example, a male psychiatrist because as an M.D. he is in a different class and has different gender markings than I do.

Although it may equalize relationships among group members, the question of access is never far from my mind. English is the de facto language of the Internet; therefore those who do not know how to write in English or who are not decent writers can be excluded. Becoming involved in online communities requires the luxury of time and money; those without either are marginalized yet again. Unfortunately, there are still limitations to clients and psychotherapists due to costs and the need for literacy and technical know-how.

My training has been fairly traditional and I use psychoanalytic psychotherapeutic models in my work. It has been a challenge to take what I know and apply it to this other medium. I would be very cautious about promoting online groups, or online psychotherapy of any kind, as the only form of therapy in which someone should participate. Psychotherapy in person is often based on many factors, including facial expressions, body posturing, vocal inflection, and, importantly, the relationship between therapist and client. Psychotherapy online is limited to one thing: text on a computer screen. We must find ways to explore online psychotherapy responsibly. Despite the numerous obstacles, all of the participants in the online groups I've facilitated have been enormously committed to the group.

Although there was a requirement to post a minimum of three times weekly, most group members posted every day, often long and thoughtful posts. They were extraordinarily committed to the group and many expressed sadness that the group had to end. Although conducting group therapy online is labor intensive and the group members and I had to connect through a medium that diminishes the senses, there seemed to be fewer emotional distractions.

Group members learned to trust each other and were willing to disclose more, making the therapy more in-depth. In online therapy, no one really comes to sessions late or doesn't pay. But resistance can manifest itself in many ways, through textual aggression or joking or silence. Psychotherapists can learn a great deal by studying the dynamics of online life. Repetition, recollection, transference, resistance, conflict, and acting out are all there. More to the point, perhaps, the single biggest thing online life can teach those in the off-line world is that language often can be more significant than action. In online therapy, and perhaps in the psychoanalytic session, language *is* action. Nothing "happens" online, or, for all intents and purposes, in therapy. There is no way to quantify what happens in an online group. And yet lives can change.

7

Virtual Facilitation:
Electronic Information and Referral,
Online Support and Self-Help

ELECTRONIC INFORMATION AND REFERRAL

Patrick is twenty-seven years old. He was adopted as an infant. Suffering from many of the identity issues common to adopted children, Patrick entered therapy. After several months, he and his therapist agree that he is ready to search for his biological parents.

Cynthia is a displaced homemaker. Two years ago, when she turned fifty, her husband left. Her two grown children were very supportive, but they were clearly involved in building their own lives. Cynthia has never worked outside the home, choosing to live a traditional family life. Suddenly, she is faced with life as a single woman, with no work skills and no idea what she might be interested in doing.

Twenty-one-year-old Bill has a college degree in liberal arts. He lives at home and works in a restaurant as a waiter because he can't decide which career direction to choose.

Catherine is a 44-year-old breast cancer patient. Twenty years ago, she had an argument with her sister and they have not spoken since. She desperately wants to speak to her again but does not know where or how to find her and is terrified that she might be rejected. Her therapist, sensitive to the issues concerning Catherine's illness, agrees that it is very important that she "make peace."

Patrick, Cynthia, Bill, and Catherine all share the need for information as part of their therapy. They need more than basic data—the information they seek will give them support and insight into their lives. Their needs vary: Patrick is seeking a biological identity; Cynthia has to adjust to an unfamiliar lifestyle; Bill must individuate and choose a direction for himself; and Catherine wants to resolve old issues. Clinical interventions of this nature ideally involve a combination of psychotherapy and information and referral. This can be swiftly and efficiently accomplished by utilizing the vast information resources of the Internet. Patrick, Cynthia, Bill, and Catherine are not actual cases but clinical models for interventions utilizing information and referral on the Internet.

The facilitation of information and referral is an important adjunct to therapy on The Online Couch. However, information exchange is both the Internet's greatest assets and greatest problem. There is a literal morass of information.

Consider some of the numbers. *WhoWhere?* (1997) offers over ten million e-mail listings, eighty million U.S. residential listings, and 500,000 personal home pages. *Alta Vista*, a popular search engine, has over thirty million pages indexed in their database (Grossan 1997). *Infoseek* (1997), self-billed as "proof of intelligent life on the net," receives over five million information requests per day from over one million Internet users worldwide. Information presents a formidable challenge in cyberspace. How do you wade through it?

David Filo and Jerry Yang, two Ph.D. candidates in Electrical Engineering at Stanford University, came up with a solution. They kept lists of their favorite sites on the Internet. In April 1994, they decided that their lists were far too long and difficult to use. So they developed software that would help them locate, identify, and edit material online. They named it "Yet Another Hierarchical Officious Oracle," or *Yahoo!* The two young men insisted that they were, themselves, "yahoos." *Yahoo!* quickly grew to serve thousands of users. Within a year, Marc Andressen, cofounder of Netscape Communications, enticed Filo and Yang to move to his company's larger computers, eventually making *Yahoo!* the number one ranked search and directory company (*Yahoo! History* 1996).

Yahoo! is one of a growing group of search engines or programs that are the digital equivalent to card catalogs in the library. Today there are more than 250 search engines on the net (Leonard 1997) with the most popular bearing names such as *Infoseek, Excite, Lycos, Alta Vista,* and *Webcrawler.* Search engines bring millions of hypertext pages into computers around the world, with text, images, and multimedia elements arranged in an accessible structure. Without these tools, netizens would drown in the flood of electronic information.

How can a clinician use these tools as an adjunct to psychotherapy?

Patrick is working through many of the issues surrounding his adoption. In the course of treatment he decides that it is time to locate his biological parents. Although he is not quite sure what he will do with this information, he knows it is time to start a search. He is reluctant to go directly to an agency that specializes in this area because he wants it to be a more private process. Patrick and his therapist tentatively climb onto The Online Couch.

Searches for adoptees, birth parents, adoptive parents, and siblings can be conducted through a variety of sites such as *Birthquest, PBN Reunion Bureau,* and *LINC Online.* They utilize a range of information—from family name, birthdate, last known address, and social security number. Patrick can also invest up to one hundred dollars to "hire" an online private investigator to search electronic databases with up to three billion different records. As Patrick begins to express more conflict related to his adoption, his therapist leads him to sites like the *Adoptees Internet Mailing List* and the *American Adoption Congress*, where he reduces his frustration and sense of helplessness by communicating with other adoptees or becoming politically active. This intervention enables his psychotherapist to provide concrete help while further exploring the deep issues that trouble him. Patrick is empowered to take control of his search and, ideally, locate his birth parents. The final decision to contact them belongs to Patrick. He also has the choice of contact medium—telephone, mail, or e-mail. Patrick's search for his biological identity is an intrinsic part of his psychotherapy.

Cynthia is terrified of computers. She knows that if she wants to enter the working world she must be computer literate. Her fears, fueled by the trauma of her divorce, have become overwhelming. She does not own a computer and is afraid that she might "break" any office machine she works with. Gently, her therapist introduces her to computers in the safety of the clinical office. She explains that Cynthia can't break a computer and demonstrates the many safeguards built into programs. Cynthia is surprised—she was terrified that her inexperience would cause massive electronic damage. Encouraged, Cynthia becomes more comfortable in the electronic environment. Her therapist takes her to the Internet, where she surfs to places such as *Project Succeed* and *New Beginnings*, two organizations that offer support groups, workshops, career development, job seeking skills, and retraining for displaced homemakers. Cynthia "looks around" in the safety of her therapist's office, learning that she is not alone in her search for a new lifestyle after twenty-five years of a traditional marriage. After several sessions, the therapist suggests that Cynthia explore the job market by browsing through Web sites such as *Careers OnLine*, *IntelliMatch*, and *The Monster Board*, which offer a wide range of information on careers, education, job searches, résumé building, and company information. Cynthia gradually feels that she has entered the information age and her fear of working outside the home diminishes. The process of overcoming her fears about the computer, "searching" the world, and examining her own needs serves as a model for future forays into working world.

Bill is having difficulty separating and individuating from his parents. He chooses to infantilize himself, working in a job that does not utilize his education or offer an adequate income to allow him to financially support himself. He is angry and frustrated over his continued dependency on his parents but afraid to venture out into a more independent lifestyle. As a recent college graduate, Bill is very comfortable with the computer. The Internet is a "safe" place where he can play, wander, and not affect his status in actuality. His psychotherapist uses the Internet as a familiar starting point to develop affiliations with young people in similar situations. They browse through *Planet Tripod*, talking about the articles, comments, suggestions, and lists for young people looking for their first jobs. They check out the local newspapers' classified ads online, discussing various jobs, what they offer, and what Bill might find interesting. They visit some of the same Web sites as Cynthia, discussing information about careers, education, job searches, job matches, and companies. Using a special program, they develop a résumé that highlights Bill's strongest assets. Bill is mildly surprised—he has not seen himself portrayed in that context. His first job applications are through Internet posts and electronic deliveries. As Bill moves into the next stage of his search—job interviews—his psychotherapist encourages Bill to generalize his behavior. They discuss corporate procedures, role play, and do online searches for information about the various companies where Bill is interviewing. During this process, Bill is encouraged to take control of his life, work through his separation anxiety, and look toward a more independent future. The Internet, as a familiar and "safe" environment, has facilitated engagement with his therapist, reduced anxiety over his job search, and served as a conduit to expressions of Bill's fears about separation and individuation.

Catherine believes that she must put her "affairs in order." Recently diagnosed with breast cancer, she is anxious, depressed, and suffering the physical and emotional side effects of chemotherapy. Her search for her sister reflects her need to take control over one part of her life as well as her fears over what she believes is impending death. Discussing how and where to search raises old unresolved family issues. Catherine talks about her mother's death from breast cancer and her fears for her own life. She recalls the argument with her sister and expresses regret over the lost years. She wonders if her sister also suffers from breast cancer. Her psychotherapist suggests that she can take control in a very concrete manner. They visit the Internet and browse through many of the sites Patrick visited, such as *PBN Reunion Bureau*. Similarly, Catherine considers online private investigative services. They try *WhoWhere* to see if anything is found under her sister's maiden name. In the course of their searches, Catherine's psychotherapist introduces her to the online support groups for breast cancer patients. Catherine is reluctant to try one in actuality, but online she can lurk, relatively unseen. Catherine learns that she is not alone—others share many of the emotions she is experiencing. Eventually, she decides to try a support group in actuality—a choice that will help her deal with the treatment and aftereffects of her illness. Catherine also finds many online advocacy groups, information about treatments, and research reports on all aspects of breast cancer. Like Cynthia, she is empowered to take control of her cancer. This serves as an adjunct to her search for her sister. When she finally locates her, Catherine and her therapist spend many sessions discussing the best contact medium. Catherine is afraid she might be rejected. Similar to Melanie (Chapter 3), she chooses a very safe e-mail dialogue. Her sister responds. They begin a gentle online reunion that eventually leads to a face-to-face reconciliation.

ONLINE SUPPORT AND SELF-HELP GROUPS

Blu877 has multiple sclerosis; KaY is struggling with infertility; FlipR does not know how to handle his overwhelming financial problems; and Jenn1288 just lost her baby to SIDS. Their issues are diverse and, to each of them, overwhelming. Yet they all have one thing in common—they have sought help from an online support group.

There is a proliferation of support and self-help groups in cyberspace. Netizens often find that they can easily talk about problems online that they can't confront face-to-face. Some believe that their difficulties don't warrant the time, money, or energy necessary for traditional individual or group therapy or regular support group meetings. Others are simply seeking information or companionship from peers immersed in the same specific set of issues. Whatever the reasons, people like Blu877, KaY, FlipR, and Jenn1288 are clamoring for online support, seeking others with similar agendas or creating new groups based on their particular problem. They often bring with them a bias that increases the probability of success: the belief that an online support group will be a caring, nurturing environment where they will find safety in people facing similar issues. Although there are no exact figures for the number of support groups on the Internet, various sites offer long lists of topics. For instance, *Emotional Support on the Internet* (Harris 1997) lists nearly three hundred different topics ranging from abuse to vitiligo (a skin disease) while *Support-Group.com* (1997) includes nearly two hundred topics ranging from Alzheimer's disease to time management, offering bulletin boards, online support groups, internet resources, and daily chat schedules. There are numerous mental health groups offering support, information, conferences, companionship, and a sense of community addressing almost every psychological condition suffered by humankind. In cyberspace, mental illness is not stigmatized the way it is in actuality. This is partially the result of the inability of others to physically observe psychological disorders in the electronic environment and the readily accepted disinhibited behavior online. "Normalcy" in the electronic environment has a far more flexible character with boundaries not set as rigidly as in actuality. In addition, anonymity provides the psychological freedom to take greater risks—whether one is the person suffering from mental illness or the person befriending him or her. Online mental health support groups range from general issues to the very specific. For instance, one can find many groups devoted to parenting, relationships, and issues such as developmental delays, disabilities, and abuse prevention. More specifically, there are groups that address depression, sexuality, and loneliness. Many groups focus on specific disorders—such as bipolar disorder, anorexia/bulimia, and social phobia. This list is long and constantly growing. If one can't find the right group, there is always the option to begin a new one. With so many people online, there is always room for a new group on a new topic.

The advantages are obvious: online support is low-cost, convenient, specialized, and can be an important adjunct to psychotherapy. Most people believe Internet groups are relatively secure. Individuals have the option to use pseudonyms, multiple pseudonyms, or simply remain unidentified through anonymous servers. Some groups request that people use their real names so as to be completely straightforward. Individuals who feel isolated or alone with their problems can find support groups that attract similar personalities, interests, or problems. In addition to emotional support, these groups offer a virtual well of information gleaned from personal experiences. Online, people are always willing to share what they know.

When Jenn1288 needs help at 3a.m. because she can't stop crying over the empty crib in the nursery, there are most likely others online who have suffered through the same heart-wrenching experience. When Blu877 is struggling with an MS exacerbation, or KaY has just completed another unsuccessful round of fertility medication, they can talk to others who know exactly what it feels like. Even FlipR can get helpful advice from other netizens on balancing his budget. It doesn't matter what time it is, where one is located, or the extent of geographical or psychological distance: Turn on the computer and there is always someone willing to "listen."

Support or self-help groups have played a significant role in mental health. In drug and alcohol abuse, most professionals believe that AA, Al-Anon, and ACOA are an integral part of the recovery process. It is estimated that these groups alone serve nine million to twelve million Americans affected by alcoholism (Phillips 1996). Traditional support groups give individuals the opportunity to join and participate in a process where they learn the behavior of others with similar problems, using interaction, information, and the incorporation of a group identity to motivate individual change. Groups nurture acceptable, universal behaviors with each member receiving support and encouragement in place of former isolation. Personal disclosure, expressiveness, and self-discovery are significant parts of the process. Individuals are validated and encouraged to experience the comfort and safety that emerges from group cohesion. What happens when this process is transposed to computer screens, keyboards, and lines of text?

In a presentation made at the Partnerships '96 conference, Tom Ferguson, M.D. (1996), Senior Associate at the Center for Clinical Computing, Harvard Medical School, and author of *Health Online*, said:

> Not all the interactions on the online support groups are . . . helpful and wise. But many of them are. I must say I've been very impressed by the ability of these online communities to provide high-quality information and support on both the emotional, and on the practical level. And they're often, though not always—quite impressive on a purely technical level. [p. 4]

Research tends to support Ferguson's statements. However, as discussed earlier, the methodology in Internet research is still being developed, consequently limiting the generalizability of results. A case in point is *Survey.net* (Perry 1996). *Survey.net* is a network of servers that polls netizens and generates all types of information concerning life in cyberspace. Survey information is automatically added to the data pool, generating immediate updated reports. Designed and maintained by Mike Perry, an independent software developer, *Survey.net* is accessible to self-selected, anonymous netizens on the Web. In the "Internet User Survey #2" (Perry 1997) begun March 21, 1997, and accessed May 31, 1997, there were, at that point, 865 respondents. The replies to the question "What do you primarily use the Internet for?" clearly illustrates why support and self-help groups proliferate on the Internet. 77.3 percent chose "communication/keeping in touch." Among the top ten choices were newsgroups, online chatting, meeting new people, and sharing interests. Other studies indicate that communication in an electronic support or self-help group setting is very beneficial. King (1994b) found that there was a positive correlation between the use of online support groups and improvement in a recovery program for addicted people. Similarly, in an analysis of an online support group devoted to sexual identity issues, King (1995b) concluded, "The growth of cyberspace support groups is paving the way for many who were without support for their feelings of gender incongruity by providing them the opportunity to reach out and type to someone. As a normative society, these groups function very well to help members place their individual experiences within the framework of others that have had similar life circumstances. The value of these groups as an adjunct to therapy needs to be recognized" (pp. 7–8).

An intriguing study conducted by Wende Phillips (1996) from Rider University compared an online chat group, online service e-mail group, Internet e-mail group, and a traditional self-help group that met in person. All four groups served adult children of alcoholics (ACOAs). Their organizations were extremely diverse. The chat group met on an online service for one hour, once a week. The group leader would "arrive," write an opening message, and discussion would begin. The meeting ended with the Alcoholics Anonymous Serenity Prayer, with most members writing "amen." In contrast, the online service e-mail list corresponded two times a month with three members taking turns to coordinate the list. Topics were posted and members would respond accordingly. The Internet e-mail group was similar except there were more members and topics were posted weekly. Phillips (1996) reached the following conclusions:

- online groups allow crosstalk, feedback, and advice-giving (this does not occur in in-person groups);
- the perceived anonymity online encourages individuals to take greater risks and makes individuals more likely to offer corrective or negative feedback to others in the group; and
- differences in communication between online and off-line groups decrease with time as online members ad-

just to lack of contextual cues by using symbols and different emphasis on their words.

Information and referral as well as online support and self-help groups can complement the psychotherapeutic process. They can also serve to help stabilize and maintain patients after treatment has been terminated. Part III offers a resource guide for clinicians that can serve as the means to establish a working base of Internet resources.

8

Reach Out and Touch Someone: Cybertherapy

The tools are simple: a computer, a good modem, and an Internet Service Provider. A website can be programmed, hosted, and publicized for the cost of a few sessions. The more enterprising cybertherapist can purchase a Web editor where he or she designs the site and the software automatically generates the program. For a few more dollars, a Web advertiser will promote the site. The cybertherapy website can be designed to be colorful, animated, and spiced with soothing sound bytes. Quiet dignity is usually preferred—the virtual equivalent of a clinician's office decorated in subtle colors and calming images hanging in frames on the walls. Put it all together and the cybertherapist is in business—with no requirements for licensing, training, certification, or education. It is called, among other appellations: online counseling, cybertherapy, e-therapy, or any combination of words that includes general psychotherapeutic terms. In other words, it is mental health's unregulated, highly disputed leap into Internet mental health.

What is a cybertherapist? It seems like a simple question but it is perhaps the most difficult to answer. Many argue that cybertherapy—or therapy conducted only through electronic devices—constitutes any clinical process that occurs in the electronic environment. Obviously, that would include telephone sessions—a relatively common practice among clinicians. Others insist that it is limited to the technological boundaries on the Internet—boundaries that expand and change each day. All agree that it is a new, tenuous modality that can stray far afield from traditional clinical practice.

In today's electronic environment, cybertherapy is a telehealth (see Part II), grassroots mental health movement in cyberspace. Unwilling to wait for more sophisticated technologies that will provide faster connections, better security, video conferencing, and standardized professional services, the cybertherapist has emerged in an electronic environment rich with self-help, support groups, and peer counseling. The ability to seek out others of similar tastes, interests, disorders, or fears enables virtual communities or populations to readily establish themselves. With asynchronous communication (the ability to communicate in one place at different times) and the belief that e-mail is secure and confidential, individuals are encouraged to share deep emotions. Perhaps the most powerful incentive to building a cybertherapeutic practice will be managed care, with its shrinking coverage, suffocating regulations, and "de-professionalization" of mental health services. Consider what has already happened in online mental health:

- Articles on "cyber-therapy" have appeared in the leading U.S. newspapers, including *The New York Times*, *The Los Angeles Times*, and *USA Today*;
- *Mental Health Net* and *Metanoia* have established an online verification center to check the credentials of therapists practicing in cyberspace ("Credential Check" 1997);
- *Online Psych*, located on *America Online* and the Internet, offers more than 50 scheduled chats per week and three chat rooms open 24 hours a day for peer coun-

seling. Its peer counseling message boards had over forty thousand posts in a ten-month period (Cohen 1997);

- *The Directory of Internet Psychotherapists* (Ainsworth 1997a) lists over 60 people providing ongoing e-mail or chats, single, in-depth responses to a one-time question, and single, in-depth responses to a one-time question in a specific subject; and
- Professional fees for cybertherapy vary from approximately $1.50 to $2.50 per minute response time or $20 to $25 per e-mail.

The cybertherapy practice is a multidisciplinary, multimodel system that covers a cross-section of mental health professionals, information, and services. Describing it, in its present state, is a difficult, ethically slippery undertaking. Essentially, cybertherapy involves communication between people, with one person taking the role of a mental health professional. Ideally, the mental health professional has training, education, and credentials appropriate to the state in which he or she is operating. However, psychotherapists online are as unregulated as the Internet. The cybertherapist does not have to hold credentials—or post any information if he or she chooses. In other words, on the Internet, anyone can hang out a shingle. *The Directory of Internet Psychotherapists* (Ainsworth 1997a) lists seven providers that netizens must be "cautious" about, with infractions ranging from lack of mental health credentials to unacceptable security. For example, "Sigmund" (No date) offers "therapeutic and life-enhancing services" from a "therapist in the field of mental health for many years" (pp. 1–2). No additional information is given about credentials. A two-way e-mail interaction costs $20—a service geared toward "normally functioning adults" who are having difficulties.

The concept of cybertherapy is so new and tenuous that there is not even a standard term to describe the interaction between a mental health professional and an online "patient." So perhaps it is easier to define what the virtual clinical practice is not.

Most online credentialed mental health professionals agree on one critical point: at this time in technology, cybertherapy is not psychotherapy. Psychotherapy involves both verbal and nonverbal communication. It relies on the process of developing a relationship. Computer mediated "counseling" does not replace psychotherapy in actuality. There are no visual cues, no audio cues, and no sense of touch, smell, or physical proximity. Text can carry great emotional impact, but it does not impart a similar sense of sharing a "safe" environment, where the living person is present. Help is not available immediately— responses come in twenty-four to forty-eight hours. There are many legal, confidentiality, credibility, and accountability issues that are regulated off-line and left untouched online (Ainsworth 1997b).

What actually happens in the virtual clinical practice? Ainsworth (1997b) refers to cybertherapy services as "interactions" or "internet mental health services" because the popular terms, such as "consultation" and "advice," "fail to fully capture the depth of humanity, interpersonal relationship and healing which *can* occur" (Ainsworth 1997c, para. 4). In contrast, Leonard G. Holmes, Ph.D., webmaster of *Shareware Psychological Consultation* (1996), views it as simply a way to gather information from an expert. He suggests that managed care has made it particularly awkward to get psychological help. Consequently, an online consultation offers the opportunity to receive helpful information without having to undergo traditional psychotherapy. Holmes offers e-mail consultation that cost $1.50 a minute. E-mailers can request that the doctor limit his time to fifteen minutes. Follow-up questions are acceptable and telephone consultations are also considered.

Evidently, e-mail is presently the technology of choice in online consultations. Other modes are also used, although not as frequently. For example, private chats serve as a more immediate forum. However, they are limited in the amount that can be written and the exchange is often awkward. Some therapists use systems such as *America Online*'s Instant Messages, where text can be sent privately, in real time, between two individuals. But *America Online* is notoriously unreliable and at any given moment a user can be tossed off-line. Obviously, these kinds of interruptions make real time psychochats capricious and undependable at best. Some websites, though, also offer forms that potential cyberpatients can complete and e-mail to the therapists.

Ainsworth (1997d) identifies two categories of online services: single interaction and ongoing interaction. She compares single interaction to a "psychological Ann Landers," wherein the therapist receives a question or problem and e-mails back with customized information or solutions. This type of interaction is suited to troubling problems that are not overwhelming or the cause of serious dysfunction. Ongoing interactions involve the formation of an electronic relationship with a trained mental health professional. It takes time, and repeated contacts, utilizing a process that Ainsworth (1997d) describes as "closer to what might happen if you met with a psychotherapist in an office" (p. 2). Ainsworth (1997b) stresses that people experiencing any sense of urgency, if they are in crisis or are having suicidal thoughts, should "get off the computer and pick up the phone" (p. 1).

It is apparent that all people are not candidates for cybertherapy. Individuals must own or lease a computer. (They can, however, access a computer through a library, school, or community center.) People must be fairly literate—able to express their feelings in words, willing to be honest with themselves, and not afraid to take the chance of an online security breach. The ability to type, write clearly, and compute are obvious prerequisites.

Keep in mind that virtual clinical practice includes more than individualized consultation. There are numerous quasitraditional forums, such as support groups and self-help, with both peer and professional facilitators. There are also highly innovative, creative modalities that are providing experimental virtual environments. Some offer therapeutic support within a fantasy, game-playing, or constructionist environment. Perhaps these are the tools of tomorrow's virtual practice. A case in point is a "game" called *The Couch* (1996).

Ralph Allora (1997) refers to *The Couch* as "true confessions, flatiron style." *The Couch* is a simulation of a simulation, a stylized psychological house of mirrors. It is an online drama series, soap-opera style, that was launched in January 1997. It takes place in Manhattan's Flatiron building where eight people are arranged on a virtual group therapy couch, led by a silent psychotherapist named Zeke. Updated daily, the serial unfolds in weekly group sessions, personal diary entries from each of the participants, and liaisons between members who meet outside the group to talk and scheme. The opening page states clearly, in insolent white letters on a black background, "We want love, success and power but our neuroses get in the way."

Allora (1997) reports that there are blurred boundaries between the characters and the writers/performers. Often, it is difficult to tell the difference between fact and fiction. This is compounded by the fact that visitors to *The Couch* can do much more than read—they are invited to enter the community discussion forum appropriately titled "Transference." In Transference, a fan can break down the barriers between "audience" and "authors" by becoming a *couch transference head.* Transference heads can be part of online discussions with the characters or with one another in topics that develop naturally from the ongoing dialogue. "Plug into Transference," Allora (1997) writes, "and you'll become aware that visitors react to the characters not as fictionalized inventions but as the real people behind them" (p. 50).

Is it gaming, role playing, or a form of online psychodrama? Or is it a peek into an alternative mental health future?

The Couch is not the only forum experimenting with new forms of electronic mental health services. Amy Bruckman's (Bruckman and Resnick 1995) *MediaMOO*, launched on January 20, 1993, was designed to created a virtual professional community in a text-based MOO. Cyberspace home to some one thousand members from twenty-nine countries, *MediaMOO* was intended to act as a forum for the casual conversation, sharing of ideas, and collaboration that spontaneously occurs at a professional conference. People meet one another, share workshops and lunches, and a social exchange occurs. In these informal interactions, people of similar interests have the opportunity to share their experiences and thoughts as well as their own special interests. *MediaMOO* was formulated for multidisciplinary researchers in media, including anthropologists, broadcasters, computer scientists, cultural studies researchers, historians, interface designers, journalists, librarians, linguists, network administrators, psychologists, sociologists of science, teachers, and virtual reality researchers. Members must be actively engaged in media research and are required to fill out an application to join.

> The world of MediaMOO is continuously being constructed and reconstructed by its members . . . people learn with particular effectiveness when they are engaged in constructing personally meaningful projects; learning by

doing is better than learning by being told. We have found that letting the users build a virtual world rather than merely interact with a pre-designed world gives them an opportunity for self expression, encourages diversity, and leads to a meaningful engagement of participants and enhanced sense of community . . . . MediaMOO challenges the boundaries between work and play, forcing one to rethink what counts as productive. [Bruckman and Resnick 1995, pp. 1, 6]

MediaMOO members create objects, build offices, and go to virtual places that reflect their cultural and intellectual diversity. In this manner, there is an ongoing exchange of ideas in a virtual community setting. In the same way, Bruckman (no date) created *MOOSE Crossing*, a research project of the MIT Media Lab. Children aged thirteen and under meet from around the world, learning reading, writing, and programming. They "build new places to hang out, and program cool objects to play with" (p. 1). They construct things such as a robot that asks people questions, an elephant that tells elephant jokes, and forests, swamps, or discos. "The world of MOOSE Crossing is built by kids for kids" (p. 1).

Cybertherapy is obviously in its infancy. It is a modality yet to be clearly defined, ready to be modified and expanded by skilled psychotherapists pioneering a new form of treatment.

9

Voices in the Circuitry: Professional Connectivity in the Electronic Environment

WITH DEAN ALLMAN

My patient's managed care company has been taken over by a larger corporation. I am not on the new provider panel that is listed as "closed." What can I do?

Medicare has changed their codes. Anyone know the latest for individual psychotherapy?

A former patient has joined my community church. How do I handle it?

My patient is moving to another state. Can anyone give me the name of a psychotherapist that specializes in grief and loss?

I am treating a child with Turner's Syndrome. Any suggestions?

How many psychotherapists do you need to change a light bulb? None. Managed care doesn't cover it.

I'm conducting research on Internet relationships. Anyone have any suggestions on how I should set up the questionnaire? Do I need informed consent?

These are some of the subjects exchanged on professional online sites. Mental health professionals, particularly those in solo practice, have long complained of feeling isolated, unconnected to their colleagues. Although workshops and conferences allow professionals to socialize, it is time-limited, unable to offer regular contact not strained by daily obligations, competition, or professional jealousy.

Professional connectivity refers to how mental health people are meeting online—discussing issues that involve them personally as well as professionally. The range of subjects varies as widely as the participants because these online forums are designed to provide a space where individuals can speak openly about their concerns, their achievements, their interests, and even their jokes.

Probably the best way to "observe" professional connectivity off-line is through the story of how one list was developed, from concept to action.

John Augsburger, LCSW, was chairman of the NetWorks Committee of the *Clinical Social Work Federation* (CSWF). The *Clinical Social Work Federation* is a confederation of thirty-five state societies for clinical social work. The state societies are organized as voluntary groups that promote high standards of practice in clinical social work. State societies and the national federation are actively involved with advocacy and lobbying, generating clinical research, and providing professional training and publications.

In 1995, Augsburger had an idea: create an e-mail list to notify CSWF members about what is going on in the legislatures, how to alert others, and how to keep in touch with one another. He believed that it would be an excellent way to communicate with one another in an organization whose members live across the entire U.S. His idea was an innovation in social work—it would be nearly two years later before NASW (National Association for Social Workers) would attempt an online presence. Augsburger's plan appealed to the CSWF, and he was given the approval to set up a comprehensive web site that received the *Mental Health Net* four-star award for excellence. In October 1995, the Board approved his plans and the website and e-mail list went online.

Augsburger began with two separate e-mail lists: one for members of CSWF and a second list for board members. As the website developed, he helped individual state societies set up their own web pages (linked to the Federation) and state e-mail lists. In addition, he received e-mail from around the world—countries as distant as Australia and Japan—with requests varying from basic information to how to set up schools of social work. The website grew quickly—it now offers, along with legislative and organizational information, a search function, help line, chat, Code of Ethics, law/forensics page, and access to several CSWF publications including *Managed Care News*. Augsburger estimates that he works at least twenty hours a week maintaining the site and responding to e-mail.

The clinical list began with fifteen members in 1995. Augsburger chose to apply social work group skills in its development. "I wanted the list to belong to the group, not to me," explains Augsburger. "So I backed off so the members would take ownership. It needed to evolve—to find its own purpose" (Personal communication, June 3, 1997).

Slowly, the list took hold. Community values began to emerge—the list was seen as a safe place for social workers where members treated one another with respect. Inevitably, one member began to test the waters. He started to flame. "I watch and read," says Augsburger. "When something has to be stopped I will step in. So when the flaming began—people were slurring one another—I had to make a rule: we don't fight, we discuss. That solved the flaming problem very quickly."

Today the list has grown to nearly three hundred members.

Dean Allman, LCSW, was one of the original CSWF list members. He has addressed both state and national audiences on the various uses of the on-line medium. When he is not in front of the computer screen, Dean reports that "I really do have a real life."

In preparation for a presentation to the membership of the *Colorado State Society for Clinical Social Work*, Dean posted a message on the CSWF mailing list requesting feedback regarding use of the Internet in social work practice. Responses to the request were varied and fascinating, and are listed below, followed by his comments:

> I am new to the Internet, but I think the possibilities are unlimited. It is helpful for me to be able to communicate with other clinical social workers nationwide about issues and frustrations that we share. I would love to be able to engage in continuing education on the web. To be able to discuss case presentations, to get feedback, and to network would be very helpful for me.
>
> *John Sivley*

* * *

> Some of my patients use the Internet for a variety of e-mail communicating. I have made selective use of e-mail with several patients by suggesting and accepting e-mail messages when they need to "talk." I have also initiated e-mail messages to two of my patients during particularly difficult times, offering encouragement and support by letting them know I was thinking about them. These communication alternatives have been beneficial and well-received by the patients.
>
> As far as the Web is concerned, I am doing some professional marketing in the Oakhurst area (near Yosemite), where I have started a weekend practice. I will be getting on-line with an Internet service there. I will also explore having my own web page
>
> *Robert Tabak, LCSW*
> *California*

* * *

I thought I would take this opportunity to say "Thanks" as well as share my thoughts. As a usual "lurker" I have found this list to be very helpful. The info you and the other contributors provide is always timely and important. I think of it as a specific news service with a personal touch, delivered to my e-mailbox, without commercials!

The information shared about many topics, the case consultations that occur . . . are extremely helpful and exciting! I haven't been able to contribute more due to lack of time, but I promise to jump in occasionally.

Bill DeLeno
New York

* * *

I work on newsletters, and I do a lot of research—most of it online. This is accomplished in two ways. The first, of course, is researching sites, topics, companies, individuals, ideas, etc. through various locations on the web. Because it is so far-reaching, I have even investigated business, legal, political, and government points of view. Equally helpful are the contacts I have made online. Each time I needed information I posted it on the Clinical Social Work Federation list and had people responding from all over the country. In this way, I was able to get a handle on what was going on 3,000 miles away as well as in my own state. The dialogue on Clinical Social Work Federation list has enabled me to listen and speak with people. I have met many colleagues and made many e-mail pals through this process. I felt isolated as a private solo practitioner. With the Internet, I have never felt more connected.

Jennifer Mutaran
Arizona

* * *

I think the subject of your presentation is exciting and frankly, I never imagined the possibility of using the computer to the extent that I now do. Although, it hasn't been helpful in terms of private practice . . . it's been extremely helpful in providing a sense of "community" with my peers. It's great to be part of a dialogue that's focused on my professional identity. It's rare to be part of the kind of humor, innuendos, and information that I've been privy to as part of the clinical mailing list.

One of my patients, who will be moving out of state, was very hopeful about the possibility of staying in touch via e-mail. I interpreted this as a defense against the process of terminating, so I did not encourage it.

Luba Shagawat
New Jersey

* * *

. . . I make my e-mail number available to clients. Many of them use it to communicate with me around scheduling, practical questions, and ideas. Many clients like the freedom to communicate their thoughts about sessions between sessions. They can do this any hour of the day and post their thoughts. They know I will read them and either respond right away or have their thoughts in mind during our next session. Members of my three groups especially like this—in one of the groups, all are online and they post on a forum between sessions. I also use e-mail as a form of narrative practice in which clients post letters to parents and I comment and make suggestions for revisions. I haven't thought out all of the transference implications of this. I have one client who lives in another city and comes to see me every few weeks. He e-mails messages from time to time. His work takes him around the country and I get postings from various cities.

As yet, I don't charge for telephone or e-mail service. I charge group members a monthly fee and perhaps I could, in the future, present e-mail availability as part of the group service. I don't do e-mail billing yet, but it is an appealing idea. Of course, the opportunity to communicate with fellow professionals is wonderful. We are at the edge of the revolution in communication and, unlike the engineers, we actually have much to communicate about.

Joel Butler
North Carolina

* * *

I have only recently joined this list. I find many of the postings informative, especially in the areas of legislation and managed care. However, I find it very time consuming to look through all the postings. Rather than have my name removed from the list I have become discriminating in what I read and I delete the rest. I am saving postings on the above-mentioned topics in a file on e-mails, hoping that if I need to find something I will be able to locate it.

Marcia Bernstein, LCSW, BCD
New York

* * *

I have been more informed on managed care issues as a result of my participation on this list. I have also been able to access and utilize a number of therapeutic web sites. I listed my practice on a site I learned about on this list. I also signed up for 2 continuing education courses with Psych Broadcasting Corp distributed via e-mail.

I have printed out a number of items from the list and shared them with colleagues at work. It has been helpful to bring up practice issues and receive responses from so many fellow professionals. I find that the only messages I don't read are the unsubscribe ones. :)

Nancy Riggins-Hume
California

* * *

Some things I use the social work list for:

1. The use that I find most helpful, are all of the listings of news articles that are relevant to our work. The fact that members forward things to us actually saves me the time of looking for things. I then send them on to the list that the CT Psychotherapists' Guild has for its members.

2. Keeping up on legislative issues and then through the Federation website being able to write to congressional representatives with such ease is terrific.

3. Thinking about clinical issues that others bring up. Even when you don't actually respond, but just lurk, you can have a good experience.

4. Staying in touch with people I work with on various committees. So much easier than six phone calls.

5. Getting other relevant postings from other lists.

Generally, with a minimum of effort, I feel much more informed. Also I get great consultation on computer and Internet issues.

Maria
Connecticut

* * *

I use the internet in two main ways—one, as an additional library resource/search engine from the Web's regular sites; & two, as a means of staying in touch with what specific colleagues are saying—through listservs like this one. The latter is harder for me to keep up with, but cer-

tainly has potential to influence my practice in a variety
of ways.

Already, I've put out requests and gotten information back, given feedback to others, and so on. I think it
has the potential to bring clinicians generally to a more
cohesive position—hopefully NOT too homogenized however.

I am also finding I correspond with colleagues,
friends on the Internet more readily than by mail . . .

Ann Aukamp, MSW, BCD, CGP

* * *

Not only do I use the Internet to gain knowledge as a clinical social worker, but the lists I am on have provided
connection and community in ways I couldn't have fore-
seen in my previous lower-tech life. I have really appre-
ciated the information listies post on managed care, privacy of information, new legislation, and I have received
helpful consultation in a couple of cases I was concerned
about, details of which I put on the list when asking for
help.

The wealth of information shared on the list has
helped me see what others are doing/struggling with and
encouraged me to consider my own options. I am going
to continue doing therapy, but make it a smaller part of
my day and add more musical performance to the balance.
Actually I believe this shift has already made the therapeutic hours I engage in even better as I continue to find
the right balance for my energies, as I believe that who I
am as a therapist is a major healing component of the relationship. Thanks for asking.

Stefani Cochran
Virginia

* * *

The Internet has proven to be a valuable tool for many social workers. Several respondents remarked on the sense of community that is fostered by the 'Net. E-mail in particular is being used in a variety of ways. I once made a remark to an on-line friend that e-mail was almost like writing to a journal that talks back to you. It is hard to imagine another intervention at the moment that has such potential to bring people together, with the possible exception of video conferencing. It raises the question—is the use of e-mail an adjunct to psychotherapy or can it be viewed as a therapeutic intervention in and of itself?

One major goal of psychotherapy is to provide support to others in times of crisis or prolonged periods of struggle in one's life. Many of the responses to the post here have identified the sense of connection one experiences from the on-line experience. If these goals can be met via an on-line experience, is this not what we seek to establish with our clients in social work? It is mildly ironic that a technology that a lot of people feared would result in isolating us from one another has actually resulted in a stronger sense of community for many, many people.

The arrival of this new technology challenges previously held assumptions about the framework of psychotherapy. Traditionally therapists sit in offices and chat with folks—hoping that they will somehow integrate what we discuss in-between sessions. We believe in setting appropriate boundaries with our clients—indeed, in many ways the setting of boundaries is seen as necessary in insuring that our clients will develop a strong sense of self.

But in some ways this framework can be viewed as a compromise between the needs of the client, the needs of the therapist, and the intentions of the insurance company. It is simply impossible to be available to clients at all times.

Something like e-mail offers an opportunity to step out of that box, if you will, and gives us an opportunity to provide support (and objective guidance) in a more immediate and ongoing way. Up until now, the telephone has been used for such purposes, but there is something more powerful about on-line communication. It provides a more immediate opportunity for deepening the connection between therapist and client. As new technologies emerge, such as video teleconferencing, this challenge to the framework of providing psychotherapy will broaden and continue.

It will be important to develop guidelines for therapists as this process continues. As previously stated, the on-line medium is a very powerful means of initiating and promoting connection between people. The popularity of chat rooms on AOL attests to a human longing for contact. As clinicians using and experimenting with this medium, what are the boundaries that we should be concerned with? When do we say it is okay to continue this relationship via this means versus viewing an e-mail connection as a means to avoid the pain of terminating a therapeutic relationship? What do we do if a client begins to abuse e-mail—filling our box with post after post that says very little but speaks to emptiness or longing that our client is struggling with? What if we are corresponding with a client out-of-state, and they become suicidal? Is it legal, therapeutic, and/or ethical to maintain contact with patients in another locale? In essence, what are the boundaries in cyberspace, how do we set them, and how do we ensure that what we are doing is indeed helpful to our clients? These and other questions will likely occupy the attention of psychotherapists for some time to come.

Dean Allman, LCSW

10

Propriety on the Online Couch: A Discussion of Ethical Guidelines for Virtual Therapy

STORM A. KING AND
STEPHAN TED POULOS

The Internet currently hosts millions of online users throughout the world, and its use is growing at a tremendous rate. Some consumers are using their Internet connection to seek professional guidance, support, or therapy. Mental health professionals worldwide are pioneering new services that offer to establish a therapeutic relationship over the Internet, sometimes on a fee basis. Existing ethical guidelines proposed by the American Psychological Association (APA) do not specifically address what constitutes responsible ethical conduct for licensed clinical psychologists who are engaged in such activities. Although the APA has formed a task force to make recommendations for such a guideline, to date there is no precedence the professional can rely upon. We will review the current information available and discuss the APA ethical guidelines and how they might apply to the use of the Internet in establishing therapeutic relationships by e-mail.

ETHICAL GUIDELINES FOR ONLINE THERAPY

The purpose of designing ethical guidelines is not to set rigid codes of conduct but to inform the professional as to what structural parameters of behavior are acceptable to one's peers.

"Ethical codes, which have been described as moral guides to self-regulation, attempt to insure the appropriate use of skill and techniques" (Keith-Spiegel and Koocher 1985, p. 2). While this tends to create an environment whereby the consumer is theoretically assured of minimal risk, an ethical guideline designed and drafted by professionals cannot help but be somewhat self-serving. Ethical guidelines and standards of conduct do not necessarily address the power differential inherent in therapeutic relationships and tend to be reactive, not anticipatory (Prilleltensky 1997). "Any set of suggested guidelines . . . will seem to over-simplify the nature of the problem they address" (King 1996a, p. 199). In particular, ethical guidelines for online therapy are yet to be clearly distinguished (King 1996b).

Given the anarchic nature of the Internet, whether or not Virtual Therapy is something that can be prohibited is already a moot point. Mental health professionals as far away as Australia can counsel a disturbed client in Belgium using e-mail as the method of communication. Licensed mental health professionals have Web sites that offer expert advice and counseling for a fee (Hannon 1996, McKeon 1997). If the payment of a fee is evidence that a professional relationship exists, then clearly some guidelines for ethical behavior ought to be defined in order to both protect the client as well as provide some framework in which professionals can offer services.

A recent survey of online professional advice and counseling efforts show that consumer satisfaction with online services is high. An initial pilot study was done by King, where recipients of online services answered questions relating to various aspects of their experience with an online professional. Of the recipients (N=30), 76 percent reported that they felt that the online therapist truly cared about them; 69 percent felt it was worth the expense. Only 14 percent had any ethical concerns about the treatment they received. These results indicate significant consumer satisfaction with online professional mental health treatment (King 1997). It is clear that the use of online therapeutic services will continue to grow according to the growth of the Internet itself.

There is a list of cybertherapy sites at http://www.cmhc. com/guide/cyber.

APPLYING APA ETHICAL PRINCIPLES
TO VIRTUAL THERAPY

Competency

The first and foremost ethical concern which arises out of a communication so "anonymous" in nature is that while one professional may be able to determine the educational background and competency of a peer, a typical online consumer may not. There is currently nothing to prevent anyone from asserting online that they are competent mental health professionals. Likewise, it is not difficult to perceive the potential for harm to an unwary consumer of these services. Whether or not the definition and professional limitations of such roles as counselor, therapist, and psycho-educational information provider have been determined by a professional standards board, the typical online consumer may perceive any of these definitions as being one and the same. However, existing online psychological service providers are not currently subject to verification of their professional status, nor is there any process for review and quality control. "The ease of communications provided by the Internet allows anyone to put out information of any sort" (Huang 1996). The consumer does not have the benefit of seeing a "shingle" hanging above the door. The Web site maintained by the online professional is the only way the consumer can determine an actual, or virtual, "location" in cyberspace. "A poorly informed consumer in crisis who has a history of mental health difficulties will be an easy target for incompe-

tent or fraudulent Internet counseling service providers"
(Sampson 1997a).

Integrity

As a means of providing self-monitoring some mental
health professionals are suggesting a service that would allow
consumers to verify the credentials of anyone offering mental
health services online. Recent discussions on the NetPsy online
group have been exploring the potential for the use of an electronic signature as a foolproof method of credential verification (Maheu 1997). This is in keeping with the APA principle
concerning the need for self-regulation (APA 1992).

Professional and Scientific Responsibility

Professional psychologists will consult with, refer to, or
cooperate with other professionals and institutions in order to
serve the best interests of their patients, clients, or other recipients of mental health services (APA 1992).

Today's online professional has been thrust into an arena
where the written word is *determined* to be evidence of the
quality of one's professional expertise. Voice tonality, pitch,
and timbre—all good qualities in telephone communication—
will no longer apply where e-mail and online conferencing are
increasingly commonplace. And with the advent of real-time
chat groups, avatars, and two-way cameras, virtual therapy is
upon us (Poulos 1998).

Respect for People's Rights and Dignity

In a survey of APA members, the most frequently reported
ethical concern had to do with issues surrounding confidentiality (Pope and Vetter 1992). It is impossible to assure confi-

dentiality in an online professional relationship when electronic communications are unsecured. In addition, the permanent record that online communication presents has created new potentials for violation of privacy. For example, a client's spouse might access, whether intentionally or not, a file of e-mail communications that were intended to be confidential. Methods of encryption and password protection should be standard practice for the consumer and the professional.

Concern for Others' Welfare

It is hard for some practitioners to show proper concern for someone in a text-based relationship. So much depends upon one's experience with the nuances of online communication. It is critical that a psychotherapist who considers offering online mental health services must be experienced with text-only based relationships. The potential for misunderstandings when people communicate solely by e-mail is considerable. In using text-based environments for therapeutic programs, some important considerations are worth bearing in mind. One concern with online support services is the potential for clients to devalue communications which appear on their computer screen.

Many people are well-equipped at communication by telephone, or even letter writing. Not all, however, are adept at writing with the intent of disclosing intimacies previously unexpressed. Text that is conversational in nature, as it exists on the Internet today, may appear colder and more impersonal than the author intended. Most people have the impression that written text represents the well-thought-out and carefully edited views of the writer; however, online communications are often the product of someone "typing off the top of his or her head." The reader may interpret these messages as being the writer's firmly held thoughts and feelings. Some research on understanding the psychological effects of substituting written word with verbal conversation has been done (Goode and Johnson 1991, King 1995).

Part of being experienced in online communication is understanding the increased potential for projection and transference in the client/therapist relationship. Because of the lack of visual and auditory clues in electronic communications, there is a tendency to idealize the other "writer." Each person will naturally use his or her mind to fill in the missing clues in the written words. An intensification loop can develop where a cycle of "behavioral confirmation and magnification" may occur.

It is well accepted that, off-line, we respond to others based largely on our expectations, despite their actual behavior. At the same time, when disconfirming social data are less available—and what does occur is selectively sent and selectively perceived—the reciprocal process of behavioral confirmation may be more likely. Such a process as this may explain how such surprisingly intimate, intense, and hyperpersonal interactions can take place. Computer mediated communications (CMC) provides the intensification loop (Walther 1996).

Social Responsibility

According to APA guidelines, psychologists "apply and make public their knowledge of psychology in order to contribute to human welfare" (1992). Online psychotherapists often include on their websites a wealth of information about psychological disorders and their treatment. This psycho-educational service is available to the public twenty-four hours a day, can be accessed by anyone—not necessarily a client—and is generally provided free of charge. To those people in geographically remote locations, online therapy may be the only psychological therapy available.

CURRENT EVALUATIONS OF ETHICS
AND VIRTUAL THERAPY

James Sampson, in a recent article titled "Counseling on the information highway: Future possibilities and potential problems" (1997b), outlines many of the ethical concerns that online therapists must consider. Sampson addresses confidentiality and writes about data storage. He suggests that securing data, preventing unauthorized access to it, and educating therapists about appropriate security measure are central issues. Sampson states that clients who receive information by computer tend to *believe* that information. Therapists are therefore obligated to ensure the validity of the information they present to the online community. If a therapist is working with a client in a remote location, then the therapist should be aware of local conditions that exist which may impact on therapist–client relationship. These may include natural disasters or political unrest. Local cultural norms vary also, and unawareness of these differences can be problematic. For example, traumatic local events may exacerbate a client's reaction to work and family stressors. "If a counselor encounters an unanticipated reaction on the part of the client, the counselor needs to proceed slowly, clarifying the client's perceptions of their thoughts, feelings, and behavior" (Sampson 1997b, p. 210). Sampson further stated that credentialing concerns are unresolved at this time, and it is not clear how any enforcement of credentialing requirements would be implemented.

The National Career Development Association Ethics Committee has a draft version of proposed ethical standards for those who offer counseling services over the internet. The draft lists the following responsibilities of the online counselor in his professional relationships:

> To communicate to the client the member's credentials and experience; the limitations of their skills; the limits

of confidentiality; the need for release of information; the length of time communications will be stored; and the potential need for making contact by telephone when appropriate;

Finding and presenting a local referral to the client in case of the need for crisis intervention;

Proper screening to insure that online counseling is appropriate;

Proper follow-up of any self-help assessment measures used;

Assuring that only current valid and relevant information is posted to the website associated with the counselor's service;

Assurance of the validity and relevance of any information derived through links to their own website;

Obligation to be aware of local conditions, cultures, and events;

If the client is not benefiting from the counseling delivered over the Internet, then the counselor has a responsibility to intervene by telephone and/or make an appropriate referral;

If the member provides counseling they must have an appropriate credential for independent practice; and

The client must be provided with an e-mail address or a website of the credentialing association that provided the counselor's license so that unethical online behavior can be responsibly reported. [Bloom 1997, April 15]

SUGGESTIONS FOR APPLICATIONS OF ETHICS IN VIRTUAL THERAPY

In 1995, the APA Task Force on Ethics adopted a statement referring to the practice of therapy as conducted over the

Internet. It reported that there has been no research done as to whether or not a psychologist can be licensed in one state and provide services over the Internet to someone residing in another state. No mention of the concerns about the international nature of Internet services was made.

We propose that the online community be classified as a "special population" similar to the ones prescribed as requiring special consideration when conducting research, for example, prison populations and people unable to give fully informed consent. If such were the case, then online psychologists would be licensed by a local credentialing agency and be certified by an association that specializes in online therapy services. Just because a method of delivering therapy services is new does not relieve the therapist from ethical guidelines (Hines 1994).

CLIENTS UNABLE TO PRESENT FOR TRADITIONAL TREATMENT

Computers can be valuable tools for counseling and conducting surveys about sensitive topics. There are many situations in which people are anxious to cover their true feelings and opinions (Sproull and Kiesler 1995, p. 133). There is a well-documented disinhibiting effect that occurs in text-based relationships (Walther 1996). This disinhibiting effect can be utilized by online therapists. Clients have been reported to reveal things by e-mail that they were unwilling to share in person (Sellu 1996). Some clients with certain psychopathologies—such as Avoidant Personality Disorder—may well benefit from e-mail therapy used in addition to traditional therapy.

CONCLUSION

The information revolution continues to bring changes to the manner in which people are able to communicate with each other. Future trends in interactive therapeutic contact will most certainly utilize real-time video connections. Currently, e-mail exchanges offer an alternative for a transformative relationship, but the exact manner that these relationships can be ethically implemented is not yet well-researched. Once a professional relationship has been established, the licensed mental health professional has a responsibility to the welfare of the client. It is unclear how this responsibility can be executed completely by e-mail. However, e-mail therapy is already occurring, and it behooves the profession to examine the pros and cons inherent in this new medium. Clear ethical guidelines need to be developed for online therapists. Future research on outcomes of "e-mail" therapy is required in order to fully understand the true scope of the ethical considerations. One thing, however, is clear: of the millions of people who regularly log on to the internet to seek information or to socialize with others, a small percentage will be concurrently suffering some kind of emotional disturbance. These people are likely to seek assistance online.

Psychotherapists who respond to this need are obligated to share information and research results and to conduct themselves in as ethical a manner as possible.

11

Dr. Rob's Story: A Day in the Life of a Virtual Clinician

ROB BISCHOFF

With today's online estimates of 30 million to 50 million people and 10 million different hosts, it is easy to forget that barely a decade ago very few people had even heard of the Internet. When psychotherapist Rob Bischoff went online in the early 1980s, it was a very different electronic landscape. The term *Internet* was used for the first time in 1982, when the loose connection of networks in the ARPAnet was first seen as a "network" of networks. There were fewer than one thousand hosts. It wasn't until 1984 that the term "cyberspace" was adopted from William Gibson's book *Neuromancer* and applied to the growing electronic environment. There was no World Wide Web, no graphics, and no multimedia.

Today, Dr. Bischoff's Internet is a very different virtual place. He is a leader in mental health online. His "day in my life" provides us with valuable insight into how computers helped shape our past, how they assist us in our current practices, and how they will inform our future. But let Dr. Bischoff tell the story . . .

A DAY IN MY LIFE: 1996/1997

Ever meet a computerized shrink? Let me tell you what my life is like.

Years ago, the very first thing I did each workday morning was to make a fresh pot of French roast coffee. Today, the process is slightly modified. First I flip the switch on my computer and then stroll off to the kitchen to begin a java preparation ritual. Having been awakened by its switch, my Pentium-166 MHz computer moves swiftly through a hardware check, making sure that all 32 megabytes of RAM are intact, the 8 speed CD-ROM drive is operational, the 28.8 BAUD modem is alert and talking, the HP-4c color flatbed scanner is alive and waiting, and the sound card and speakers are chirping. During the boot up, the Pentium is also aware of the IBM Voice Type hardware card and runs its diagnostics, readying it for a day of voice-activated dictation. It's a bit different than simply brewing some coffee.

It all began back in 1983, when John Doonan, a good friend of mine, invited me to his home to share his prized new computing machine, a *Commodore 64*. I was really curious about the new machine. In those days, there was much talk about computers. Movies like *Tron* and *War Games* and media hype about hackers and phreakers breaking into government computers, driving the phone company absolutely crazy and putting great stress on the legal justice system, were stimulating curiosity. Predictably, I was intrigued by John's tiny machine. We proceeded to play a computer text adventure game named *Zork*. My images of huge computers that filled entire rooms with thousands of punch cards flowing like a raging paper river through hundreds of gears and gizmos were shaken. How could this computer be so interesting, challenging, and *small*? Suddenly, my fascination was muted. I felt an overwhelming sense of apprehension—rapidly approaching fear. Maybe I would do something "wrong." Maybe I would break my dear friend's new "toy." Maybe I would be too stupid to figure it out and feel hopelessly inadequate.

The fear never totally subsided. In subsequent years, new software, operating systems, and computer models—particularly those with less-than-friendly parts—have intimidated me. I have been unnerved by the intangible nature of the information entered into the computer. When you create something with a typewriter, you have a tangible end result: real paper with words. It's highly unlikely that it will disappear suddenly into the ether, stealing hours or even days of work in the process. A computer demands much greater faith. The development of trust, through understanding and learning about "those television typewriters" helped me overcome many formidable barriers to electronic information.

John and *Zork* had me off and running. I was determined to have my own computer. In 1983, the prevailing wisdom for the correct way to purchase a computer was to first define the task, find the software to do the task, and then buy the computer hardware that would run the software. Actually, this is still a good piece of basic wisdom, since needs identification is almost always the best place to begin. My first thought was that I had always hated the idea of paying a bookkeeper to do the highly repetitive task of balancing my books and completing monthly insurance billing forms with mostly identical information. I wanted software that would do this for me and save a good deal of money in the long run. I quickly recognized that I needed to educate myself on the fundamentals of computers.

My coffee is brewing and my computer has also completed its morning ablutions. It's time to log in and check my electronic mail account. I use a local ISP (Internet Service Provider) that charges a flat rate of $30.00 per month for unlimited connect time and a variety of services which allow me to run my own Web site (different from a Web page).

Thirty-five e-mails are waiting. Only half of them really interest me. A few of my friends have written since last night. The remainder of the e-mail is from a variety of listservs, users of my Web site who are looking for answers to questions about psychology or computer use in mental health. There is even some advertising from a few online companies where I have accounts. I always look forward to their product notices.

My friend Sam Gabby, a school psychologist in Wisconsin, has e-mailed me to say that he and his wife are coming out to California for vacation. They want to hook up with us, see the sights, and stay at our home. I quickly consult my old fashioned "paper" *Week-At-A-Glance* to avoid any social collisions. Sam's dates are fine. I hit the reply button on his e-mail and dash off an enthusiastic note confirming his visit. The next e-mail is from a couple whom I'm currently treating in my private practice. She writes that they are in the final throes of publishing the second edition of their book and must meet some deadlines. Can they please reschedule their appointment for later in the week? I check my appointment book and confirm the change. I move on to a message from a listserv (online e-mail conference line) for the Rorschach list. I had asked a question about a particular scoring on a protocol. The answer is in the e-mail. It saves me a phone call to a local colleague. The remaining e-mail is from other lists discussing Internet addiction, treatment of a child who had been electrocuted, and the latest in electronic gizmos. There is also an invitation from Ivan Goldberg to join him in the "online lounge" of *Psycom.net*. I like Ivan. He is also one of the "ancients" who have been online for the better part of twenty years. Ivan started the highly acclaimed online site *Depression Central.* His energy and enthusiasm have always been an inspiration to me.

It wasn't always that easy.

In the early days of PCs, it was a very lonely existence for a mental health professional who was interested in computers. One of the original reasons I started my BBS (Bulletin Board System) was with the hope that I would meet other mental health professionals online.

For many years, I searched the telecommunications land-scape looking for other mental health types who shared my interest and enthusiasm for computing. It took several years before I found Sam, in Wisconsin, along with a psychiatrist in New York, a psychologist in Nashville, Tennessee, and a neuropsychologist in Indian Springs, Alabama. We were con-nected through the budding telecommunications services of the day: *CompuServe*, *Delphi*, *American Peoplelink (PLINK)*, and *Genie*. I still value these friendships today, over two decades later. Yet I have only met one of these men in person. I also made many friends with other general computer users from all walks of life—from welders to college students to cops—and have enjoyed every moment.

In those days, the Internet belonged to the military and academia. It was called ARPAnet. Bulletin Boards were one of the most popular ways to communicate. Sam, like me, was an avid BBSer (Bulletin Board System user). He had found my BBS, *ShrinkTank*, through Ed Delgrosso's *Black Bag* BBS. Ed, the psychiatrist in New York, was one of the few national sources of information in the medical and human services area. Today, Ed still runs the *Black Bag*, with an awesome collec-tion of program and text files for downloading.

Communication was different, too. If a user were too shy to page me for a chat, I would often receive e-mail with spe-cific questions. Since there were many users who could log in under pseudonyms, I also had available a forum for mental health questions both on *ShrinkTank* and another BBS called *The SharksHead*, where I was a remote SysOp (System Op-erator). In these online forums, users would leave questions for me to answer. Many others would comment and continue a par-ticular line of questions. Questions about sexuality were always a favorite followed by questions about dating and self-esteem.

Finished with my e-mail, and eagerly awaiting my first cup of coffee, I start my ritual backup of files from the past twenty-four hours. All it takes is inserting a tape into the drive. One should always back up all files (actually it only involves backing up modified or added files) on a daily basis. You never know when someone is going to send you a virus. It happened to me last week.

I have used the computer for years to test, research, and create my own testing and interviewing instruments. Only last week I sent a young man off with a diskette containing several programs that do the testing and then encrypt the data when completed. This enabled me to conduct tests out of the office without compromising the instruments or having the subject see the results without professional supervision.

The testing was completed and the diskette returned via snail mail. I put it into my computer and *McAfee*, my fairly sophisticated virus monitor, blasted me from the screen: The NYB or B1 virus was attempting to contaminate my system. I had several options, so I took the most obvious—I ZAPPED the little intruder, or, in more proper computer-speak, cleaned up the mess. There went another little nasty virus, written by a testosterone-driven pubescent, into an electronic black hole. I quickly consulted the *Symantec* online database and found that this particular demon virus is fairly common, doing little but annoying the end user. With this in mind, I e-mailed the young man and told him the disk was infected and that he should warn the owner of the computer he used to do the testing that the system was contaminated.

It was also in the 1980s when I began to clarify some of my interests outside direct clinical practice. I felt the need to do more than engage in long and detailed discussions about computers and their myriad applications in clinical practice. I knew that computers could be used to help a great many people. You see, after I figured out how to do my insurance billing, I picked up the manual for the Commodore 64 and realized that it had some native abilities when using the built-in *GWBASIC* language. For example, I typed on the screen the following:

```
10 PRINT "Hello World"
20 GOTO 10
```

When I pressed the RUN command key and "Hello World" quickly streamed down the left-hand side of the screen, I was delighted! From *GWBASIC*, I moved to *Microsoft BASICA*, and then to *Borland*'s fledgling version of *Pascal* (a more structured programming language), and finally to *Borland*'s attempt at declarative languages with *Turbo Prolog*. Since those early days of learning by reading weighty computer reference books along with and trial and error research, I have acquired two U.S. copyrights—for my own billing program, *The Office Manager* (TOM), and *Knowledge Base*, version 2.0 (which is now at version 5.0). My current interest is in object-oriented programming and *Borland*'s latest incarnation of *Delphi*, version 3.0. Writing programs has helped me to better understand the computer's capabilities and allowed me to make the machine do my bidding. I suppose it's no surprise that I don't really care for computer games. However, John still keeps on trying—he only recently gave up on buying me a computer game for my birthday.

Ahhh . . . the smell of the coffee has made its way into my office, and I move like a heat-seeking missile for the kitchen to enjoy my first java of the day. On the way upstairs to deliver a cup to my bride, I pause to send the computer on another remote mission of collecting data from my Internet Web site. One can create what are called scripts or batch files that will put a computer through its paces in a variety of ways. This particular script logs into my Web site, downloads an ever-appending list of users who have visited my site, and then loads the results into my word processor for viewing. Knowing where people have been visiting and what pages they tend to choose is valuable to me in a variety of ways.

By the time my wife has finished her coffee and I've shaved and completed dressing for my trip to the office, the computer's task is done and waiting. Meanwhile, there's some more e-mail. The wife of the couple I mentioned earlier has written back, confirming their appointment and thanking me for allowing them to reschedule. About half of the people I see in my clinical practice have e-mail and prefer to use it for scheduling or asking questions between sessions.

I log off the net and use the modem to do a few lesser-known, but equally powerful, functions. The first is to use *PCAnywhere* to log in at the hospitals where I consult. I will download the latest testing files so I can review them and advise the staff later in the week. This process is automated. It's a simple one-keystroke command and the log-in is complete, the files are transferred, and the working files at the remote computer (in San Jose—a city 12 miles to the south) are cleaned up. The computer logs off the remote, directs the archive to be opened, and prints everything on my Canon Bubble Jet printer. I smile, even now, as this program runs, remembering how much time this has saved me over the years—as well as enabling me to be more productive. I stuff the printouts into my bag and I'm off to the office.

Now, don't think I turn off the computer. There is still more remote work to be done while I'm seeing patients at my clinical office across town. I have scheduled a facsimile (FAX) to be sent to a physician with whom I'm working on a case. He will be returning a color scan by facsimile. Since my printer is a color Bubble Jet, this will be a snap to print.

The "good" computer is in my home office, but I have another in my clinical office for word processing, accessing the net and my other phone networked computers. I prefer to do my psychological and other computer-based testing in my clinical office (the young man mentioned earlier is the exception), and today I have a new patient to whom I administer a few tests to screen for depression and chemical dependency. He arrives, and the testing takes about twenty minutes, during which time I walk to the post office down the street and retrieve my paper mail.

After several hours of seeing patients, I make a few telephone calls before returning home for lunch. The telephone numbers are stored in my automated database of addresses and phone numbers (which moves easily between my computer and hand-held organizer). I hit AutoDial, and the computer does the dialing, including the long distance carrier designation when needed. One of the calls is to Norm, a colleague who is having me train his staff person in the use of data mining on the Internet. This is a fancy way to say that I'm instructing her in the art of searching the net for the vast amount of information that's readily available on almost any topic. I'm reminded of the *Yellow Pages* ad that goes, "If it's not in the Yellow Pages, it probably doesn't exist." Well, this really applies to the net! I return Norm's call and agree that I'll e-mail him a copy of the information about professional online search engines, the free *MedLine®* search engine, and the *Dialog* search service. There are many different ways to go about using these search tools. Each one carries a different price tag, ranging from free to $25.00 per hour. It's important to know which is which.

Once at home, I cut and paste the URL (the equivalent of an address) for the various sites to an e-mail to Norm and I send it off. Recalling that a friend of mine is relocating and looking for a job in California, I run *Web Compass* to find several good Web sites which deal with both employment and location. Sending off e-mail to these sites via their Webmasters, I ask for some assistance. When it comes back, I'll send the information to my printer and put it in the mail. Unfortunately, not everyone I know owns a computer or has e-mail.

On the drive back to my office, I think about a program on which I have been working for the past several years. It's a computer program that will allow anyone who is contemplating entering psychotherapy to first check their symptoms against an extensive database of many medical illnesses which usually present first as psychiatric disorders. There are a wide variety of physical problems that can cause the symptoms associated with depression and anxiety. I'm working with *Delphi 3.0*, a development computer language, which will make this program a reality. The key to any program is in the planning and logic, hence there is a long gestation period for ideas in my "other" computer—my brain.

Back in my clinical office, I learn that the fellow who owns the test publishing house back East has finally had a chance to examine one of my computer programs and is interested in contractual talks. He has e-mailed two sample contracts for me to review.

They will have to wait for a real-time conversation with my friend and financial advisor—over dinner and after a detailed discussion about our son's new girlfriend. I'll have to get back to him later. I send out a quick e-mail, copy the message back to myself at my home computer, and print out the contracts. I send a copy of the contracts to an attorney friend of mine. It's now time to begin seeing my afternoon patients.

When my clinical hours are complete, I return home to find the facsimile from the doctor. I send it to the color printer and wait expectantly to see what a P.E.T. scan looks like when printed on my bubble jet. The scan is a cross section of brain from an A.D.H.D. young man who had a paradoxical calming response to stimulant drug. While that's printing, I knock out a few e-mails, scan some color photos for use on my Web site, and make notes on the program I was thinking about earlier in the day.

ANATOMY OF A VIRTUAL PRACTICE

There are many different ways to utilize computers in clinical practice. Here are some of my primary uses:

Self-Referral for Psychological Testing

I have had a number of individuals refer themselves to me after reading my curriculum vitae on my Web site. Two recent self-referrals involved a man who wanted an evaluation and recommendation for clinical depression and another who was interested in pursuing a psychotherapy relationship.

Therapy

Virtual practice can enhance communications through writing online, risk taking, and chats in virtual environments. There are a number of patients with whom I have used the BBS and later e-mail or other Internet functions. I find that this encourages patients to both communicate with me as well as others in writing and to take more risks. This can be of tremendous therapeutic value. There are also some dangers inherent in this process. One must keep in mind that an online professional contact might be supportive and encouraging but it is, by no means, "therapy." When it comes to offering advice on psychological issues, I would, in almost every case, attempt to refer the individual to a community resource for follow-up evaluation and possibly therapy or counseling.

E-mail Contact for Support and Scheduling of Patients

This is an obvious application of the net. I schedule and reschedule patient appointments, give support, answer quick questions, and provide information to patients through this medium.

Communications with Other
Mental Health Professionals

Here is just a brief list of some of the different ways to communicate with colleagues:

- Listservs;
- Online chat or forums in secure chat rooms;
- Private or "moderated" lists with specific focus, neuropsych, MMPI; and
- Rorschach and similar lists.

WHAT DO PEOPLE SAY?

Here are a few examples of actual online advice requests:

Correspondence 1

Dear Sir:

I am not sure whether this question is appropriate to ask in this forum. If it is not, I would appreciate your directing me to a more suitable resource. I am talking with a close friend who is undergoing tremendous stress at this time which involves the loss of a spouse about 10 months ago and several upcoming "anniversaries" that naturally are triggering her emotions even further. I believe that she is going through the grieving process in a very healthy manner, although she is somewhat embarrassed sometimes when she gets sad and cries. But I am not terribly concerned with her grieving. What I am concerned about is her reluctance to take care of herself in terms of getting enough rest.

* * *

Correspondence 2

Hi, my name is X and I'm taking a psychology class at the Community College and I need to find a psychologist with a masters or Ph.D. and ask them a few questions (that would be you:) Well, on to the questions . . .

What is your current job?

If it's not as a psychologist then how does psychology relate to it?

Which psychological perspective do you believe in? (like behaviorism, cognitive, etc.)

What is the most important thing psychology has done for you?

What is the most important question that psychology still has to answer?

Thank you for the help.

* * *

Correspondence 3

Dr. Bischoff:

I am a graduate student at West Virginia Graduate College, and am ready to start working on my thesis. I am having a great deal of difficulty coming up with an appropriate topic. Would you have any ideas/suggestions? thanks

* * *

Correspondence 4

Subject: OnLine Search of Psych Abstracts?

Hi: Found your "name" & adrs on Usenet and thought you might be able to tell me of a resource for searching Psych Abstracts (esp. 1955–1972) on line and at little or no cost.

I'll appreciate any help you might be able to provide. Peace.

X

Professor of Psychology

* * *

Correspondence 5 (e-mail from a past patient)

Subject: help!

Robert,

Hello again.

I know e-mail isn't a regular channel of therapy, but I've got to ask for your help with something. Twenty-four hours ago I was the happiest man alive . . . I enjoyed my work, my friends, and the young lady I was seeing. Well, last night I went to pick her up for a date and the first thing she said when I saw her was that while she was away in Nevada for the past week she wound up getting close to this guy she knew from college. She said she wasn't sure how close or serious I wanted to get with her and she didn't mean for it to happen but the two of them just fell in love and became very close in that short amount of time. So, naturally, we are now "just friends" which is KILLING me because I had such hopes for us. The clincher is that she said if she just would have known how strongly I feel, she wouldn't have let anything happen with that other guy. Why am I always a day behind on these things??? I remember someone's advice: find out where you're going, then find out who you'll take with you. How can I calm down and deal with this?

I appreciate any cybertherapy you could provide. Thanks.

* * *

Correspondence 6

Subject: Anxiety disorder
To: wizard@shrinktank.com
X-URL: http://www.shrinktank.com/

Hello Doc! I am a 44-year-old woman and have experienced anxiety disorder for most of my life. The person I am living with has little or nor patience with this basically because she can't understand fear. Any useful suggestions??

MOVING ON . . .

Some of the men I mentioned earlier also did programming. For instance, Sam Gabby in Wisconsin and I collaborated on various projects over the years, using my BBS as a transfer point for sharing code. More recently, I do my programming with engineering friends who work as professional programmers and have a local group of friends and business associates who have formed Therapy Enhancement Associates (TEA). We have been developing instruments which will be presented to the world market via the Internet fairly soon. If you check my Web site, *ShrinkTank* at http://www.shrinktank. com/tea.htm), you'll see how some of my ideas have found their way into reality. I am also one of the founders of Psyjourn, Inc., specialists in computer-assisted psychotherapy aids, at http://www.psyjourn.com.

Now the really exciting stuff is just around the corner with the advent of virtual reality (VR). At the VR World convention in San Jose, California, in April 1997, the hardware is still woefully inadequate or prohibitively expensive for the kinds of neuropsychological tasks I have in mind. Only the U.S. Government can afford this technology right now. In the future, VR can be used in mental health for treating phobias, performing complicated diagnostic tasks by coordinating bio-measures with psychological parameters, and treating stress disorders. But new and wondrous capabilities are not without their price.

I have some very strong concerns about how this technology will impact on people. What kinds of problems will emerge in addition to the wonderful tools that will be created? Problems with compulsive behavior, addiction, social and emotional isolation, and machine obsession can easily surface. As neuroscience becomes even more adept at mapping regions of the brain, when the feedback loops are better isolated, and the hardware becomes more sophisticated, I see the potential for more people to opt for relationships with their machines rather than the more difficult, inconsistent, selfish, and moody people who might be in their lives. As sound is better incorporated into the VR experience, the emotional connection and dependency will grow to awesome proportions. The need for real-life connections will diminish. Sensory and intellectual experiences designed and delivered endlessly and without hesitation by the computer will tear at the need for real-life relationships. Egocentric needs and desires will not have to be mediated by the individual and satiation will be delivered automatically. In this information age, conscious experience will be for sale and the neurochemicals in the brain will be manipulated for profit. Heroin, cocaine, and other potent drugs will be completely unnecessary and "black market experiences" will be for sale through your phone line. The power of these experiences will be mind boggling. My notions about using the computer to design the most potent phobic response object by reading bio-measures while presenting various shape, color, or texture, objects in real time could be used to enhance and sharpen other physiologic responses. The possibilities are enormous. Virtual reality—and the future—can be both blessing and abuse.

And so, another day in the life of a computerized shrink draws to a close. When I operated the twenty-four hour Bulletin Board System years ago, I would not think of turning my old 386-workhorse computer off at the end of a day; however, my pet Pentium receives its well-deserved rest. Reversing the switching order, I begin the shutdown sequence, which ends with *Win95* telling me that it's safe to turn off my computer.

As the after-image fades from my monitor and the power supply fan whirls in an ever-decreasing pitch, I think about my productivity, my patients, and most of all about my friends. I am grateful that the computer revolution has continued to bring fascinating people into my life, allowed me to be more productive with each passing year, and given my imagination so much space in which to run about. I worry some about the future and hope that I am truly up for the challenges that I'm sure I will face—but my excitement and curiosity will have it no other way.

PART II

QUESTIONS AND ANSWERS FOR EMERGING TREATMENTS IN PSYCHOTECHNOLOGY

Part II is an introduction to the new inquiry of psychotech-nology. It is arranged in a question–answer format that ad-dresses the essential issues. Obviously, an important role of any inquiry is to reflect both sides of the argument. In this primer, *Cyberlibertarians* represent advocates who tend to speak about the positive effects of the electronic environment, predicting greater equality, widespread global access to democracy, im-proved social relationships, and a "brave new world" of unlim-ited human potential. They are named for the liberals in human society—the individuals who are deeply committed to free choice, free will, and social, political, and economic equity. In contrast, *Cyberluddites* reflect an important adversarial role. They are named for the Luddites, a group of skilled craftsmen in England who, in 1812, physically attacked the machines they felt were threatening their livelihood. Cyberluddites talk about things such as the dangerous scattering of self, identity, and privacy. They suggest we are entering a precarious psychoso-cial environment that threatens to remove us from physical and spiritual life. They warn against the substitution of virtuality for actuality. Both Cyberlibertarians and Cyberluddites have much to say. Likewise, both sides are a little right and a little wrong. As in any human environment, the truth is found primarily in the gray areas where boundaries are blurred and accurate forecasts painfully difficult to make.

What is Psychotechnology?

Psychotechnology represents a new phenomenon in search of an identifier. The concept of psychotechnology emerges from the need to describe and codify human behavior in the electronic environment. It constitutes a "new" psychology, where patterns of interaction evolve from electronic concepts rooted in simulation. Commonly used terms such as community, self, and identity take on new meaning when paired with virtual, online, or electronic. Our roles as individuals, community members, netizens, facilitators, and mental health professionals shift along with the often tenuous landscape of cyberspace. Understanding why the words "psychology" and "technology" originally emerged and where their combination will take us is perhaps the best definition of psychotechnology.

Psychology began as the combination of two disciplines: philosophy and physiology. Since the beginning of civilization, philosophers have been exploring the human condition, questioning emotions, thoughts, and behavior. Similarly, physiology had been slowly offering a new way to look at the brain, the nervous system, and how they affect behavior. The combination reflected a natural marriage of ideas (Dworetzky 1985). The result was what *The American Heritage Dictionary* (1995) defines as a science that deals with both human mental processes and behavior.

Today, "psychology is a large, sprawling, confusing human undertaking" (Leahey 1987, p. 3). It emerged as a discipline separate from philosophy in the late nineteenth century. William Wundt and his contemporaries were searching for a way to utilize the empirical methodology of the natural sciences in answering philosophical issues of the mind. Wundt established a psychological laboratory in Germany to study conscious experience. Using a machine he called the "thought meter," Wundt attempted to measure "the time of the swiftest thought" (Dworetzky 1985, p. 9). In the century since Wundt's research, psychology has "sprawled" across countless theories and systems to explain consciousness as well as the unconscious, building a vast body of knowledge that complements many human disciplines.

The concept of technology is somewhat harder to define. The need for a new term emerged in the nineteenth century during a period of enormous mechanical invention, including such things as locomotives, streetcars, the transition from iron to steel, and vastly increased mechanized factory production. As a construct, it is a neonate in the history of humankind.

Technology initially referred to the practical arts or applications of scientific discoveries (Marx 1997). Physicist and philosopher of science Stephen Toulmin (1990) proposes that it was the result of "revolutions in natural sciences and history" where Newton's science and Descartes philosophy created a "world of physical theory and technical practice" (p. 15). The idea of technology raised the status of mechanical invention, applying an abstract concept to a very practical, concrete process.

Obviously, the concept of technology existed long before the word. Armed with a new way to describe the human condition, many historians began to view human development as the story of technological progress. Technological time periods are identified, such as the Stone Age (stone tools), the

Bronze Age (bronze tools), the Industrial Revolution (machines), and the Information Age (computers). Yet technology involves far more, reflecting human innovation as well as the re-weaving of social realities, the demand to adapt to technologically new environments, and revising of such seminal questions as how, where, and why we live together.

Arno Penzia, nobel laureate (1997), remarked in his keynote speech at the New School for Social Research symposium on *Technology and the rest of culture* that technology is essentially the use of organized knowledge, a specific body of information produced to solve whatever problems we have. Technology tends to move relatively slowly, garnering information from scientific discovery. Although computer technology moves at a breakneck pace, it actually reflects an evolutionary process, albeit rapid, that began in the 1950s. Ironically, technology represents the best—and worst—of human endeavors, with medical "technology" sitting in the same category as nuclear bomb "technology."

How does "technology" mix with psychology? As history has so clearly demonstrated, dramatic changes in technology lead to dramatic changes in human behavior. Consider the impact of technological innovations such as the invention of writing in Mesopotamia, circa 3000 B.C.E.; the Greek discovery of using marble columns in architecture, circa 5 B.C.E.; James Watts' construction of the first steam engine in Scotland during the 1760s; and Alexander Graham Bell's telephone in 1876. What would life be like without that technology? Present-day technological innovation in the Age of Information has nurtured a population of potential "cyborgs" created from both physical and psychological mergers with machines. Along with this new exposure to cybernetic experiences come psychological changes—significant alterations in how we view our objects, our realities, and ourselves.

The need for a psychotechnology is now upon us.

Is Psychotechnology Actual or Virtual Reality?

Humans create, adapt, and eventually create-to-adapt. If this is possible in both *actual* and *virtual* reality, then inevitably we arrive at the question: What is reality? An anonymous post made on the Internet states it succinctly:

> I don't like to relinquish or cancel my reality, but I don't like to reveal it either. Instead, remaining faceless is very safe.

Humans have been trying to determine the nature of reality since their brains developed the capacity for abstract thought. One of the most significant separations between human and animal is self-consciousness and the subsequent awareness of existence. People know that they are alive. Thinking, acting, and feeling are a uniquely singular experience. It is as if there is an entity *within* that accomplishes these feats. This entity is very different from taking a step, breathing, or eating. Knowing that others have similar inner entities, most people generally assume that these internal processes are made up of something other than the physical body (Carlson 1986).

The psychic division between these internal and physical processes underlie much of philosophy and religion. It was, and continues to be, the struggle to understand the nature of mind and body.

Ernest Becker (1973), in his classic work *The Denial of Death*, proposed that the human constitution is actually an "existential paradox" (p. 26). People have a basically symbolic nature, using thought, speculation, creativity, self-consciousness, and other abstract processes to explain, explore, and understand the world. Yet at the same time, people are organic.

> This is the paradox; he is out of nature and hopelessly in it; he is dual, up in the stars and yet housed in a heart-pumping, breath-gasping body that once belonged to a fish and still carries the gill-marks to prove it. His body is a material fleshy casing that is alien to him in many ways— the strangest and most repugnant way being that it aches and bleeds and will decay and die. Man is literally split in two: he has an awareness of his own splendid uniqueness in that he sticks out of nature with a towering majesty, and yet he goes back into the ground a few feet in order blindly and dumbly to rot and disappear forever. [Becker 1973, p. 26]

The paradox or duality is terrifying. Yes, the mind or spirit stands apart from the body. But in actual reality it dies along with the cells.

Becker interprets this as a horrifying psychological dilemma. Beneath the greatest joys, the wildest adventures, and the most intoxicating dreams crouches the inevitability of biological death. In order to survive this devastating knowledge, humans *create*. Society itself is a system that draws a living, ongoing legend of the significance of life. Religion establishes a power greater than biology, a spiritual world with heaven, and a God, or system of Gods, that allows humans to partake in their own immortality. Every culture has established dramatic methods of heroism to elevate self-worth beyond mortal parameters. Individually, people use social games, psychological parodies, preoccupations, and obsessions to avoid the truth of biological destiny. Even narcissism, Becker points out, compels one to feel that everyone is expendable but *I*. These psychosocial behaviors all serve the essential biological need of an organism to protect itself against anything that might threaten harm or death. And the fear of death is so horrifying that it, in itself, can psychologically strangle the individual.

"Is it not for us to confess," Freud asked, "that in our civilized attitude towards death we are once more living psychologically beyond our means and must reform and give truth its due?" (Becker 1973, p. 11).

The essential human paradox can be denied in a cyborg metaphor of human-is-better-with-machine. The machine in actual reality affords the illusion of replacing the biological system. The more machine, the less organic material. Mr. Data, the popular android in *Star Trek*, doesn't die. Robocops, too, live forever. When devices and environments are created from and for machines, humans can maintain the illusion of moving further away from their biological destiny. Adaptation then involves lessening one's hold on nature in exchange for the machine or technology. Obviously, the best illusion of spirit that allows the most effective denial of biological duality is in a world of simulation, totally removed from physical or actual reality. It is called cyberspace.

Cyberspace is not a revolution but an evolution, a space humans have craved since the first tool replaced an organic human resource. Can a more desirable environment be created to suit these psychological needs? Online, people venture into simulations where they can assume multiple identities. Games can be played where you can be killed, resurrected, or put to rest at will—and you always exit alive. Your voice can carry over tens of thousands of miles at the flick of a keyboard, or the click of a mouse, as if there were no limitations in space. Time becomes a relative phenomenon, easily manipulated. Information explodes in colors, words, and symbols that dance

across a screen providing access to an environment metaphori-
cally titled *windows*. Individuals assume the nomenclature of
their browsers, such as *Netscape Navigator* or *Internet Ex-
plorer*. Some have referred to the Internet as similar to falling
through the looking glass into a fanciful world where backward,
frontward, up, and down are all equally plausible. The power
is heady, diving into the past, present, and beyond, creating new
and inventive ways of simulation. Many believe that we have
finally discovered the mythic *noosphere*.

Where is the Noosphere?

In the mid-twentieth century, Teilhard de Chardin, a pale-ontologist as well as a Catholic priest, predicted that a "single, integrated, and evolutionary view of reality" would emerge (Pesce 1996). The phenomena within the new reality would define a totally unambiguous shape that would be impossible to view as a whole. De Chardin called it the *noosphere*.

Pesce (1994) contends that the noosphere (pronounced no-o-sphere) is a collective of the total human knowledge, created by the explosion of intraspecies connections. These connections occur in holosthetic space, or "any medium which produces the perception of an event through several (or all) sensory modalities in a self-consistent manner" (p. 2). A prime example of holosthetic space is virtual reality, where the intent is to create human perception of actual reality from a simulation.

Essentially, these ideas maintain that by connecting millions of humans in a nonphysical or virtual space a collective phenomenon—the noosphere—emerges. In other words, the sum of these connections is far greater than its parts. Luba Shugawat, LCSW, talks about these collective phenomena:

> There are significant changes online. You find blurred boundaries, changes in the sense of self, experiences that highlight fantasy and anonymity. It's as if there is an es-

sence or entity emerging—a kind of collective consciousness—that blends all those things we view as separate into
a group think. [Personal communication, January 6, 1997]

Carl Gustav Jung (1934) described a similar entity when
he introduced the concept of the collective unconscious. He proposed that there was a second "psychic system" that was collective, universal, impersonal, and identical in all people. The
phenomena contained in the collective unconscious are the
archetypes or universal forms in the human mind. Many disciplines recognize these forms and have called them by different names, including "motifs" (mythology), "representations
collectives" (psychology of primitives) and "categories of the
imagination" (comparative religion) (Jung 1934). Jung suggests
that the very fate of "great nations" is nothing "but a summation of the psychic changes in individuals" (p. 3).

The noosphere can be seen as a collective *consciousness*
created by the summation of externalized human archetypes in
cyberspace. Simply put, all the human connections in
chatrooms, e-mail exchanges, bulletin boards, fantasy games,
websites, and so forth are beginning to coalesce into identifi-
able virtual archetypes. If the fate of great nations is determined
by the collective unconscious, then the noosphere may be determined by the collective virtual consciousness.

Pesce (1995, 1996) refers to this concept of collectivity in
describing the three distinct phases in the development of
cyberspace. The first phase involves a period of *connection*
where individuals move into a single space that will enable
collectivity. The best example of this are the years 1969–1989,
when millions of people were brought into one single, connected "global village," the Internet. The next phase is *collectivity*, the inevitable result of bringing individuals together on
a large scale. This is when people work together and begin to
display properties that are archetypal and greater than the sum

of their parts. Creation and success of their creation exemplifies this phase—with millions of individuals participating in a well-delineated space owned and controlled by all without a single dominant entity. The World Wide Web defies restriction and authorship, stubbornly maintaining equal access. Pesce's third phase involves the emergence of *corrective* behaviors, where the collective begins to monitor, modify, and correct its own behavior. The corrective goal is to protect the collective without prejudice and without conscience. As Pesce (1996) describes it, "The corrective has no prejudices and willingly eats its own children or the children of others."

The end result is what Pierre Levy, French philosopher and University of Paris professor, calls *l'intelligence collectit*—collective intelligence.

While many of these concepts may appear strange, they are perfectly consistent with the postmodern zeitgeist.

Is "I" Lost in Cyberspace?

The modern self was seen as having a single identity that was fixed and rational. Although an individual could play many roles in life, the essence remained intact, centered, and uniquely defined. Postmodern culture in the noosphere contradicts the order and structural limitations of modernism. Poster (No date) suggests that the postmodern identity might be the direct opposite to those of modernity. He maintains that the most apparent effects of technology—new forms of communication, the information superhighway, and ultimately, virtual reality—have created a new cultural space that forces us to redefine and multiply the various realities that humans enter. This shift to decentralization must be accompanied by a readjustment in the self.

Meet Kim.

The computer sits like a monolith on her desk. Wrinkled clothing, papers of all colors and sizes, and books are scattered across the floor, bed, and every available surface in the small room. Two young women live in this college dormitory room, the artifacts of their life tossed haphazardly around them. Makeup, perfume, and hair clips share space with philosophy, statistics, and Western civilization texts. Half-written essays lay buried beneath flyers advertising college bars and dance clubs.

The air is filled with the lingering scent of strawberry—from a fat pillar candle now melted into a shapeless mass of red wax.

The only order is around the computer. The desktop machine is carefully placed, the keyboard perfectly aligned, the mouse resting quietly on a pink mousepad. All the cables are hidden behind the desk, the printer waits patiently on an adjoining perch.

Kim sits down at the desk.

She is a junior, majoring in psychology. Kim works hard—and plays hard—doing all the things that are expected of a 20-year-old college student. She has good grades and, next year, as a senior, she will be applying to graduate school. When Kim gets tired of being herself—studying, thinking, socializing, and looking for significant relationships—she goes online and becomes someone else.

Today, Kim will be a man.

She logs on to her favorite chat room and describes herself as a 35-year-old man. There are seventeen other people in the chat room and no one responds to her introduction. Kim decides to raise the stakes. She reports that she is in trouble with the law. Some people begin to take notice. They want to know what kind of trouble she is in. Enjoying her infamy, Kim embellishes her story. She tells them that she is actually typing from a prison computer.

Suddenly, the screen is filled with responses. Several women ask "male" Kim for a date as soon as she gets out. Others tell her they always fantasized about making love with a convict. One woman excitedly explains that she is married, has two children, lives in the suburbs, is a good girl, but wants to explore her dark side. Is Kim interested?

No one knew—or let on if they did know—that the 35-year-old male convict was a female psychology major in a cluttered college dorm room.

There is a classic cartoon poking fun at the Internet. It is a picture of a dog sitting in front of a computer talking to another dog that is watching. The animal at the computer is explaining to the canine observer that when you go on the Internet, "nobody knows you're a dog" (Steiner 1993). The message is clear. You can be whoever and whatever you want online. You can be yourself, you can be another "self," or you can be many different selves.

The postmodern "I" is a plural and decentralized self; it breaks into many parts and roles, constructing a flexible reality that involves superficial manipulations in time, space, and ideology. Nobody knows you're a dog, a cat, a man, or a woman. Movement between psychological places is eased through a conscious dissociation of self.

Dissociation has been receiving increasing attention in mental health. *DSM-IV* (1994) defines the essential feature of the dissociative disorders as the sudden, gradual, transient, or chronic disruption in what are usually integrated functions of consciousness, memory, identity, or perception of the environment.

Putnam (1989) suggests that there are three principles that characterize *pathological* dissociation:

- The individual experiences a change in personal identity;
- The individual experiences disturbance in memory; and
- The vast majority of dissociative disorders result from trauma.

These principles emerge from the premise that dissociation "is a normal process that is initially used defensively by an individual to handle traumatic experiences and evolves over time into a maladaptive or pathological process" (p. 9). As such, dissociation is believed to be a highly adaptive function that can be measured on a continuum that runs from normal to pathological. "Normal" dissociation can involve behaviors such as daydreaming, light trances, and meditation, while pathological dissociation, to its extreme, is manifested in behaviors such as fugues, amnesia, and multiple personality disorder.

Is the postmodern "I" a form of adaptive dissociation?

Adaptive dissociation is a natural and necessary psychological process in cyberspace. Online, people can experiment with their identities, going to a variety of environments where different names, personalities, personal information, and entire personas can be forged without anyone being able to confirm or confront their confabulations. Anonymity protects the individual, enabling him or her to create a flexible, multiple self that can explore all aspects of inner reality. "Dark" sides can be as viable as "light" sides, names can be changed at will, roles can be played, personal icons or avatars drawn and manipulated in many distinct ways. Not only do we find ourselves in a virtual environment, but also in a virtual *self* that simulates bits and pieces of conscious and unconscious fantasy.

These behaviors have been found throughout human history and legend. Human transformations have always fascinated people. The story of Adam and Eve begins with the creation of two identities from one: woman created from Adam's rib. Much of ancient mythology told stories of opposing characters within one God. Ovid wrote *Metamorphoses* (1992) in the early years after the birth of Christ, explaining that:

> My intention is to tell of bodies changed
> To different forms; the gods, who made the changes,
> Will help me—or I hope so—with a poem
> That runs from the world's beginning to our own days.

Perhaps one of the most famous human transformations came in Robert Louis Stevenson's famous story *Dr. Jekyll and Mr. Hyde* (1987), written in 1886. It is the dramatic portrayal of what Stevenson believed to be the good and evil sides of people housed in one body.

> Think of it—I did not even exist! Let me but escape into my laboratory door, give me but a second or two to mix and swallow the draught that I had always standing ready; and whatever he had done, Edward Hyde would pass away like the stain of breath upon a mirror; and there in his stead, quietly at home, trimming the midnight lamp in his study, a man who could afford to laugh at suspicion, would be Henry Jekyll. [p. 100]

Stevenson suggested that each individual is made up of many identities, a "polity of multifarious, incongruous and independent citizens" (p. 104).

Freud was the first to legitimize these "fictions" by theories that postulated a decentralized view of the self. The model of the psychic apparatus of the mind—the id, the ego, and the superego—proposed that these were structures that represented specific mental processes and contents functionally related to one another (Brenner 1974). Moving away from Freud, Jung saw the self as the meeting of archetypes, while object relations referred to the many internalizations of people and things (Turkle 1995).

It took technology and cyberspace to create an environment where multiplicity could be clarified, accepted, and acted out within acceptable parameters of dissociation. Turkle (1995) maintains that people "cycle" through many selves online, moving from one virtual community or environment to the next, mixing and matching roles, surfing the Internet as if it were a "social laboratory" filled with experiments that construct and reconstruct the self (p. 180).

Where Exactly is Cyberspace?

On the very shores of the eastern oceans lies the great and ancient cityport of Parrius. It is ruled by the Lady Augustine and is home to many mariners and seafaring folk. Parrius has traditionally enjoyed a close relationship with its sister cityport, Mercinae, and the trading routes between the two are well established and usually safe to travel. The merchant of Parrius has a shop just east of Hellespont Square, an excellent place to trade unwanted items for gold pieces. Also, when in Parrius be sure to visit the stalls of Chapman's Square in the north of the city where some of the finest produce of Avalon can be found on sale. [*Avalon* 1996, p. 7]

Parrius is in *Avalon*, a MUD (**M**ulti-**u**ser **D**imension) on the Internet.

Our lives in actuality are defined by spaces that follow the laws of physics. There is up and down, above and below, gravity and inertia—a long list of highly recognizable physical attributes. To move in actuality, there is an expenditure of energy with a corresponding response: you take a step, a wheel turns, and the jet engine propels. Similarly, time structures our lives. Distance is often defined primarily by time: miles per hour, revolutions per minute, light years. The rhythms of our bodies, our daily lives, our cultures are connected to concrete concepts such as eating, sleeping, birth, and death.

In contrast, electronic space is intangible, measured primarily by *psychosocial* constructs. Time, distance, and place are determined by simulation, not physics. Gravity and inertia don't restrict or enhance electronic space. The laws of actuality apply only when complex programming and increased system power can simulate them (Suler 1996a).

Electronic space can be understood more easily in a psychosocial context. "In reality," observes Dean Allman, LCSW, "there is no such thing as cyberspace. It is what we project."

Chip Morningstar and F. Randall Farmer (1996), two designers involved in the creation of Lucasfilm's *Habitat*, a large, commercial multi-user environment, found Allman's statement to be true. Their goal was to create a virtual world where users "communicated, played games, experienced adventures, fell in love, got married and divorced, started businesses, found religions, waged wars, protested against them, and experimented with self-government" (p. 1). Ultimately, they found that cyberspace "is defined more by the interactions among the actors within it than by the technology with which it is implemented" (p. 1). Naturally, defining cyberspace in psychological terms raises more questions than answers. If electronic space is constructed through human projection, then what are we creating? Are we entering an altered state of consciousness: A dream state, trance state, or conscious fantasy somewhat akin to daydreaming? Where do we actually "go" when we e-mail, chat, research, play, or work on the net? Do digitized psychological projections produce only simulation or are we going beyond the third dimension into virtual locales that challenge our present comprehension?

Shirky (1995) attempts to answer these questions by de-

fining cyberspace as "the space where electronic entities interact" (p. 59). The space sits on a continuum that presently ranges
from "literary" to "architectural." Literary space is created with
words and text, while architectural space organizes information
into a visible, interactive, and virtually transportable medium
that some refer to as 4D (4-dimensional).

Today's version of the Internet operates mostly in literary
space. This includes arenas such as e-mail, chats, and
newsgroups. We use language to give the illusion of physicality. For example, *America Online* calls its chats "rooms" and
holds online, real time interviews in "auditoriums." *Netcom,* a
large Internet service provider (ISP), refers to its first screen
as "homeport." Individual electronic spaces are called "home
pages," and electronic search programs are referred to as
"search engines." As more graphics and multimedia are added,
literary spaces use even more powerful physical metaphors.
CyberTowers Professional Center describes itself as "the premier, virtual professional center for professionals and execu-
tives" that operates in a "virtual office building" (CyberTowers
1997). They offer Web-hosting services in packages identified
as standard, deluxe, executive/professional, and presidential
suites. CNET's *MediaDome* (1997) offers activities such as live
concerts, videos, interviews, and other media events in their
simulated hall.

Shirky (1995) notes that electronic spaces are intrinsic to
virtual communities. "Because a community needs a place to
organize," he writes, "it is something of a chicken and egg
proposition to know whether the space creates the sense of an
organized community or if the community creates the sense of
organized space" (p. 61). Beneath it all—the words, the graphics, the illusions, and the communications, the essence of
cyberspace is the extension of us—a psychosocial mirror of
humankind.

Are All Netizens Created Equal?

In late 1996, Serbian dictator Slobodan Milosevic annulled the results of local elections won by the opposition. It resulted in daily protest demonstrations. The government tried to block news of the rapidly escalating violence caused by the demonstrations. But they were unable to control the Internet. The following excerpts were taken from the *University of Belgrade Protest* (1996–1997) site on the World Wide Web:

> [accessed December 29, 1996] 22nd day of the protest begins with a song "To Belgrade" . . . The sky is totally blue today, and it has no intention at all to throw some rain at us. There are people beside us—they are selling chewing gums and whistling lollipops, workers are smiling at us from the second floor of some half-built building. The carnival of anger, although with basically good vibrations, is reaching its peak . . . People are thrilled, they are throwing balloons from their balconies, they love us, encourage us to continue, to be persistent & brave. They "finance" us with their smiles. They are the only ones we depend on, that we live for. And they live for us . . .

> [accessed February 9, 1997] Shortly after midnight, on February the 3rd, strong police forces resorted to violence to disperse peaceful demonstrations of the opposition in Belgrade. Using batons and water cannons the

police brutally injured a number of people. Meanwhile, a few members of the police force burst into the building of the School of Philosophy, severely violating the autonomy of the Belgrade University, and injured several members of the students' security staff.

As long as this dramatic situation is taking place in Belgrade, on this page you will be able to find the latest news about the happenings here, so reload this page often.

In the days before the Internet, information like this often never left the country. If it did "leak," supporters had to organize themselves to find ways to aid the protesters. Moore (1995) refers to this as part of another Internet culture: "the international online freedom fighters" (p. 137). Instantaneous communication has enabled the messages of oppressed, misunderstood, protesting, angry, rebelling, need-to-be-heard groups heard around the world. Due to the structure of the Internet, the only way to shut it down is not have it in the country in the first place. Although many governments have tried some sort of censorship, it is nearly impossible to succeed. The Internet has no centralized government, no net headquarters, and no main office. It is an assortment of hundreds of thousands of networks linked together, bypassing every boundary previously known to humankind. To remove all access in a country might mean banning computers or shutting down the telephone system. No country or region can afford such drastic isolation or economic limitations (Moore 1995).

So the world "heard" the Serbian students. And responded in kind. The following is a sample of e-mail sent to the *University of Belgrade Protest* (1996) site:

We, the Romanian students from Timisoara, have found out about your action for democracy and justice. That's why we would like to tell you that you can count on us. If you think we could help you please feel free to e-mail us. Waiting for your answer, we wish you good luck and DON'T GIVE UP!

Herzovi Olimpiu
Pop Adrian
Campian Mircea
Technical University of Timisoara, Romania
Students League from Computer Science Department

* * *

Friends,

This is to let you know that you have the full and unambiguous support of the student population of Stanford . . .

Tom Soule
Stanford University
Palo Alto, California, United States

* * *

Your e-mail message to the world has just been passed onto me through the LEARN Network . . . it is important for you to know that millions of people around the world understand what is happening in Serbia . . .

Allison Armstrong
Information Services Manager
Victoria, Australia

* * *

BE STRONG AND COURAGEOUS!!!! WE SUPPORT YOU.

Senato degli studenti
Architettura Venezia (IAUV)
Raccoglimentia, Venezia (Italy)

* * *

All over the United States, the citizens are with you in spirit . . . For your interest, I attached copies of the original American Declaration of Independence and also the Bill of Rights from the American Constitution written in 1789 . . . Your students may be interested to see the similarities between their present struggle and the one that was carried on here 220 years ago . . .

Frederick Sweet, Ph.D.
Professor
School of Medicine
Washington University
St. Louis, Missouri (USA)

Equalization of status is one of the favorite features praised by Cyberlibertarians. They talk about the "netizen"—the online citizen. They argue that all national, racial, religious, ethnic, ideological, physical, and mental boundaries are neutralized in cyberspace—unless one chooses to identify him- or herself as such. In fact, the only disabilities or discriminations that theoretically exist online are things such as slow modems, old computers, poor Internet Service Providers, old video cards, limited access, and other technological confines. English is the standard language. However, there are sites in almost every language spoken on the globe. Social hierarchies do emerge, but they are usually dependent on the type of site. For example, on an e-mail list, individuals with the best communication skills, expertise, or stamina tend to predominate. On a newsgroup, the hierarchy might depend on different qualities— such as verbal assertiveness, working knowledge, and frequency of posting. In MUDs, people who developed the highest skills in playing and manipulating the environment tend to garner greater status. Commitment to the virtual community, generally measured in frequency and stamina, is always critical in cyberspace where surfing is a natural form of "travel."

Notwithstanding, Cyberluddites are quick to point out that equal status is not always the rule. McAllester (1997a) writes that the Netizen creed says "On The Internet, I have an equal voice. People listen to my opinions. It's a place where it doesn't matter what race I am, how rich I am or whom I sleep with. We are all the same . . . so what's with the title of this book that's been sitting on my desk . . . 'Digerati: Encounters with the cyber elite'?" (p. A42). He asks how a classless society can have a book about the elite?

Who are the Digerati? John Brockman (1996), author of the book, describes them as constituting a "critical mass of the doers, thinkers, and writers, connected in ways they may not even appreciate, who have tremendous influence on the emerging communication revolution surround the growth of the Internet and the World Wide Web." Classless and elite cannot exist in the same culture. Cyberluddites also note that if the Internet is classless and egalitarian, why are there so many fascists and other hate groups online to disrupt the spirit of cyberspace? Acknowledging their right to exist does not mean the same thing as questioning the need for their existence.

How Do People Interact in an Electronic Environment?

Identity, flexibility, and anonymity constitute a postmodern concept of multiple, cycling selves. There are many choices in the electronic environment. For example, when one registers with an Internet Service Provider (ISP), there is the option to use several screen names. Those "names" can be female, male, celebrity names, nicknames—the list is as long as the imagination. The Web sites often define how much of any chosen "self" is revealed. On an e-mail list, individuals are often required to use real names while the same person in a newsgroup might use a screen name and in a virtual reality habitat have an identifying set of avatars (personal graphics). Chats by definition encourage logging in regularly with a set of names (and identities), playing different roles in different role-playing games and designing colorful icons or avatars as "physical" representations in graphic virtual environments. What is the psychosocial effect of digital multiplicity and anonymity? Randy, a 16-year-old high school student, offers her opinions:

> The Internet is good in some cases and makes one feel more isolated in other cases. For example, when I write e-mail sometimes it is very frustrating to realize I am staring at a blank screen in my computer room. It is very one sided. When I talk to other people on the Internet, it is

very strange because all I am seeing are words. At least on the telephone I can get a feeling of what a person is like through their tone of voice. Yet, at the same time, the Internet is a true communication hub. I can talk to people whom I would not ordinarily talk to, become involved in causes and groups that would not otherwise be possible. It fosters a sense of community because essentially, nobody knows whom they are talking to. Everyone can start anew and not worry about what anybody else thinks of them. [Personal communication, February 10, 1997]

The concept of anonymity is closely linked to flexible identity, adaptive dissociation, and altered views of reality. Suler (1996a) speculates that cyberspace emulates a dream state: an extension of the mind and of all the facets of an individual's mental environment. It results in an entrance into an altered reality where unconscious thoughts, fantasies, and impulses can be acted out safely. No one knows who you are. Consequently, no one will connect "you" to your behavior. Suler (1996a) proposes that this "may explain some of the sexuality, aggression, and imaginative role playing we see on The Internet" (p. 13).

Anonymity reinforces dissociation, subsequently releasing individuals from the confines of a unitary self. *You can be anyone because no one knows who you are.* In due course, two psychosocial controls that dramatically determine behavior in actuality are diminished: social constraint and social consequence.

Social constraint refers to the set of norms and values that restrict, limit, or regulate individual behavior. We use social constraints to guide ourselves as well as predict the behavior of others. Social constraints tend to become more fluid with multiple identities and anonymity. Consequently, a system of social constraints online, called *netiquette*, has developed to provide guidelines. Virginia Shea (no date), author of *Netiquette*, lists the ten core rules:

1. Remember the human;
2. Adhere to the same standards of behavior online that you follow in real life;
3. Know where you are in cyberspace;
4. Respect other people's time and bandwidth;
5. Make yourself look good online;
6. Share expert knowledge;
7. Help keep flame wars under control;
8. Respect other people's privacy;
9. Don't abuse your power; and
10. Be forgiving of other people's mistakes.

Netiquette notwithstanding, many have found an excess of anger and aggression on the Internet. The loosening of social constraint allows for flaming (hurling electronic insults) and flame wars, sexual disinhibition, psychological experimentation, and many of the more disturbing behaviors discussed in *Can virtual crime be real?* A loosening of social consequence further reinforces these behaviors. In real life there are clear, linear consequences for inappropriate behavior. A breach of etiquette is usually met with relatively swift repercussions. In cyberspace there are few, if any, consequences. If one does something "wrong," he or she merely logs off, changes identity, and returns to the same site. No one gets thrown out of cyberspace—they merely recycle.

How do these social "facts" of cyberspace affect interaction? Do people experience mass communication or interpersonal relationships? Should electronic interactions be considered intimacies, correspondences, friendships, or narcissistic mirrors? These questions attempt to understand the nature of the many "connections" being made between people in cyberspace. Contact can be transient, occasional, long-term, or anything in-between. They can occur in a vast range of environments. But do they have any long-lasting emotional or psychological effects? Can interaction in the electronic environment fulfill human social needs?

Cyberluddites and Cyberlibertarians are polarized on this issue. Cyberlibertarians extol the advantages of having numerous relationships accessible so people can connect with others that share their specific interests. In actual communities, the prevailing commonality is geographical space. Online, people have more choices. Netizens can share their most intimate ideas, behaviors, and interests—finding others with similar tastes. Thus a quick look through the IRC (Internet Relay Chat) finds chats as common as "families," "grow-your-own-business," and "cheerleaders" and as esoteric as "planeteers," "darkWolves," and "innerspace." Removal of physical identifiers such as height, weight, race, ethnicity, attractiveness, disability, and so forth further neutralizes relationships, freeing participants to relate solely to the words, ideas, and written thoughts of the other.

Cyberluddites contest this assessment. They insist that online "relationships" divert people from significant and necessary human physical contact. These connections encourage a brand of superficial communication that enable people to avoid the harder-to-establish social interactions in actuality.

Obviously, interactions in the electronic environment presently lack the visual and contextual cues that characterize actuality. However, people can and do adapt to the absence of these cues off-line. If they didn't, then the visually, hearing, or physically impaired would never be able to establish intimate relationships. Clearly, that does not happen. One only needs to consider the experience of the multiply impaired Helen Keller and the depth of her relationships with so many people in her life to observe the ability of humans to compensate. Walther (1996) agrees, finding that people will adapt when cues aren't present. The critical factor is time. Where there is adequate time to establish communication, the negative effects of the lack of cues is greatly reduced. The time factor gives individuals the opportunity to adequately compensate for physicality as to enable electronic relationships. Again, this finding is not particularly surprising. Consider the relationships that have been forged, historically, through media such as letter-writing and telephone calls. In pre-computer days the concept of pen-pals was strongly encouraged, particularly for young people to experience a different way of life. Letter writing to soldiers, lovers, travelers, distant friends, and relatives is a practice that can be found in almost every literate society. Is e-mail very different?

Evidently, as people become more adept in these forms of communication, they require less time to compensate. Experienced netizens "fill in the gap" faster than newbies (new users), who are still struggling to compensate. Nonetheless, there are numerous devices netizens use to compensate for the limited social dimensions of cyberspace. One of the most popular means is through the use of "smileys" or "emoticons." These are characters created on a keyboard that emulate the facial expressions and emotional responses found in actual reality. For example, a happy or smiling face appears as the following (turn your head sideways to "read"

:-)

Hundreds of smileys enhance net communications, expressing a wide range of human response.

;-) winking
:-(frowning
8-) smiley with sunglasses
:-{) smiley with a mustache
:-p sticking out your tongue

There are also many emoticons that provide psychological shorthand. For example, you can have a drink _/, toast a friend _/! or say cheers _/ _/! When the drinking is over you can sober up with a cup of coffee _/3.

Altering the appearance of text is used to imitate the "nonverbal" messages of 3D. Capitalizing all the letters means that you're SHOUTING, particularly popular in flame wars. Embedding words in text can express specific emotions such as "grin" or "frown". <VBG> or "very big grin" and <VBF> or "very big frown" can further enhance communication. A warm embrace is a graphic (((((((((hug))))))))).

For a more detailed listing of electronic shorthand, see the various glossaries in the Appendices.

Information about an individual is often imparted in specific details. Many of the large ISPs offer free personal Web pages. For a relatively small fee, one can set up their own home page, complete with photos, stories, pets, favorite links, and preferred ice cream. Many of the chats, virtual communities, MUDs, and other sites where people gather provide profile pages where pertinent information can be made available at the click of the mouse. Even e-mail, with its strict text format, now offers "signatures" or statements, quotes, or aphorisms that are printed at the bottom of every message (see Glossaries—Menno Pieters' Signature Museum). The following are sample signatures used by Rob Bischoff, Ph.D.

> Great spirits have always encountered violent opposition from mediocre minds . . . Albert Einstein

> DENIAL is NOT a RIVER in EGYPT

> Noteworthy Bible translation error: Satan's mark was thought to be 666 by the translators; however, it actually read 101010

Malcolm Parks, Ph.D., associate professor of speech communication at the University of Washington, and Kory Floyd, a doctoral student in communication at the University of Arizona (1996), conducted a study with the goal of providing "an empirical reference point for evaluating conflicting visions of social life in cyberspace by exploring the prevalence and development of personal relationships in one large, online environment, *Usenet* newsgroups on the Internet" (p. 10). They found that 60.7 percent of their subjects formed personal relationships with someone they met online. These relationships involved regular communications, with over half of the respondents reporting that they had connected at least once a week. Parks and Floyd identified a developmental pattern for online relationships that evolved from impersonal to personal, with *increases* in the following psychosocial dimensions (p. 6):

1. Interdependence;
2. Breadth and depth of interaction;
3. Interpersonal predictability and understanding;
4. More personalized ways of communicating;
5. Commitment; and
6. Convergence of social networks.

They concluded that for the majority of their subjects "the ultimate social impact of cyberspace will not flow from its exotic capabilities, but rather the fact that people are putting it to ordinary, even mundane social use" (p. 11).

Cyberspace may not be the egalitarian utopia that the Cyberlibertarians predict. It may not be the threat to the intimacy and integrity of the human species that the Cyberluddites predict. It may simply be the next step.

Why Do People Love to Hang Out in Cyberspace?

Why do so many people get involved in the electronic environment . . . and stay?

In cyberspace, people are meeting other people. They are talking, they are laughing, and they are communicating their feelings. They are also disagreeing, arguing, and sometimes even hating. To wit, people are forming relationships through the words exchanged in e-mail, newsgroups, chats, and other Web forums. In a seminal study by Parks and Floyd (1996) to determine whether humans actually connect online, they concluded, "our primary finding was that personal relationships were common in this environment" (p. 11). Using a random sample of 176 newsgroup members, they found that 60.7 percent reported they had formed a personal relationship with someone online. There was only a small difference between opposite-sex relationships (55.1 percent) than same sex relationships (44.9 percent). Most of the relationships reported were less than a year's duration. Women were more likely to have an online relationship (72.2 percent) than men (54.5 percent). However, the best predictor of whether or not a subject developed a personal relationship was the length of time and frequency or participation in the newsgroup. "Although much more extensive research is necessary," Parks and Floyd write, "it may be that developing personal relationships online is more a function of simple experience than it is of demographic or personality factors. As people get used to and involved with their favorite newsgroups over time, they appear to start developing personal relationships with one another" (p. 6).

As discussed earlier, people enhance online relationships by various techniques, including emoticons, personal codes, special words, and "private" online meetings. Interestingly, people involved in online personal relationships tend to move to other modes of communication. Parks and Floyd (1996) found that even though all their subjects *began* their relationships in newsgroups, 98 percent also used direct e-mail. In addition, 35.3 percent used the telephone, 28.4 percent used snail mail, and 33.3 percent met face to face. Overall, nearly two-thirds of the subjects used other means of communication than the computer to contact their friends. This is particularly interesting when one considers the emerging audiovisual technology. When the technology becomes widely available, will people be satisfied to conduct their relationships totally in cyberspace? Or will the need for physical contact increase? If Parks and Floyd's assessment is correct, is cyberspace just another meeting ground, a safe-sex, safe-friend locale where people can feel, although not necessarily be, less vulnerable?

In a study on people who engage in sexually explicit online communication, Witmer (1997) found that none of their fifty-two subjects felt that they were taking any risk in their behavior. They generally felt secure, believing that their behavior would have no impact on their careers or other relationships. People tend to be less inhibited in an environment where they are not forced to take personal responsibility through social constraints and consequences. In a postmodern environment where multiple identities and multiple spaces are the rule, mistakes are readily rectified. If one commits a grievous netiquette sin, he or she can log off, assume a new identity, and return unscathed. With a click of the mouse, one can transform from transgressor to citizen, philosopher to laborer, peacemaker to hate monger. This is reinforced by the reality that most electronic groups have a customized netiquette often expressed in the group's FAQs (frequently asked questions) or in the members' online comments. Some groups will accept flaming and others will immediately reproach any offender. Many discussion groups consider heated discourse that often leads to harsh criticism of others part of the intellectual foray while others maintain an almost pristine civility. Breaking rules, however, is not a very serious crime. The perpetrator can simply leave— or change. The other members can take all the posts in a newsgroup or mailing list by the transgressor and send them to the "trash" or "kill" file. In a chat, a transgressor can simply be "blocked out" from one's screen. Reproach in the electronic environment is very different than making a social faux pas while among a group of people. In real life, words, body language, aggressive criticism, or isolation reproach the transgressor. Interestingly, the electronic environment empowers both the transgressor and his or her victim. The transgressor can never be fully reproached and the victims can never be fully offended.

In a study on conduct control on Usenet, Smith and McLaughlin (1997) confirm this postmodern view of breaches in netiquette. They found that Usenet participants usually do not respond publicly to offenders—and when they do, there is a tendency to use wit and humor that inhibits or softens the attack. Flaming and other "language improprieties and group norm violations" (p. 10) are not tolerated in online groups, with reproaches varying by individual newsgroup and by the nature of the offense. "One of the unique aspects of remedial episodes in an asynchronous communication context like Usenet," writes Smith and McLaughlin, "is the ease with which offenders can 'duck out' of accounting for their behavior" (p. 9).

Rafaeli and Sudweeks (1997) hypothesize that *interactivity* is an important ingredient in understanding the social cohesion apparent in computer mediated communication (CMC). Interactivity is a construct that looks at specific elements in CMC: captivation, fascination, and allure. "Interactivity is a variable quality of communication settings," write Rafaeli and Sudweeks. "It expresses the degree to which communication transcends reaction" (p. 2). They propose that interactivity engages people and, accordingly, leads to socialization. As a process, interactivity "merges *speaking* with *listening*" (p. 3), and involves all forms of CMC. In a random sampling of 40 lists, with a total of 4,322 messages, they found the following:

- Interactivity is a variable in CMC, with messages, threads, and groups more or less interactive;
- As a variable, interactivity represents a specific quality, rather than a dichotomy between two types or styles; and
- Interactivity impacts on the behavior of groups.

Rafaeli and Sudweeks conclude that groups that contain little interactivity tend to have unstable or constantly changing memberships. Groups with high interactivity are more likely to sustain memberships and have more desirable outcomes, including such things as "symmetry in contributions, creativity and productivity, agreement, humor, and sense of belonging" (p. 12).

Does this fully explain why people love to hang out in the electronic environment? Much of the research is seminal, extrapolating behavioral and communication theories from actuality. Virtuality, as it matures and changes, may present an entire new dimension in communication. It is here, where postmodern metaphors of multiple, simulated identities and ideas become most viable. Is cyberspace a simulation of actuality-communication or is actuality-communication a simulation of cyberspace? When one examines popular media, literature, and the arts, the increasing presence of cyberspace is obvious. The language of computer mediated communications has permeated the spoken tongue; the behaviors are becoming increasingly generalized and overlapped. The psychology of cyberspace—psychotechnology—may, in a few short generations, become indistinguishable from the psychology of actuality. That does not require a leap of the imagination but merely a conservative projection into the early years of the new millennium.

What is a Disembodied Gender?

Morf is a popular word found mostly in live chats and one-to-one encounters online. It means *Male Or Female?* Generally, Morf is used as a question: "Are you male or female so I know how to continue this digital affiliation?" As with most words, the definition of Morf does not fully explain its content. Morf signifies a pervasive aspect of digital life—the confusion about gender and gender boundaries.

Peter Steiner's (1993) classic cartoon states, "on the Internet, nobody knows you're a dog." Likewise, no one is supposed to know gender. Virtual space is disembodied—a space without physical bodies. Consider the implications. Humans are defined by their physical bodies. One of the most primal human identifiers is based on the type of genitals that the body possesses. We know that this definition goes beyond physical appendages into an intricately balanced system of internal organs, biochemical processes, and neurological connections that control both mental and physical processes. The concept of gender is intrinsic to how we think, feel, and negotiate the environment consciously and unconsciously. What happens when these physical facts are removed from social life? When gender is disembodied?

Cyberlibertarians like to believe that it allows us to approach a higher level of consciousness where discarding physicality frees the individual to focus on a Cartesian identity: "I think, therefore I exist." In this idealization, human physical reality is totally sublimated to the mental experience. Cyberlibertarians often ignore the fact that people must drink water, eat food, expel wastes, sleep—attend to the physical body whether or not they are in cyberspace. The old issues always surface: hungry or not hungry, thirsty or not thirsty. As Abraham Maslow (1954) argued, there is a hierarchy of needs characteristic of the human organism, beginning from basic needs such as food and shelter that rise toward more abstract, less physical requirements. Thus, self-actualization is a lofty goal, but essentially impossible if there are too many basic needs left unfulfilled. Maslow points out that the human who is very hungry has no other interest but food. As much as humans might *want* to leave behind the physical body, when entering cyberspace, is it possible? Staunch Cyberlibertarians will respond with an emphatic "yes." Classless virtuality means disembodied space. Julian Dibbell (1993) writes, "you've read Foucault and your mind is not quite blown by the notion that sex is never so much an exchange of fluids as it is an exchange of signs" (p. 4).

What is Morf online? For that matter, what is Morf off-line? And is any of it *really* plausible?

Off-line, human beings have a well-defined actual body that dominates daily life. If all is intact, most bodies are biologically equipped in a similar fashion: We have two legs, two arms, a heart, a brain, lungs, and so forth. How these various biological features *function* differ in every human being. There is one pronounced, defining distinction in human biological bodies: gender. Male bodies look and perform differently than female bodies. Female bodies conceive and nurture new life while male bodies provide the catalyst. Obviously, gender is a primary determinant in behavior. Vander Zanden (1993) argues that "all societies have seized on the anatomical differences between men and women to assign gender roles—sets of cultural expectations that define the ways in which the members of each sex should behave" (p. 221). Whether biological, psychological, cultural, or a combination of all, genders have adapted to diverse thinking and behavior in actuality.

When genders move into the metaphorical space of virtuality, the issue can be readily obscured. If gender is primarily a physical manifestation, then its signifiers should fall away in disembodiment. However, if gender is more than physicality— a set of signs, a critical element in identity, an organizer of behavior—it will naturally transfer to the digital self. This raises some intriguing questions: What characteristics of gender accompany the virtual self and how does it affect acts of disembodied sex and sexuality? Does the existence of gender online make the Cyberlibertarian Internet an oxymoron? Can any space be classless when, in fact, two classes exist?

In concrete terms, there is a quickly diminishing delineation between digital genders in the electronic population. The Internet began as a man's world, although recent trends indicate that it has nearly equalized. Since 1994, GVU, a public service group, has conducted surveys of World Wide Web users. In an attempt to keep up with the rapid change, surveys were posted every six months. Accordingly, GVU has been able to document demographic trends. However, one must keep in mind the problems inherent to online research that dramatically affects the large disparity in numbers. For example, estimates of Internet usage can vary widely from as low as 5.8 million (O'Reilly Research 1996) to 50.6 million (CommerceNet/ Neilsen 1997). Simply put, with increasing numbers of netizens, cyberspace population mirrors the demographics in actuality.

Yet online gender remains disembodied. Or does it? Susan Herring (1993, 1994) asked this question in her research on gender differences in online communication styles. Herring, a linguist, academic, and researcher, investigated computer-mediated communication in the context of gender. Her 1993 paper, "Gender and democracy in computer-mediated communication," addresses the issue of whether electronic communication is as free and uncensored as Cyberlibertarians maintain. Democracy, agues Herring, is the state where all participants have equal access without external or internal constraints that censor discourse.

> CMC [computer-mediated communication] is power-based and hierarchical. This state of affairs cannot however be attributed to the influence of computer communication technology; rather, it continues pre-existing patterns of hierarchy and male dominance in academia, more generally, and in society as a whole. [p. 10]

Herring draws her conclusions from a content analysis of a yearlong investigation into two academic electronic discussion lists. Essentially she explored two basic assumptions:

1. Men and women have different posting styles on the net contrary to the belief that cyberspace neutralizes gender; and
2. Men and women have different values concerning what is suitable and rewarding discourse online.

In analyzing differences between male and female online communication styles, Herring (1994) found that males did most of the "talking"; held onto most of the attention; tended to dominate discussions; and generally trivialized female contributions. Males tend to be more authoritative, self-confident, and willing to take control. Herring concluded that male online style is "adversarial"—containing more derogatory remarks, strong, opinionated statements, long and/or frequent posts, self-promotion, and sarcasm. In contrast, female online style tends to be supportive toward others while often expressing self-doubt. A female style might affirm appreciation and encourage community building while at the same time apologizing, hedging, expressing doubt, and offering ideas in the form of suggestions rather than statements. Herring (1993) compared the following features in online language:

Female Language	Male Language
attenuated assertions	strong assertions
apologies	self-promotion
explicit justifications	presuppositions
questions	rhetorical questions
personal orientation	authoritative orientation
supports others	challenges others
	humor/sarcasm

The following posts serve as examples of Herring's differentiated online gender styles. They were written in a professional e-mail list in response to a lengthy discussion on Internet addiction.

I get sick of the anal retentiveness here—your ideas of what's proper are so narrow. I've already shut up about post modernism and other approaches to the Net—now that some people are going on about internet addiction you want to drive them away as well. ["Re: Internet addiction" (e-mail list), 1996, November 11]

* * *

For clinicians to go out with no research and without the knowledge of numerous case studies on the subject and create pathological categories on their own seems to me irresponsible. ["Re: Internet addiction" (e-mail list), 1996, November 11]

Obviously, the first post was written by a male and the second by a female. Savicki, Lingenfelter, and Kelley (1996) supported Herring's findings in a study conducted on a randomly selected set of thirty online discussion groups. They concluded that groups with a higher ratio of men were more likely to be impersonal and use fact-oriented language as well as more frequent calls for action.

Gender differences are by no means limited to style. Herring found significant variations in frequency, communication ethics, and netiquette. She reported that "the most striking disparity in academic CMC is the extent to which men participate more than women" (1993, p. 4). Herring found that in theoretical discussions, only 16 percent of the participants were female–even when the group was 36 percent female and 42 percent male. In addition, the female's messages tended to be shorter and less frequent. Herring noted that when women did post, they received fewer responses and their topics were less likely to be taken up by the entire group. Herring likens this to results of research conducted by Spender in 1979 (Herring 1993) that found that women are perceived as talking more than men in mixed gender conversations even though they only speak 30 percent of the time. Herring concludes that men are more successful in their topics, responses, ability to garner attention, and their tacit compliance to encourage women to participate less.

Hoai-An Truong (1993) wrote in a paper compiled in conjunction with the Bay Area Women in Telecommunications (BAWiT):

> Despite the fact that computer networking systems obscure physical characteristics, many women find that gender follows them into the online community, and sets a tone for their public and private interactions there—to such an extent that some women purposefully choose gender neutral identities, or refrain from expressing their opinions. [p. 1]

What follows women online? Truong suggests that these qualities are both personal and political, grounded in actuality, where socialization, economics, and reluctance to indulge in the technical world prevent them from finding an equal footing. "Online environments," she adds, "are largely determined by the viewpoints of their users and programmers, still predominantly white men" (p. 1).

These sex-based differences go beyond technology. Males are socialized to be more assertive, promote themselves, use more adversarial means to communicate, and seek to dominate social situations. Males value freedom from censorship; open, direct discussion; and aggressive debate as a means of communicating and advancing knowledge. In contrast, women are socialized to be uncomfortable with confrontation or direct conflict; they seek means to establish community and are comfortable with discussions that involve more self-disclosure and exchange of mutual emotional supports. Females value consideration for the needs of others and sensitivity, often finding aggressive behavior as rude. While men will be more inclined to tolerate flaming, use humor and sarcasm, women will shrink from that style of confrontation. "The norms and practices of masculine net culture," writes Herring (1994), "codified in netiquette rules, conflict with those of the female culture in ways that render cyberspace—or at least many 'neighborhoods' in cyberspace—inhospitable to women" (p. 8). This can be exacerbated by male harassment, further widening the gender gap. However, even if men and women choose names that don't identify their gender, their styles and ethics continue in the virtual world to be many of the discrepancies and attitudes that cause so many problems in the actual world.

Is There Love in Cyberspace?

In many ways, virtual relationships epitomize postmodern life. Online human connection is an information exchange, albeit one that involves emotion and fantasy. It offers freedom from the cumbersome weight of nontechnological awkwardness. The entire issue of physicality is conveniently removed enabling participants to manipulate people and superficial emotions. Multiple recycling of selves is a natural electronic behavior that leads to experimenting with disembodied gender within and without oneself. Language shifts and softens: offline "meat" bars become online "meets"; almost everyone goes on "blind" dates (unless video or photos are available), and the number and frequency of potential relationships is limited only by global population. The frequency, general safety, and diversity of contacts easily replace contextual depth.

Women and men have found countless ways to relate to one another in cyberspace—everything from virtual friendships, courtships, and passionate Net.sex are in vogue. The disembodied gender has tacit permission to experiment with sexual fantasy, gender, and relationships. There are those who indulge in gender switching, often a precarious game, while others happily conduct virtual weddings, inviting all of cyberspace to experience their nuptials. Newlywed and young families have their place online, in groups that talk about everything from recipes to cravings during pregnancy. Love and romance is as popular in cyberspace as in actuality.

> I met my wife via America Online, and we had our "courtship" via online writing. We corresponded via e-mail and chatted for about 4 months before we met in person. After that time, we "dated" for over 13 months using AOL while we lived in different cities.
>
> One of the interesting aspects of our online courtship is that, thanks to America Online, my wife and I could use the online chat rooms. As you can imagine, online chat is a much more fluent and sensitive way to exchange text, and I really believe that it facilitated the growth of our relationship. Online chat allowed us to essentially have the equivalent of an oral conversation, albeit in reading and writing mode. Since my wife and I entered our relationship as good typists, we found we could type to each other, in real time, close to the speed with which we could talk.
>
> I happened to keep an archive of most of our online relationship—it amounts to over 25 megabytes of AOL files, which equals several thousand print pages, perhaps over 10,000 pages.
>
> We did eventually marry, and now we both live in New York City. [Anonymous 1996]

A popular Internet search engine, *Excite* (1997), found 1,146,776 documents on love, 106,159 documents on dating, and 98,768 documents on romance. Each postmodern step of the virtual relationship is replete with digitized aids, from meeting strategies to automated problem-solvers. The discovery of love can occur serendipitously in a variety of virtual locales, including newsgroups, e-mail, and other discussion lists, MUDs, MOOs, and chats. For those seeking more structured, less postmodern encounters, there are thousands of matchmaking services designed to suit all tastes, from basic heterosexuals to highly specific fetishists. For example, one can indulge in the many choices offered by sites such as *Match.com* or the more circumspect *Cyber-Yenta*. Clinging to the trappings of actuality, the Internet offers a wide variety of personal ad sites, such as the *Web Personals* and *The Internet Personals* (No date), which wisely advises, "just because you aren't seen online is not a reason to lie about yourself" (p. 1). Naturally, there are those one-stop shopping sites that extend a whole range of services, with appealing names such as *Cupid's Network* and the *Single Christian Network*.

Once hooked, digital lovers have an assortment of aids to guide them through romance. Virtual flowers, postcards, teddy bears, valentines, and kisses are among the "love" gifts offered online. For those in a bind, one can access *Joe's Amazing Relationship Problem Solver*, *The Official Hopeless Romantic's Home Page*, or even *Mark's Apology Note Generator* (1995), that might produce a customized "I'm sorry" like the following:

> I humbly beg for your forgiveness for neglecting to say Happy Birthday the moment you woke up. I was sleeping and thought it could wait. So I'm writing in my Franklin, hoping you don't banish me to the couch for a month. Please, let's cool off for a while.
>
> This is a familiar pattern in my life, and I'm working on it with my therapist. [Mark's Apology 1995]

On a more serious note, virtual lovers might seek the advice of the many purported "experts," such as Dr. Sherree Motta and Dr. Michael Adamse, Florida clinical psychologists who call themselves "Cybershrinks" and say that the "anonymity of the online world is a perfect setting for the mystery that begets romance" ("Love.net" 1996, February 2). Motta and Adamse believe that online relationships begin with a friendship and develop into romance using language to spark a relationship that might have been overlooked in person. They stress the thrill of the virtual unknown, where secret online identities lead to the mystery, intrigue, and anticipation that feed romance. However, the "do's and don'ts" of online dating often have a striking similarity to safe sex. For example, Deborah Baumrucker (No date), contributing editor for Love@AOL, lists some critical rules:

1. Remember, people online are strangers—even though he or she might feel like that "special someone";
2. Don't give out your telephone number or address;
3. Don't believe everything you read. It's very easy to misguide you online;
4. Ignore all obscene e-mails;
5. Don't meet people off-line. If you insist on face-to-face, use common sense. Meet in a public place, preferably a group setting; and
6. Online should be fun and entertaining. Use good judgment and be sensible.

Online romance, just as in actuality, can have mixed results. Although it is a disembodied act, the more serious relationships tend to follow the pattern described at the beginning of this section: informal chatting, private chats, telephone calls, and if all goes well, face-to-face. Contrary to what netizens may believe, each step is fraught with emotional and psychological risk. Face-to-face, of course, presents the very real danger that the virtual lover is far more lethal than his or her words implied. Situations where women have been physically or sexually assaulted by men met online are popular stories in the media. Although these situations are relatively infrequent, it is simply another indication that cyberspace can conceal dangers that are more immediately apparent in actuality. While virtual "happiness" and marriage do occur, virtual heartbreak is perhaps more common. After all, the same search engine, *Excite* (1996) found 231,288 documents on "breaking up." Much advice is given on dissolving relationships. Consider the flamboyant *Cyrano Server* (1997), for those who need an instant "love or dump" note, allowing one to customize a message such as the following:

> I have enjoyed our relationship for the past few months, but fear that we have soared to exuberant heights only to alight upon a plateau of sadness. It would have been better to have just remained friends, but alas, our passion prevailed.
>
> Now, it is time for you to remove your heart-wrenching jeans from my closet and to detach your annoying pet pit bull from my leg.
>
> I will mourn the loss of your lips, as they are etched in my mind forever. [Cyrano Server 1997]

In postmodern virtuality, emotions can run deep on superficial playing fields. For example, in a post to a newsgroup, one woman wrote about her extreme hurt and humiliation resulting from an online relationship conducted over the distance of thousands of miles. It is a story heard frequently on the Internet. They met in a chat room and graduated to a intensely "romantic" e-mail communication. Poetry, words proclaiming deep, everlasting love and intense passion were exchanged over the wires. They spoke on the telephone and met face to face on several different occasions, both traveling significant distances for each of the impassioned rendezvous. As the relationship approached the yearlong mark, he began to make demands of marriage. She was reluctant. In a frenzy, he drove the thousands of miles that separated them to confront her. She wasn't home, so he left and went somewhere to e-mail her.

The e-mail came from another woman's home. Suspicious, she began to look through online personal ads and other chats.

He was all over cyberspace, with his passionate words and demands of marriage.

She asked the same painful question over and over: "Why did he do it to me?"

Although it was a virtual affair, her hurt was no less than if it had been in actuality. Many believe an individual online has a *greater* tendency to reveal himself or herself, thus becoming more vulnerable to emotional injury.

Similar to actuality, there are many "prowlers" online looking for a quick "hook up" before they move on to the next adventure. Without contextual cues such as facial expressions, dress, and body language, these individuals are more difficult to identify, particularly if one does not acknowledge the emotional risks online.

Sometimes fact can be far stranger than fiction, particularly in a world of disembodied gender. In May 1997, Margaret Hunter, a twenty-four-year-old administrative assistant from Alexandria, Virginia, won a bizarre court case. Hunter met a person online who called himself Thorne Wesley Jameson Groves from Bryan, Texas. Groves told Hunter that he was a "jet-set" businessman dying from AIDS. Hunter was convinced she had met the love of her life. They married—knowing that there would be no sexual intimacy. However, after four months of marriage, Groves did not get sicker—nor did he receive any medical bills. Suspicious, Hunter decided to locate her husband's birth certificate. Thorne, who wrapped bandages around his chest because of "rib" injuries, turned out to be "Holly" and very much female. Hunter sued and was awarded $264,000 in damages (McAllester 1997c).

What Do People *Do* When They Have Net.sex?

Net.sex, or sex in the electronic environment, raises a host of interesting questions:

- If a woman has Net.sex with a man and later finds out that *he* is really a *she*, is it a heterosexual or homosexual experience?
- If a gay man has Net.sex with another gay man, and finds out later that his lover is a female, how would they be classified?
- Is it adultery for a married person to have an online lover?
- Is it promiscuity, deception, or normal behavior to carry on "affairs" with several people online at the same time?
- Can rape occur in cyberspace?
- Is it child abuse to unknowingly have Net.sex with an underage (adolescent) partner?
- Is Net.sex really sex?
- Is Net.sex love?
- Are virtual sexual relationships based on intimacy or narcissism?
- What constitutes intimacy in virtual sexual relationships?

To answer these questions, it is necessary to define exactly what happens during a virtual sexual encounter. Turkle (1995) explains it as an online experience where two or more people type descriptions of physical actions, verbal descriptions, and emotional responses pertaining to their virtual sexual activity. Alt.culture, an online site, refers to net.sex as "computer-enhanced masturbation or computer-simulated copulation" (No date, paragraph one). Others use it as an umbrella term, referring to the entire spectrum of sexual activity in cyberspace. Slouka (1995) views it as "phone sex without the voice. Also known as [cybersex], tinysex, and, [my personal favorite] teledildonics" (p. 154). Whichever definition one might choose, net.sex provides one of the most popular attractions online.

Net.sex, like so many other issues in the disembodied gender, raises many questions about the nature and location of human sexual activity. Is sex primarily a physical act, a psychological act, or an equal combination of both? How much gender stretching is possible before emotional or psychological damage is risked? Does digitizing a biological function shared by all animal species further separate humans from their theoretical ancestors?

"Does net.sex boil down to a lifeless, soul-less thing that has lost the luster and depth of humankind?" asks Herbert Michelson, Ph.D. "Maybe we have lost our soul and are trying desperately to replace it with a poor imitation" (personal communication, January 20, 1997).

There are far more questions than answers. We do know, however, that net.sex is as diverse as human imagination and technology will allow it. The disembodied gender twists and turns net.sex into at least as many different forms as the embodied off-line gender. Cyberlibertarians might argue that it allows individuals to experiment with the "safest" sex known to humankind. Cyberluddites might return with the possibility that virtual sex is merely a form of universal, customized pornography. Whatever the ideology, the simple fact is that virtual sex has arrived and entrenched itself in cyberspace. How net.sex will develop and whether its popularity will continue with changing technology remains to be seen.

Can People Be Addicted to Computers?

Can a disembodied "cyber" space lead to a entirely new class of disordered behavior? This question is presently part of a furor surrounding the question whether IAD—Internet Addiction Disorder—actually exists. It's being argued on chat lines and professional e-mail lists; reported in print publications around the world; analyzed on television; and debated in almost every university with an Internet hookup. Perhaps the genesis of IAD, material for future legend, is the best indication of its validity.

The "disorder" was first identified in 1995. According to David Wallis (1997) in *The New Yorker*, it originated with "Dr. Goldberg, a burly, bearded Upper East Side [Manhattan] psychiatrist [who] allots two hours each day to browsing the bulletin boards of *PsyCom.Net*, a cyber club for shrinks" (p. 28). Ivan Goldberg, Webmaster of *Depression Central* and *PsyCom.Net*, is a seasoned netizen, navigating the electronic frontier since the early 1980s. In an attempt to make a statement about the rigidity of the *DSM*—and how mental health professionals took things too seriously, Goldberg came up with what he believed was a parody of DSM criteria—Internet Addiction Disorder. Goldberg facetiously defined the malady as:

> A maladaptive pattern of Internet use, leading to clinically
> significant impairment or distress as manifested by three

(or more) of the following, occurring at any time in the same 12-month period. [1995, p. 1]

Sound familiar? He continued the joke, referring to tolerance, withdrawal, overuse, inability to control use, reduction in social, occupational, or recreational activities, and the inability to stop. Dr. Goldberg never thought that anyone would take it seriously.

A lot of mental health professionals missed the punchline. Instead, Goldberg received e-mail from colleagues confessing to "netaholism." Somewhat askance, Goldberg set up the Internet Addiction Support Group. "Word of the group spread faster than a computer virus," writes Wallis (1997). "Hundreds of self-described addicts—some claiming to surf the net twelve hours a day—posted their pain." A new movement had begun. It spread out of control—reaching the far corners of the electronic globe. To illustrate, a psychology student from Brazil requested information, noting that he read about it in a local newspaper who reported that IAD was in a catalog produced by a Canadian Medical Institution. From England, a psychotherapist questioned whether IAD was really an addiction or a compulsive disorder. From the U.S. a young woman initiated research that would eventually be featured in some of the leading international English publications such as *The London Times*, *The New England Journal of Medicine*, and *The Canadian Medical Journal*. Clinics, online support groups, and a rush of research studies sprang up around the world.

Ivan Goldberg had to take a stand. In response to my e-mail requesting a statement, Dr. Goldberg explained his position (1997, May 27):

> Computers and the Internet are about as addicting as work. While we call some people "workaholics" it is clear that they are overworking to escape from some unpleasant reality in their lives. They do not overwork because of the addicting qualities of work itself.

People overuse computers or the Internet for the same reasons that other people overwork. Their interpersonal relationships are unsatisfactory, they are depressed, they are anxious about their future, etc. etc. etc . . .

Internet Addictive Disorder (IAD) is a poor name for a disorder involving the overuse of the Net. If such over-use needs a *DSM-IV*-type name it should be called "Pathological Computer/Internet Use Disorder."

BTW, the "criteria" for IAD, may be found at: http://www.cog.brown.edu/brochure/people/duchon/humor/internet. addiction.html

It is not an accident that the word "humor" is part of the URL.

Unfortunately, Pathological Computer/Internet Use Disorder is not as sexy as IAD. So, the battle continues to rage. Yet there are people who spend too much time online, abandoning actuality for the chats, discussions, and MOOs of virtual reality. Consider some of the things that have already occurred:

- Dr. Kimberly Young, psychologist and Director of the Center for Online Addiction, is described on the Center's website as "an international expert on the subject of Internet Addiction" ("Notable research" 1996);
- A young man in college gives up all his friends, stops going to classes, and spends his days and nights online, surfing the chats (Personal communication, January 14, 1997);
- A medically disabled young man constructs an online life that is far more exciting than his physical reality, spending at least forty hours a week on various MUDs (Turkle 1995);
- A husband comes home from work each night and spends the entire evening online, avoiding his wife. In

a week's time, he spends more hours online than at work or with his wife or friends (Personal communication, February 12, 1997);

- Dr. Mark Griffiths, a psychologist at the University of Plymouth in England, found that in a study of one hundred internet users, twenty-two reported a cocaine-like "rush" when online (Egger and Rauterberg 1996).

Numerous studies have been conducted to determine whether IAD actually exists. In a small survey conducted by Steve Thompson (1996), he attempted to determine what happens to people that describe themselves as Internet addicts. Seventy-two percent reported an addiction or dependency to the Internet with 33 percent viewing it as a negative force in their lives. Interestingly, 47 percent reported a physical response such as blurred vision or sleep problems. Thompson concludes that IAD or technology dependence is a very real phenomenon that has the power to disrupt individual lives. He predicts that this will increase as the size of the global Internet community grows.

In a much larger study by Egger and Rauterberg (1996), 450 responses to a questionnaire on the World Wide Web were analyzed. Most of the responses came from Switzerland. Ten percent of the respondents identified themselves as addicted or dependent on the Internet. The authors concluded that there was a strong indication that Internet addiction does, in fact, exist.

Kimberly S. Young, Ph.D., Director of the Center for Online Addiction (COLA), is as well-known for IAD as Ivan Goldberg. She has appeared in print, online, on television, and on radio. In an audio interview on Ann Online (Young 1996a), Young describes the Internet addict as needing to "have it" every day, spending forty to sixty hours online a week. She suggests it goes beyond obsession, beyond information or communication, into a deep emotional attachment that allows the individual to access forbidden parts of himself or herself. Utilizing this access, the addict plays out fantasies that are not generally accepted in daily life. Young investigated the case studies of 396 dependent Internet users, extrapolating from the seven criteria Substance Dependence in *DSM-IV* (American Psychiatric Association 1994):

1. Tolerance or the need for increased amounts to achieve the desired effect;
2. Withdrawal or the maladaptive behavioral change that occurs when heavy use is suspended;
3. Dependence or the need for increased amounts than was originally intended;
4. Persistent need to reduce or regulate use;
5. Investment of time to obtain, use, or recover from the effects of usage;
6. Important social, occupational, or recreational activities may be reduced or given up; and
7. Withdrawal from other activities to spend more time with the addiction.

Sound familiar? Young (1996b) found that "people can and do become addicted to the Internet," with "significant academic, social and occupational consequences similar to those problems that have been well-documented for other established addictions such as pathological gambling."

Of course, for every study there is one of those quirky Internet jokes. Richard Scott (1995), founder of *Interneters Anonymous*, begins his online story with the following anecdote:

Hi, I'm Rich, and I am an Internet Addict . . . I gave up eating to find time for my HTML tutorials, neglected my kids for the sake of a good URL. My wife decided celibacy for the sake of a 17" monitor was not right for her, and my neighbors thought I had moved to Brazil. My lawn started to look like a meadow and my boss wondered why I left the office at three in the afternoon. Suddenly it hit me, I was an Internet Junkie, a social dropout. I knew I had to get my life in order . . . [p. 1]

Interneters Anonymous (Scott 1995) even offers twelve easy steps to solve your problems. Surfing further, one can join *F12 Online Anonymous*, a.k.a. "netaholic modemheads" (Baird 1996) or venture into the *World Headquarters of Netaholics Anonymous*, where for a mere twelve dollars you can own the official T-shirt.

Is IAD a serious disorder, good joke, or something in-between? Are we still too new in cyberspace to make that assessment? Is it simply another obsession manifested in vulnerable personalities? It seems that one can discuss the issue endlessly, with both sides offering reasonable arguments. Perhaps it merely reflects a range of human behavior that is measured along a continuum with light use on one end, heavy or obsessive use on the other, and most falling in the large space between. And perhaps the battle of its existence has become an entertaining exercise in defining pathology, occupying the time and attention of individuals who are struggling to identify the role of cyberspace in daily life. On one professional e-mail list, *Psychology&Research*, the debate is refueled periodically. Here are a few responses:

It is unfortunate that our addiction to patholization invites us to conjure up yet another "disorder" to add to our geometrically expanding DSM taxonomy.

Tom Conran

* * *

There are several people doing research on Internet Addiction . . . Kimberly Young at University of Pittsburgh,

Keith Anderson at RPI, John Aiello at Rutgers, Howard Schaffer at Harvard Medical School, Mark Griffiths in England. I am about to start a co-morbidity study.

Maressa Hecht Orzac

* * *

While we are at it, why don't we establish the following as possible DSM pathologies:

ATM Addiction Disorder (overuse of cash machines)

Vending Machine Disorder (habitual use of Coke Machines)

Car Addiction Disorder (habitual reliance upon automotive transportation)

(add your own modern convenience disorder here)

Of course, these would first need intensive working groups to study the phenomena for a couple of years before placement in the "disorders warranting further consideration." Or we could just make them V codes. . . :)

J. N. Browndyke

* * *

Is There a Difference between ADD and Life in Cyberspace?

Jason sits at his computer, logged on to America Online. On his screen are four Instant Message (IM) boxes—he is having conversations with four separate people. One is another teenager in his community, the other three live in states thousands of miles away. In the background, the television is tuned to *The Simpsons*. Jason follows the television rerun as he flips from the IMs to his homework, a composition for his high school English class.

In front of another computer, Jan answers her e-mail with *Nine Inch Nails* wailing from a CD in her stereo. As soon as she clicks on the "send" icon, Jan is surfing, looking for a beach resort where she can spend her vacation. She flips to an airline Web page and quickly moves on to a travel site. She spends a minute or two there checking out several vacation options and then is surfing once again, looking for islands in the Caribbean. Her computer beeps, telling her she's just received e-mail. Jan checks the message, sends a short reply, and resumes her surfing. Fewer than five minutes has elapsed.

Are Jason and Jan suffering from ADD? Or is the computer nurturing it? Which comes first—the virtual chicken or the egg?

In *Self-Help & Psychology*, Gobbo and Bolaski (1997) offer their views concerning attention disorders on the Internet.

What better place for a person with fluctuating attention span and the impulse to move from topic to topic quickly to collect information than on the Internet. One can move from site to site with the click of a mouse and in a very brief span of time take in a variety of information that is interesting, provides frequent, immediate, consistent, reward that increases attention and performance while reducing impulsive restless behavior. [p. 1]

Most Web designers are well aware that pages must be short. If they're too long, surfers simply won't read them. Not surprisingly, *GVU's WWW 6th User Survey* (1996) found that 77 percent of Web users view slow speed as the number one problem online. *GVU's 7th WWW User Survey* (1997) found the same results. However, only 66 percent in 1997 viewed speed as the top problem—probably the result of advances in connect speed technology. Speed, in both surveys, is rated more problematic than issues such as finding information, organization, and cost. Cyberspace is oriented toward the quick-action and short attention span style that we observe in television commercials, action movies, and popular television shows such as *ER*. Gergen (1991) maintains that the dilemma of contemporary life originates in a self saturated with different roles, identities, events, opportunities, and so forth. The more conveniences that technology introduces to "save time," the less time we have. Consider those devices designed to ease our lives— such as cellular telephones, answering machines, fax machines, *and* computers—and ask whether they have saved time or added new opportunities to take on additional chores. The cellular telephone, for example, "follows" us into our cars, onto the beach, as we walk along the street, and enables us to make more telephone calls than ever before. The laptop computer brings work onto airplanes, into hotel rooms, and on commuter trains. The concept of saving time has been translated into doing *more*, not less. "Saved time" feeds the multiplicity intrinsic to the saturated self, opening new avenues for activity rather than rest or leisure. Does that, along with the media, necessitate an *intellectually* manic approach to daily life that emulates attention deficit?

Whether ADD, ADHD, or intellectual mania, it tends to look the same online. For the people who suffer from attention disorders, the Internet provides a comfortable habitat, not only from its structure but also because impulsive, short-focus, quick-moving behavior is a standard. With an Internet chicken, it really does not matter which came first—the virtual chicken or the virtual egg. They all play the same.

**What is Inappropriate Behavior
in the Electronic Environment?**

Social transgressions are readily adapted into the electronic environment. They are directly related to the technology, appearing and disappearing along with upgrades. Presently, the most common social transgressions involve spamming, spoofing, and flaming. Clearly, more serious crime is also increasing, mirroring human social behaviors in actuality.

Interestingly, many of today's inappropriate behaviors may disappear with the advent of widespread audio and visual applications. The impact and severity of inappropriate behavior is relative to the sender, the receiver, and the context in which it was written. Technology provides new protection for the offended. The utility popularly known as a *bozo filter* or *kill file* allows a netizen to block messages from another person. In other words, if you don't like what someone is saying it is relatively easy to "turn that person off"—somewhat akin to hanging up the telephone.

What are these inappropriate virtual behaviors? Lee-Ellen Marvin (1994), in *The Journal of Computer-Mediated Communication*, defines spam and spoof in terms of communication. "Spam" is an "excess of communication," while "spoof" is "unattributed communication." Spam is when the Internet is flooded with multiple copies of the same message, forced on people who do not elect to receive it. Spammers reach individuals, groups, and communities in the electronic environment. A single message is designed to reach thousands—even tens of thousands—of people with one delivery. Made notorious by junk e-mailers, spamming is also used by individuals (as well as ISPs) promoting products and services. Spamming is not limited to electronic commerce. People trying to get any message across to large numbers of receivers also spam. They can range from proselytizers, hate mongers, or mischief-makers trying to start flame wars.

Consider some numbers. Sanford Wallace, President of Cyber Promotions, perhaps the most notorious "professional spammer" online, claimed his company sends out almost two million messages a day (Wallace 1997). L-Soft InfoCenter (1996), the people that license LISTSERV software, claim that with their software and ten thousand to fifteen thousand dollars in hardware, one could deliver five million messages a day. Before getting a court injunction in 1996 to stop the onslaught, America Online reported receiving nearly two million spams from Cyber Promotions *per day* (Mueller, no date).

Although closely related to spamming, spoofing is a much more personal and intrusive act. Spammers usually follow cultural (commercial) traditions in their race to make money. Their disregard for privacy and electronic rights is loathsome. Spoofers take this transgression in another direction—they steal digital identity. Spoofers attack attribution, snatching ownership and control in malicious forgeries that can leave victims angry, confused, and without retaliation.

The spoofer manipulates the technology to imply that a message or post is coming from someone other than himself or herself. In this "unattributed" communication, individuals can be "framed" for statements, threats, actions, and even more serious computer crimes made by savvy techies. Spoofs can range from simple, humorous statements to serious attacks on individual privacy and Internet security. Perhaps the most common spoof is posting false or inflammatory messages to newsgroups. One of the best examples of this type of spoof was with Bob Rae, the former premier of Ontario. His e-mail address was spoofed, used to post sexually explicit messages and politically embarrassing statements on Usenet groups (Ferrell 1997). In an even stranger spoof, the former girlfriend of Larry Ellison, CEO of Oracle Systems, was brought to court in what was referred to as a "Silicon Valley soap opera" (Pimentel 1997). In 1995, the ex-girlfriend, Adelyn Lee, won a $100,000 settlement in a wrongful termination suit. She claimed that she had been fired from her job as an executive assistant after she refused to have sex with Ellison. A key piece of evidence was an e-mail message that had been supposedly sent to Ellison from Lee's former boss, Craig Ramsey. The e-mail informed Ellison that he had terminated Lee according to the CEO's request. Two years later, Lee was accused of forging the e-mail to sue Oracle Corporation. She was found guilty of perjury and falsification of evidence (Pimentel 1997).

In contrast to spamming and spoofing, "flaming" is communication that insults, chastises, argues, or directly attacks. Obviously, this behavior adapts well into the technology and content of cyberspace. In a classic article published in *The New Yorker*, John Seabrook (1994) describes "My First Flame":

> Now, for the first time, I understood the novelty and power of the technology I was dealing with. No one had ever said something like this to me before, and no one *could* have said this to me before: in any other medium, these words would be, literally, unspeakable. [p. 71]

It is easy to flame. Holland (1996) suggests that the computer alters the nature of communication. Computer mediated communication is a transformation into cyborg identity—

netizens "exist" in a half-human, half-machine state. This leads to ambivalence. On one hand, the computer is the good parent and does wonderful things for the user—it balances checkbooks, plays games, spits out tax forms, and, of course, brings one through the looking glass into the electronic world. On the other hand, it is mindless, without common sense or human intuition—it can fail at any given time, the victim of a long list of mysterious maladies ranging from viruses, bugs, glitches, and human error. This is compounded by the paradox that a user's control over the computer is at odds with the computer's control over the user. When the computer is down, an individual's digital "life" ceases. When lines are "unavailable," a few minutes set aside for surfing can stretch into hours waiting for repairs, less traffic, or entry into the system. What at one moment appears to be a willing partnership can quickly turn into an adversarial relationship with mixed feelings of complicity and rage. According to Holland, this ambivalence is projected onto others online, compelling individuals to act out their emotional responses.

Not all agree. Herring (1994) argues that "a popular explanation advanced by CMC researchers is that flaming is a by-product of the medium itself—the decontextualized and anonymous nature of CMC leads to 'disinhibition' in users and a tendency to forget that there is an actual human being at the receiving end of one's emotional outbursts" (p. 5). She maintains that these ideas have ignored the impact of gender style, asserting that "the simple fact of the matter is that it is virtually only men who flame" (p. 5). Gender notwithstanding, the conditions of textual CMC lend itself to inappropriate behavior. Digital anonymity leads to a loosening of social constraints and accountability. CMC transgressions can and do flourish in such an environment. Herring (1994) maintains that if it these behaviors could be completely attributed to the medium, than females as well as males would be involved.

Kozma (no date) offers another possible, if not quite plausible, explanation. He views flaming as the Internet's way of regulating itself. Kozma argues that there is no central authority that enforces netiquette, no longstanding social traditions to guide behavior. Consequently, individuals take over. These individuals, nicknamed the *net police*, publicly highlight offending behavior, often giving suggestions on more socially appropriate alternatives. Flames can range from simple corrections to harsh, punitive attacks. They may utilize irony, humor, sarcasm, name-calling, and expletives to get their point across.

Who Commits Sex Crimes in Cyberspace?

Perhaps the most lethal aspect of the electronic environment is the creation of a new playing field for sex crimes. Sexual predators freely wander the dark virtual streets of cyberspace. There are stalkers, sexual harassers, pedophiles, and other online sexual abusers. Clearly, the Internet mirrors actuality in abuse and obscenity. What is so unclear is how to work with it. In the 1997 Supreme Court hearing on the Communications Decency Act, Schwartz (1997) wrote, "The real question isn't what's on the Net, but rather what is the Net" (para. 1). The search was for a metaphor that would enable boundaries to be established. Is the Internet like telephone, radio, print material, television, or a public park? In order to ascertain First Amendment Rights, the judges have to know exactly what they are dealing with. And no one has yet been able to define the parameters of cyberspace. One wonders if there are—or will ever be—measurable boundaries to an ever-expanding technologically constructed environment. Consider the virtual possibilities for one type of sexual predator: the pedophile.

The Internet provides a compelling environment for pedophiles. Individuals can find networks and share fantasies and pornographic materials with others of similar interest. It is easy to exchange information using pseudonyms or maintaining anonymity. Sexually explicit material can be traded, sold, or simply shared worldwide. Direct contact with children can be established in children's chat groups, bulletin boards, newsgroups, and e-mail lists. Most ominous, these connections can be used to nurture trust and curiosity in future victims, leading to rendezvous all over the world. When one considers that an estimated 6 million children under age eighteen regularly use the Internet (Witham 1997), the possibilities for abuse are sobering.

Father Adrian McLeish was a forty-five-year-old Roman Catholic priest from St. Joseph's Church in the United Kingdom. McLeish was known in his presbytery in Gilesgate, Durham, as " 'a helpful, loving priest' with a fatal flaw in his attraction to children" (Stokes 1996, paragraph 23). The priest sexually abused young boys and participated in an international pedophile ring on the Internet. McLeish took pictures and wrote descriptions of his victims, collecting and disseminating a voluminous amount of child pornography. Ironically, his behavior began when he was a junior priest in another parish. In 1991, burglars broke into the presbytery in Wallsend, North Tyneside, and later contacted police to say they had found pornographic videos. By then, McLeish had moved to Durham, claiming there was no link between the break-in and his decision to change churches. Five years later, when he was arrested, police found a library of computer disks with 11,000 images and evidence of participation in a ring of at least nine other pedophiles in Sweden, Germany, France, New Zealand, and the U.S. Justice Moses, the Judge at McLeish's trial, said to the priest:

> For six years you sexually abused four young boys, some of whom you groomed with a view to indulging your future desires. You had a vast collection of child pornography and, in four months, you spent 143 hours building up your collection. It is difficult to stop such distribution

of these pictures. Users are rarely caught but it is the active part you have played in the distribution of these pictures, which is the real crime. It is also clear you lived up to your fantasies, fueled by pornography to which you had access through the Internet. [Stokes 1996, para. 7]

Father McLeish was sentenced to six years in prison. He is not alone. Online sexual abuse is increasing. Although federal child protection laws in the U.S. make it a felony crime to create, possess, or disseminate child pornography, punishable by up to ten years in prison and a $10,000 fine (Meyers 1995), "proof" of online criminal activity is difficult to obtain. To arrest a pedophile, one must be able to prove that the perpetrator transmitted obscene images of minors or actually left the keyboard to solicit sex from a child in actuality. It is perfectly legal for an adult to *write* sexually explicit messages to children online or impersonate other children in sexual exchanges in chatrooms (Witham 1997). These distinctions were exemplified in an FBI operation called "Innocent Images." In September 1995, the FBI raided 120 homes and arrested a dozen people—the culmination of a two-year investigation into child pornography on America Online. The FBI said it had collected pornography involving children ages two to thirteen, in photographs where they were nude or having actual or simulated sex. The investigation was the result of the 1993 kidnapping of a ten-year-old-boy in Maryland who was believed to have been lured by computer pedophiles. The boy was never found (Meyers 1995).

> # Is Something Missing?: Three Essays

Perhaps the following essays that juxtapose three different ages and viewpoints to understand the potential dangers that
lurk behind the screen can best answer this question.

Herb Michelson is a retired psychologist. Storm King is a
baby boomer approaching middle age. The youngest writer,
Russell Fink, is a college student. Although separated in age
by as much as half a century, these three essayists have a
strange, haunting similarity. There is a pervasive sense of loss—
something missing—that permeates their words. The question
lingers behind their words: Is cyberspace nothing but a poor
substitute for that intrinsic human quality so readily exchanged
for computers, televisions, and cellular phones? Or is it, in a
very sinister sense, more than meets the screen—lending itself
to the manipulation of the human spirit?

"THOUGHTS ON CYBERSPACE"
Herbert Michelson

It's 5 A.M. in Amherst, Massachusetts, and it's undecided
outside, snowing, sleeting, and freezing all at the same time.
Since I'm in New England, I can't predict what will happen
out there in the next ten minutes. So I commence my morning

routine: SAD—preventing lights to combat the psychological blahs of winter and coffee to wake the rest of me to the business of fighting off my knee jerk daily reactions that could result in doing combat with the PC mavens of "happy valley." It is my ongoing effort to survive the 1990s still sentient, remaining a rational being with real feelings. I am attempting to resist the automation of my spirit and mind in an "elevated" technological age without becoming a raging conservative in all the important ways.

I turn to my trusty NEC to read the latest in *The New York Times*, *CNN,* and *Slate*. In the process I paste myself on the screen with the identity: "herbm@". And then, with only a few clicks, I give myself my very own cyberspace soul. Damned if I will! Cowardly, I muddle through the Web, peeking but never committing, fearful of downloading lest I become virus ridden, careful of what I write lest it be vandalized—or even worse. And I never expose my flanks to attack so I do not reveal my credit card number, my social security number, or my exact residence address.

Is this consensus reality or is it Cyberspace? I think that we need to know the difference and keep the distance between the two.

Why Cyberspace? I have been through a lifetime of events—a medic in World War Two; clinical practice when the first piece of furniture in the office was an analyst's couch looking like an electric chair for some and a womb for others; a time when transference and countertransference were supreme and hadn't been replaced with a prescription; and a time when one could admit to liberal views and browse "head shops" without shame.

Now the 1960s have become the politically correct fiction of the 1990s. None of it prepared me for cyberspace and what I see on the current screen as fast becoming a fearsome monster threatening to devour the Reality we have all agreed upon—replacing it with an intricate array of data that can be manipulated and can manipulate the Human Spirit.

Is there really a need for cyberspace? It is a very new concept to most of us mortals, perhaps best understood by those anonymous, bizarre, or unfulfilled folks who wish to create a reality apart from ordinary reality or who have not found it possible to function in the real world. Some have applied this escapist style to both life and death. Now we have entered the era of virtual cemeteries and one can buy a "plot" in cyberspace for the right fee. I wonder if one day "death" will happen when there is a widespread power outage and our computers lose the electrical power that animates them?

It might sound like I'm talking from that ever growing segment of our species that we gingerly label as psychotic, "out of touch with reality," or just plain silly. Why worry, some might wonder, "it's the new wave, the future." From certain perspectives it would not be hard to view cyberspace as a flight from reality. Then we could talk about a new universal disorder: cyberpsychosis, suggesting that once again we have found a means to escape from ourselves and the world and failed in our duty to improve ourselves and the world.

This "improvement" of oneself and the world has been called "tikkun" in the *Kaballah*, the mystical underpinning of Judaism and much of Christianity. "Fixing" oneself and fixing the world are not part of some grand healing effort, rather it refers to preparing one's soul to receive and contain the divine light that is basic to many spiritual philosophies as well as prominent in Jewish mysticism. Similarly, "fixing" the world refers also to the positive preparation of the world for the great peace and healing that is postulated as part of the future of humankind.

"Tikkun hanefesh" and "tikkun olam" (fixing the soul and fixing the world) are not issues in cyberspace. Cyberspace in-

stead seems to provide a forum of expression for some of the
nastiest and degraded aspects of the Human Condition while
at the same time leaving a window of opportunity for the more
elevated and decent aspects of our nature. Sadly, few really active participants in Cyberspace are able to resist the temptation
to express the negative to find personal and often psychopatho-
logical satisfaction and profit. The problem doesn't lie in the
synthetic reality called Cyberspace—it lies squarely with us!
This has been the case with many of our discoveries and innovations. We have not adequately prepared ourselves to cope
with this new "light," we haven't attended to "tikkun hanefesh,"
and we find ourselves launched into a new and unexplored
world that we are able to create as we like it. Heaven help us!

Cyberspace leads away from the real world and the real
organism that is humankind. It has the potential to replace the
Human Spirit (the soul?) with an electronic space described as
a "cyber" world. The vacuous cyberworld is less than real, replete with a frightening sense of finality. Ultimately, it departs
from what I and many others define as the unknowable God.

The parallel between cyberspace and its mixture of real,
unreal, and unimaginable is fascinating. With the fascination
comes the risk of allowing ourselves to get too deeply en-
meshed in the nooks and crannies of a world that exists only
on the level of the electron and ends when the switch is turned
to off. There is now a language called "Cyberbabble" that has
been imposed upon us by a jealous G-d still mindful of the old
days when HIS "creations" got too ambitious and attempted to
invade the celestial realms with their arrogant little tower.

This is a not so subtle movement to replace HIM with a
Cybergod—in direct violation of a very old commandment
against idol worship and "other" gods. I suspect that cyberspace
puts us in a danger similar to the time-honed habit of anoint-
ing heroes and demigods. For example, through the ages our
need to medicate our ills, malaise, and neuroses has elevated

the healer to the lofty plateau of DOCTOR and ultimately to the embittered heights of "ordained Doctor" whose dictates we follow under penalty of pain, suffering and yes, even death. Unless we remain humble and rational in the electronic hodge podge, we may find ourselves spelling cyberspace in capital letters C-E in much the same way some traditional folks spell G-D (since the many names of G-D may not be spoken). Analogously, since we give our DOCTORS a great deal of freedom when it comes to our bodies and minds, their "ordination" is a predictable outcome of the deference that is shown for their high (above human) station. Recently, Dr. Kevorkian has made us more than mindful of the doctor's direct participation in death; cloning has brought the wonders of human replication into our doctor's armamentarium; and genetic engineering offers a panoply of heavenly alterations. Just pick and choose what you like!

Is there a language we can use in Cyberspace that bypasses all this heresy? A language I can understand? The folks at my Internet service provider speak only in the alien "Cyberbabble." I fear communicating with them in real English lest I offend the cybergods, much less C-E. Yet I refuse to kneel at the altar of C-E . . .

But wait . . . I just looked out the window. A world is there, just behind my monitor's screen. It might be snowing, sleeting, and freezing—but it's really there!

I can't help but think of Woody Allen's old movie, *Sleeper*. Remember the "orgasmatron"—the magical sex box with the plain outside wrapping? A human + machine masturbatory interaction? Imagine the science fiction-type android complete with programmed feelings and the appropriate plumbing.

What about that nebulous thing we call the "soul"? Is it there? Does it exist? Is it necessary? I'd rather not know the answers. I like the mystery. We need the mystery. If we forget this, it's all over for us.

A journey into a politically correct, cyborg-dominated world reveals what I see as a lifeless, soul-less, affect-less experience devoid of the human luster and depth that has been apparent everywhere in our history, even in our worst depredations and bloodlettings. We will have lost our soul and replaced it with a poor imitation. Sure, some day we may invent computers that can think and create. We may even become enslaved to them as doomsayers. But we will never create and insert a soul. That is ultimately where the real danger in cyberspace lurks—the fact that there are already too many of us who cannot leave their computer screens and celebrate the real world. And it will get worse. Whatever you choose to call it—addiction, obsession, or play—the pathology is only in its infancy.

We need to see through the rose-colored glasses we all wear when we enter uncharted realms. I find cyberspace and its attendant bells and whistles very interesting and provocative, but I have many fears regarding its potential. It is very unlike your run-of-the mill uncharted realms such as the human psyche, the moon, and the depths of the sea, where we enter into what is *there*. In cyberspace, we create what's there from the very beginning and before we realize it we come face-to-face with ourselves, particularly the dark side of the Human Condition.

I don't fear for those folks whose feet are rooted in reality and find relief from cyber-activities by seeking real life and its inhabitants. Those are the folks who find passion, life, and people—who know and nurture love. But what about the vast body of those who uncritically participate in the replacement reality of cyberspace? What about the growing numbers of computer nerds amongst us? Are they to be the next high priests?

The ordained cyberfreaks? Are they the folks who have already gotten caught up in the substitution of cyberspace for the real— or are we?

Most of these people see themselves as moral individuals just having "fun." They ignore the growing numbers of those who can't leave the Web—its chat groups and other delights— for time to sleep. For time to eat with other people. For time to love. For time to write a song, paint a picture, or talk face to face, smelling the pheromones. They are experiencing life less and less, encased in their private technological window on the world. It is in the nature of our species to play silly or per- haps sinister games walking the edge of the abyss, confident that we won't totter and fall. Shades of the nuclear bomb. In a moment of passive resistance, I attempted to taunt the G-D of cyberspace. With all the snow and sleet outside, I turned to cyberspace to send some mail, read the headlines, and find a bit of ancient philosophy. I could not get online! Cussing and ranting, not to speak of tempting the Cybergod who reprised with silence, my computer seemed to be near death. After a few days, I finally decided to e-mail the server with my complaints (expressed in the most observant PC language) because my telephone calls for help were unanswered. To add a little per- sonal satisfaction to my plight and to rattle some cages in the realm of the cybergods, I changed the rules. I ventured onto the server Website to complete the online "help" form. Instead of writing "Help" or "Problems around disconnection while I write scripture in my e-mail" in the Subject section of the form, I put the body of the letter there—leaving the appropriate space blank. The response was immediate—I wrote my defiant, im- properly formatted letter on Sunday and on Monday morning I received a lengthy response in which the Cyber-PC monitor spent half the letter politely, but firmly, suggesting that in the future I should use the expected format to ease "their" reading of e-mail. It was the first time I had been scolded by a Cyber-PC monitor.

Interestingly, in my letter I had specifically stated I was using this format to GET THEIR ATTENTION SINCE NOTHING ELSE SEEMED TO WORK. That message had been ignored.

Unfortunately, it spreads beyond my own simple mischief. A UMass college student, and customer in my son's automotive business, had spent too much money on his partying. When he came to get his car, he couldn't pay the bill. Trying to get something for nothing, he wove a fabric of lies. But it was very clear: he had contracted for the work and then couldn't—or wouldn't—pay the bill. My son insisted he make good on his debt. Unsuccessful in his attempt to manipulate the situation, the student turned the battle over to daddy who, via long distance, defended the lies of his child. My son explained the agreed-upon work, faxed an invoice to the irate father, and insisted that he be paid accordingly.

Daddy, taking a cyber-extortion stance suggested that if his demands were not satisfied he would post a warning on the Web advising people to boycott the business. Daddy added darkly "a college community takes the Web seriously. And word moves fast on the electronic grapevine." I wrote a brief note to him about the realities of libel—using his letter as my illustration—and he backed off. However, it made me realize that the typical Web extortionist can't be scared off as readily because he can so easily remain anonymous.

Two weeks later a similar cyber-extortion took place with a far more sweeping impact. Two kids in Amherst brought pipe bombs to school and placed them in their lockers. They were live bombs. Their bragging alerted someone, the police came and carted off the bombs. The kids made the papers but their identities were "protected" because of their age.

The debate over their fate began in earnest in the local PC community, with the following statements repeated over and over again as though they were valid excuses for the kids' behavior:

"They were just fooling around."
"They're only kids."
"The bombs didn't go off."
"They learned how to make the bombs on the Web."

The majority of people in the community supported this stance on the basis that no one or thing was actually harmed by the bombs. The minorities were folks like myself who felt that the response should be fast, just, and convincingly punitive. In any case, it eventually boiled down to a liberal versus conservative battle—a popular pastime these days. Sadly, the implications of the behavior and the affect of the PC debates were never really addressed.

One Amherst resident loudly came to the defense of the would-be bombers. He threatened, nay beseeched people to put their objections to punishment on the Web. He advocated retribution against those who persisted in their insistence that the boys be punished according to the law. Online punishment? Democracy on the Web? Justice? The Human Condition remains unchanged—only the metaphor of expression is different.

The point remains that we need to avoid the creation of a C-E, or Cybergod. We need to prepare the vessel (ourselves) for this new challenge/toy/tool.

Cyberspace can quickly blur the lines between reality and virtual reality, further tainting the human condition. We must guard ourselves against the changes until such time comes that we can handle the creature and not get carried away by its charm. I don't think that will be very easy. It appears that our species is beginning the new millennium like a two-year old child throwing a temper tantrum—with a loaded gun in hand and without the knowledge that there is a difference between the trigger and the muzzle.

"THE IMPERSONAL NATURE OF INTERPERSONAL CYBERSPACE RELATIONSHIPS"
Storm A. King

I couldn't get to sleep tonight. Something kept turning in my head. For the last year and a half, I have spent considerable time at this keyboard. Participating in virtual support groups. Reading thousands of notes from discussion groups devoted to topics relating to psychology and virtual communities. And writing about how valuable it is to feel connected to so many others that share similar interests. Some things happened this week to conspire and caused me to realize the true nature and effect of what is missing in this medium. We don't really know each other, because we don't tend to share the kind of information that brings people close and fosters a sense of community. Even in the virtual groups where that is part of the stated purpose for participation.

What happened is that one person died, one person got very angry with me, and another shared about meeting a lover for the first time that they had come to know over the Net. All on different e-mail lists. As I tell these three stories, think about what you know and do not know about the people you have met here.

Mr. Gerald M. Phillips, among his many other accomplishments, was a regular contributor to a list I am on. This list is devoted to discussions of the interpersonal nature of cyberspace communication and has over a thousand subscribers. When he died this week, what I knew about him was based on my reading the near daily notes that he posted to this group over the last year and a half. As the tributes to him came pouring in, my impression of this man was filled in. I learned about who he truly was for the first time. People wrote about how he had helped them, about how he had been a friend and a mentor. They spoke of his goals and ideas and accomplishments in a way that made me realize that I had in fact barely known this person at all. I knew his ideas, and a bare minimum of his situation. Since this list is not an emotional support group, it is quite appropriate that I had known no more than I did. But, having been given this new insight into the personal nature of someone who had been an influence so many lives, including mine, it caused me to reconsider the insight I think I have with others [with] whom I share cyberspaces that are designed to be support groups. And to contemplate what it is I use to feel close to someone here.

Telling this next story is a bit tricky. I want to talk about something that went on in a private, closed group, in a way that I can share with that group and others. The nearly 200 people on this list value the privacy of it and often post notes that are very self-disclosing. An incident occurred last fall. One of the members of the group was in trouble, and this caused great stress and anxiety among the other members, who tried their best to help. As someone doing research into and writing about the value of such support groups, I saw this as an example that could be used to explain to others the nature and depth of the interpersonal bonds that form in such cyberspace groups. I wrote an article, and shared it with the group. There was a misunderstanding regarding permission to tell this story in the way I did. The member who had been at the focus of this incident became very upset with me. The group sharing was disrupted, and emotions ran very high. I concluded I had made a mistake, and agreed not to try to publish that article. This person and I are net.friends again, because we care about and respect each other. This all had several effects on me. One was to sharpen my awareness of the ethics involved in writing about what goes on in virtual communities. That is a whole separate subject I am looking into. The other effect was to make me realize that it is too easy to think that I know someone here because I have read a lot of notes they post.

It is all the small details that are missing. Cyberspace relationships are truncated versions of real life ones. The exchanges are short, and the awareness of others' true nature is illusionary. Even in the closest of groups, the notes posted represent such a small fraction of the person writing, that intimacy and interpersonal bonding occur only if someone unilaterally chooses it. Behind every one of the notes I read daily from even my best net.friends, there is a life, filled with houses and cars and wives and kids and jobs, of which I am mostly completely unaware.

One more illustration. One of the lists I am on is an open list, but the subject matter is very personal. I have met in person a half dozen of the approximately 100 people on this list and feel very close to all the rest that post regularly. Last night, a member told the story of what happened when he traveled across the country to meet, in person for the first time, a lady he had fallen in love with by e-mail. In an 8k message to the group, he talked about his trip and his hopes and anxieties and fears. The little details were there. A traffic jam on the way, the color of the night, a light in her window. I could feel it all because it was concrete, not just the ideas and emotions, but the context and situation they occurred in. I realized that what fosters insight, produces emotional attachment, and promotes the sense of community in virtual environments is the completeness of the picture in my head of the other people here. Not just how they feel about the important issues we share in common, but what the world looks like from their eyes.

The media continues to hype the Internet for all its worth. Membership in commercial interactive services is at an all time high and rising ever faster. What are all these millions of people doing here? Asking inane questions? Lots. Having meaningless chat sessions where the underlying attraction is to try to flirt? Yes. Sifting through unimaginable piles of information organized in a random fashion? Indeed. Arguing and yelling and calling each other names? This happens a lot in some forums. Falling madly in love? This happens way more than anyone I know has been able to account for so far. And forming lasting, important friendships based on interpersonal bonds that are mostly illusions. Yet, somehow, for so many, the cold impersonal presence of the words and the ideas expressed on a computer screen are being translated into emotional connections and exciting adventures into long-distance relationships. When real lives touch each other, things change. What makes it real is the connection to the real life behind the ideas, as expressed in the little details. The picture of others is only completed in its context, form, and colors. We come alive through the knowledge that the other has grandkids, drives a certain kind of car, likes a particular type of breakfast cereal.

Well, it is after 5 A.M., and the muse that wouldn't let me sleep is leaving. I plan to post this to groups where the purpose is not one of fostering intimacy or exchanging emotional support, but, as a bit of an experiment, allow me to share some details and see if you agree with this assessment.

I live in a one-bedroom apartment on the second floor. I just stepped out on the balcony to stretch and get some fresh air. Even without my contacts in, I can see that the sky has a few clouds, just turning pink. The birds have started their pre-dawn chirping. It is still in the room, except for the sound of the exhaust fan on my computer, sitting on my big wrap-around desk, and the tapping of these keys. My desk is its normal mess. Organized piles of half-sorted papers, notes to myself, and yesterday's mail strewn on top of that. I am alone, because my wife has been working out of town for a few months now. I do not like kicking around this apartment by myself, but the new shag carpet feels good under my bare feet when I end up pacing and thinking like I did tonight. The second cup of strong coffee since midnight got cold before it was half gone some time ago, but I drank it anyway. I have no doubt that the struggle to write this and the lack of sleep will seem well worth it later, for my fascination with and attempts to explain interpersonal computer intimacy is a big creative outlet in my life. I hope it helps others. Now, to take a hot shower and sleep a bit. I have to drive an hour to be at my mom's at noon for a family get-together.

"REALITY?"
Russell Fink

Who is "I"?

Traditionally this pronoun has represented a person's singular, stable, identity. The *American Heritage Dictionary* (1995) defines identity as "the distinct personality of an individual regarded as persisting entity; individuality." Identity is what defines us, it creates "who and what we are." Identity has always been seen through the philosophy of the "I."

For example, the Romanticists of the nineteenth century described human identity as coming from the soul or how we existed on the inside. Twentieth century Modernists changed that view, stating that identity was how we existed in relation to others. Computer screens and the simulation of reality in cyberspace has changed the human equation of "I." "I" becomes a simulation in the electronic world. As we move into the twenty-first century we enter a period of postmodernism where the philosophy distorts "I" even further. The argument shifts from one simulated "I" to many with each single human consisting of multiple identities rather than a single identity.

We say "virtual reality" and "real time"—drawing clear lines between the two. But are they so different? Haven't they become like my many "I"s—separate but the same? On a daily basis, we attest to the postmodern media age as a simulated culture. Since these words are no longer jargon and have become standard English, cyberspace is able to change the very thing it represents. In other words, cyberspace, with full support from the media, is able to transform the original. The original becomes multiple until simulation becomes the overriding force in our society. From the invention of the radio to the extension of the Internet, these forces rule and control our culture. As the media becomes more complex, we become more complex and subsequently, isolated. Our original sense of self becomes skewed and our identity shifts into multiple identities instead of the singular "I" to which we were accustomed. Our culture becomes like the media, merely a simulation. Once culture is solely based on simulation rather than concrete reality, human identities are fictionalized and more readily dispersed into multiples.

The creation of such terms like "virtual reality" and "real time" support this point even further. Postmodernists create oxymorons to define the most obvious, further blurring the boundary between reality and simulation. Through accelerating technology, we have created an "advanced" society where each of us holds multiple identities but no stability. There is no central core—no singular "I." Our identities replay like computer loops or frames in film, each somewhat different from the other. When "I" sits at my computer screen, several "I"s dance before me. There is the "I" that reads a class assignment, completes it, and e-mails it to my professor without ever meeting her eyes. There's the "I" that plays online, changing electronic faces at the whim of a mouse click, metamorphosing from a serious NYU student to a not-so-bright guy searching to hook up with as many girls as willing. And in the background the old "I" always lurks, e-mailing friends around the country or writing my brother in Israel, sharing stories about high school days or the Italian restaurant at home that suddenly closed down. Who is the real "I"?

We have made the simple into something complex,

changed a concrete world into a simulation and in the process lost ourselves.

Now that we have entered an age of simulation, there is a different vantage point that must be studied. Simulation is more than the loss or confusion of identity. It goes far deeper, touching a fragile mechanism that diminishes the control of ourselves. By doing so, we automatically increase the control that society has. The freedom in cyberspace is ultimately controlled by the machine you use. And the machine is controlled by business people, assigning prices, designing marketing campaigns, telling us exactly what we need. When Microsoft fights Netscape we are caught in the middle, waiting for their battle to be resolved. We lose our control because we seek to split ourselves into fragments, wandering in a postmodern cyberspace where others predict, map out, and control our needs and desires. With such control, postmodern society steps up its embezzlement of my "I"—demanding that I believe in their design for social simulation. Nothing is real so we're easily controlled, ready to believe is stated in their social simulation and not seen by our own eyes. We lose stability, reality, and identity.

Does this new postmodern environment completely destroy my sense of stability? Is it possible for multiple identities to be stable? Does the level of stability create confusion or social control? These questions are the ones left unanswered and debated by many different philosophers and scientists. They are also the questions that plague me every day. I know that we have entered an age of mass media and simulation. Postmodernism is equivalent to simulation and identity defined as multiple. As a film student I am both part of the simulation and separate from it. But I don't have to like it.

It is my life. Cyberspace and reality are increasingly blurred. I did not see this transformation but was born into it.

I have known nothing else but a postmodern world. Also, on top of everything, I am 19 and in the dead center of what is labeled "Generation X". I have no singular identity—and neither does my generation. How nice to be called a baby boomer, to have one name you can call your own. Generation X doesn't even warrant a name—only a single, anonymous letter. Does that mean that my generation has only one identity, multiple identities, or no identity at all? Where does that leave me? Do I have one identity, multiple identities, or no identity? How ironic to write an essay on postmodernism, identity, and reality when I lack a single definition for all three.

Ironically, society prefers the company of a simulation to the harshness of a reality. Maybe simulation has become our defining reality—making the copy more meaningful than the original. It makes sense. Any Generation X-er would rather go to DisneyWorld than Tucson; play a wargame on *Sega* than join the Army; or watch a television medical drama than talk to a doctor. Is a trip to DisneyWorld less real than a trip to Jones Beach or is a movie any different than watching the people in Washington Square Park? How do we distinguish between reality and simulation? Where is the line that one crosses to move from reality to virtual reality? We have all learned that "I" is a plural pronoun.

The second question begs to be asked: When you lose a stable identity does it lead to confusion or social control? Since the mass media is the primary focus of postmodernism, the best way to illustrate this is to study the Internet. The Internet is the epitome of postmodernism. On the Internet, I have no single identity; I am what I want to be and how I want others to perceive me. I love simulation, I hate simulation, and I accept simulation. My identities are images on a screen. That has becomes my reality. Supposedly, these multiple identities are stabilized because of the control of the Internet. What control? Where does this control originate? There is no one at the top of this. For that matter, there is no one at the bottom or the middle of this. The Internet is amorphous, like the gelatinous special effect that turns a *Star Trek* shapeshifter into a pulsating liquid at the bottom of his bucket.

The Internet can complicate things. There is no way to keep an accurate count of someone's different identities. "I" can be a series of Internet code names, a set of colorful characters, or an individualized collection of different personalities. It may change so quickly that confusion sets in, with no control or stability. Since no one knows any of the identities that someone contains, it leaves us in a simulated guessing game.

Simulation and reality have intertwined. I am images and words on a screen. I am a multiple-identity simulation unable to "find" a single self. I am a bundle of RAM caught in a never-ending Cyberspace. The blurring of the boundaries between simulation and reality has becomes a constant—a normal part of daily life. Identity has no meaning in an era of postmodernism. These words no longer exist in the same way they used to. There is no longer stability or individuality. There are only layers, and plurals, and multiples. We change and blur so quickly! Simulation and imagery are non-distinct. My computer is human and my human-ness is computerized. I am assorted bytes and life is just a couple of pixels on a screen. I am not "me" at all; I am Coolguy101, a victim of Generation X, or the first born in a postmodern simulation.

What is Virtual Healthcare and How Does It Work in a Managed Care World?

Want to lower health care costs? Simple, just keep people away from doctors.

Davis 1995

Virtual healthcare has been around for quite awhile. It is called telemedicine or telehealth and has become an intrinsic part of the system used by practitioners in a wide range of fields.

The Telemedicine Information Exchange (TIE) (1997) broadly defines telemedicine as the use of "electronic signals to transfer medical data (i.e. high resolution photographs, radiological images, sounds, patient records, video conferencing) from one site to another. This transfer of medical data may use the Internet, Intranets, PCs, satellites, video conferencing equipment and telephones" (p. 1). In their 1997 report to congress, the Joint Working Group on Telemedicine (JWGT) (1997a) used the term "telehealth" to "refer to a diverse group of health-related activities, such as health professional's education, community health education, public health, research, and administration of health services" (p. 1). The report noted that nearly all of the federally funded telemedicine projects have broader telehealth applications. Consequently, the term "telehealth" is used to refer to both telehealth and telemedicine applications.

Telehealth works by using a "hybrid" technology that utilizes components of television, telecommunications, computers, and engineering. Most applications use interactive voice and video. At one end of the scale is the use of telephone conversations. Using conventional telephone lines to transmit audio and visual images can expand the applications. Generally, there is a handset, camcorder, or built-in camera at one end and a monitor at the other. Obviously, the Internet provides a platform for this type of telehealth transmission, with data, text, still images, and limited full motion video (Swett and Holaday 1996). As technology improves, the Internet will be better equipped to provide telehealth services. Easily accessible video conferencing has the greatest potential in this area. The biggest obstacle to Internet telehealth is reliability, security, and speed of transmission.

At the higher end of telehealth technology is dual monitor video conferencing (one monitor displays the outgoing image, another the incoming) with microphones, cameras, and user interfaces. Digital scanners, microscopes, VCRs, electronic medical instruments, and home health care monitoring equipment all contribute to high-tech transmissions. Once again, the speed determines the quality and accuracy of the image. To get full broadcast quality telehealth, satellite communications must be used (Swett and Holaday 1996).

Telehealth is used worldwide in a vast range of applications. Rural patients who have no access to specialty care may go to general practitioners that work with telemedicine doctors in large urban centers to help in diagnosis and treatment. People in Third World countries or populations without access to medical care use telemedicine to get the same quality treatment that is available in the cities. Prison inmates, patients on ships, and victims of natural disasters are now being linked to physicians through telecommunications. Telehealth is also being used in education, research, community health education, public health, and administration. In a report by a forty-member advisory committee from the Council on Competitiveness (1996) analyzing the impact of the National Information Infrastructure on the health care system, today's three most common practitioner scenarios were identified as (p. 2):

1. a physician at one location seeking a consultation from a specialist at another location;
2. a non-physician practitioner consulting with a remotely located medical practitioner; and
3. a patient consulting with a medical practitioner such as a primary care provider, a specialist referred by a primary care practitioner, or a monitoring nurse.

The report also notes that telemedicine has enormous potential to meet the needs of patients who could benefit from home care services requiring time-limited monitoring for a specific illness or chronic long-term care.

According to the Telemedicine Information Exchange ("What is telemedicine?" 1997) "telemedicine is a high-tech solution to the universal problem of access to health care" (p. 1). In this context, telehealth can offer a dramatic improvement in the healthcare system. However, insurance companies seeking to cut costs rather than improve the quality of healthcare can also abuse it.

Although still establishing itself, telehealth is booming. There are professional telehealth organizations, journals, and research on technology, feasibility, and future applications. The Yale Telemedicine Center (1996) reports that there were ten telemedicine programs in 1992, twenty in 1993, and presently, nearly all U.S. hospitals plan to implement some form of clinical or administrative program in the future. In a survey conducted by the Joint Working Group on Telemedicine (1997b) for their congressional report, they found that nearly 30 percent of rural hospitals are using telemedicine technology in patient care, with 68 percent offering *only* teleradiology. The very existence of the Joint Working Group was the result of the 1996 Telecommunications Reform Act where the Secretary of Commerce and the Secretary of Health and Human Services were asked to compile a report on using telecommunications in health care. They concluded, "telemedicine . . . is still in its developmental phase. It has been estimated that more than sixty percent of the current non-radiology telemedicine projects have been established in the last three years, mostly with the investment of Federal dollars" (1997c, p. 2).

While most telehealth projects are of recent origin, the concept has been around for over thirty years. The first inkling of its future was actually revealed in 1959. The New York World's Fair unveiled the first video phone. Physicians began dreaming about the possibilities of "healing by wire." At the time, however, it was impossible to transmit a detailed image over a thin copper cable ("History of telemedicine," no date).

One of the first mental health facilities to use closed-circuit television was the Nebraska Psychiatric Institute, which initiated it in 1955. In 1964, they received a grant from the National Institute of Mental Health to establish a link between the psychiatric institute and Norfolk State Hospital—112 miles away. They used the connection for education and consultations between specialists and general practitioners. They later linked with three veterans administration facilities in different locations ("History of telemedicine," 1996). Interestingly, telepsychiatry was one of the earliest specialties in the field.

The 1970s saw increasing interest in the utilization of telemedicine while improved technology in the 1980s stimulated greater interest in global telemedicine. The goal of the North-West Telemedicine Project, for example, set up in 1984 in Australia, was to provide healthcare to people in five remote towns south of the Gulf of Carpentaria. Two-thirds of the healthcare recipients were aborigines or Torres Strait Islanders. The project used conference telephone, fax, and free-frame transceivers. It was found that the telemedicine improved healthcare for people in remote regions and reduced the need for the transport of patients and specialists for routine consultations as well as emergencies. NASA (1997) established the first international telemedicine program in 1989. The Space Bridge to Armenia/Ufa was in response to the massive earthquake that leveled much of the then Soviet Republic of Armenia. The U.S. offered to conduct telemedical consultations from the earthquake site to several major centers in America. NASA used one-way video, voice, and fax to connect an onsite medical center in Yerevan, Armenia, and four medical centers in the U.S. The program was so successful that it was extended to Ufa, Russia, to help burn victims after a devastating railway accident. It was the first time that telemedicine was used to cross political, social, cultural, and economic borders to share medical resources.

Today, telemedicine centers are located in some of the best facilities in the U.S., such as the Mayo Clinic, U.S. Army Medical Research Center, University of California Davis, Kansas University Medical Center, Los Alamos National Laboratory, and the National Cancer Institute. This list is growing longer each day.

Essentially, telehealth is a managed care bargain. It was originally established to enable underserved populations to get quality healthcare without making long, expensive trips into high-tech medical facilities usually located in urban centers. In this capacity, it is an excellent alternative. But something happened on the way to the bank. Healthcare business people began to ask the inevitable question: Why not use telehealth in place of traditional healthcare for all patients? If technology costs can be contained, the potential to dramatically reduce healthcare costs across the board is sobering. And that's where managed care comes in.

David Balch (no date), Director of Telemedicine at East Carolina University School of Medicine, defined a new model of telemedicine known as the "bridge." "The bridge is not a physical thing. It's a conceptual model of telemedicine for managed care. It's all about putting the most appropriate health care at the exact place it needs to be . . . it's all about moving information not people . . . ."(p. 1). The model attempts to construct a bridge between patient and provider—regardless of distance, level, or type of care—or geography. Balch refers to it as "scaleable" or adaptable to a wide range of technologies, needs, and treatments. A bridge might be a system that links the home, the rural practice site, ambulatory clinic, or small hospital to a "DOCking" station or tertiary care center. In other words, it is the means to conceptualize a healthcare system based on communication, information technology, and treatment. Of course, another way to translate the bridge model is fewer doctors, more employees that are considerably less expensive to pay, fewer hospital and office visits, and more localized health care. As Davis (1995) said so aptly, one of the best ways to lower healthcare costs is not to see doctors.

Telehealth advocates believe that these new technologies can work with managed care to ease the problems in healthcare. They maintain that the higher quality, patient-centered care received through telemedicine will dramatically cut costs. Market analyses from Feedback Research Services (1996) have projected dramatic growth in the U.S. Telemedicine market, with an estimated $283 million from equipment sales alone.

IntelMed (1997), a telemedicine services company, claims that they "combine the best choices in medical care, with second opinions from top specialists and discounts of nearly fifty percent off the standard fees of physicians and hospitals, diagnostic and laboratory services" (p. 1). The Council on Competitiveness' Report (1996) notes that early predictions have suggested that the potential market opportunity might be as high as $100 billion. Although these numbers have not been substantiated, it opens a very friendly door to managed care. The report clearly states that the motivations behind one of the leading areas in telehealth—radiology—is driven by business interests:

> Business strategies behind the establishment of teleradiology sites are propelled by a desire to increase patient volume, lower cost, and obtain a greater market share. [p. 3]

It is no surprise that there was a great deal of support from managed care companies to the California Telemedicine Act of 1966, which requires reimbursement for telehealth services (see p. 261, this volume). Telehealth is simply good for business.

Is Mental Health the Next Telehealth Target?

Unlike some specialties such as cardiology, mental health telemedicine applications do not require a high degree of image specificity, thus the technology can be simpler and costs can be lower. Moreover, initial evidence indicates that telemedicine works well for group therapy as well as individual consults.

As noted in the OHRP/A Report, Mental Health Care ranked among the top five telemedicine applications in terms of usage. [Joint Working Group on Telemedicine 1997b]

Where does mental health fit into the emerging telemedicine industry? The above quote appeared in the Joint Working Group on Telemedicine's report to Congress. After all, mental health is probably the easiest form of telehealth to establish. Psychiatry has been using telehealth since the 1950s. Most psychotherapists are already involved in some form of telehealth: talking to patients on the telephone, consulting with colleagues on the telephone, managed care telephone "case conferences," using beepers and pagers to be alerted in emergencies. In the near future, psychotherapists might abandon their offices to home spaces similar to the one advertised by *CU-SeeMe* (1997a,b), a camera, fixed on a face, with a soothing or therapeutically appropriate backdrop. Patients might compose similar spots in their homes. Clinicians might be compelled to interpret patient "backdrops" or choice of home "setting" as a diagnostic tool. (Why does Mr. G insist on a night scene, with black storm clouds and no stars? Is Ms. R's choice of "kitchen" backdrop related to her struggle with an eating disorder? Why is the children's "space" so neat?)

Maybe there will be a "home visit" in this virtual treatment, where the patient, armed with a video camera, gives a forty-five minute tour of his or her house and the people who share it. But why stop there? A wireless remote camera can bring the therapist to work, play, or simply to observe the patient's social behavior. Virtual reality exercises can be used to teach new social skills or overcome phobias. Talk therapy might be an audiovisual process and transference might be a function of bandwidth. In this Orwellian vision, what is seen as well as what is not seen on the monitor will be the ultimate assessment.

Similarly, another question might address what lies beyond the parameters of the camera. Patient records could be a collection of annotated moving images rather than unforgiving words on digital forms. The effects of time and distance will be diminished. A New York therapist who likes to work late hours can work at midnight with a California patient, whose appointment falls at 9 p.m. California time. A politician, afraid of public exposure, can be assured of confidential treatment by using a psychotherapist halfway around the world. Psychotherapists seeking to fill those unpopular morning hours can simply look for patients in the appropriate time zones. And travelers, whether on business or pleasure, can bring their sessions wherever they go.

No one knows whether virtuality will be a better—or worse—therapeutic environment. Although a giant leap from the safety of the analyst's couch, teletherapy will probably be very acceptable to the postmodern citizen in the third millennium.

What Happens to Confidentiality?

Whether you see telehealth as an exciting foray in the future, a devastating blow to human connection, or simply an inevitable occurrence, it arrives with a serious problem that undermines the essence of all health and mental health care: confidentiality.

Technology carries a heavy price. Better, more efficient health care, telehealth, and managed care all demand detailed records of patients. Patient records are compiled when individuals go for health, mental health, or alternative treatments or to related facilities such as hospitals, clinics, and wellness centers. All medical and mental health professionals are required to maintain patient records. Patient records are stories of who a person is—physically, emotionally, and socially—along with their family, lifestyle, work habits, and, in some cases, the genetic probability of an individual's future.

Consider some of the sources for compiling today's patient records (Tuckfelt et al. 1997):

- Mental health practitioners;
- Medical practitioners;
- Related practitioners such as chiropractors, dentists, nutritionists, physical therapists, etc.;
- Medical and psychiatric hospitals;

- Outpatient treatment centers, clinics, agencies, community health and mental health centers;
- Employee assistance programs;
- Testing laboratories;
- Pharmaceutical retailers and drug plans;
- Managed care 800-numbers;
- Managed care gatekeepers;
- Managed care case managers;
- Wellness groups; and
- Consumer questionnaires.

Now add the more efficient "total" telehealth systems—complete with stored video and audio images and patient records—and psychotherapeutic telehealth can become a sobering Orwellian reality.

Yet the facts are clear. Arthur D. Little, a prestigious Massachusetts consulting firm, conducted a study on the computerization of patient records (Flower 1994). They concluded that the United States could save $15 billion dollars every year if the medical records of every man, woman, and child were put online.

While much of this information is presently scattered throughout the files and databases of individuals and organizations that patients have contacted for various physical and psychological needs, technology is quickly changing the landscape. As technology improves, networks and centralized databases are connecting various patient record sources, thus easing accessibility to the "whole story." Many large information management companies are aiming toward the business of maintaining "cradle to grave" records of every man, woman, and child. These records are housed in huge databases that operate most efficiently when they are centralized and readily available to practitioners. That means patient records will be stored in computer databases or archives, accessible to all that need them. Many groups are advocating placing patient records in "secure" sites on the Internet. However, technology has been unable to design a system that is totally secure. The "good" guys, as well as the "bad" guys, will have potential access to the archived amalgam of an individual's life. As all of us know too well, no computer is invulnerable (Tuckfelt et al. 1997).

Consider the Medical Information Bureau, financed and run by the insurance industry, with over 750 firms using their services for information on insurance applications. They maintain a database of patient records for approximately 15 million Americans. Other information systems management companies that have built their business on the storage of huge amounts of information on national, centralized databases are entering the patient records industry. For example, Equifax is one of the country's largest compilers of credit information with data on more than 119 million people in the United States. A typical Equifax credit report offers a list of credit cards, bank loans, student loans, and payment histories (i.e., how many times you were late and how many days you were behind). They will include unpaid bills, notes on credit information such as how many times an individual reported a lost or stolen credit card, and demographics such as employment history, marital situation, and whether one rents or owns his or her home. Financial judgments, whether settled, still disputed, or incorrect, are kept on record. The information is gleaned from banks, stores, and other businesses that send all reports, good or bad. The Big Three companies that store this type of information are Equifax, TRW, and Trans Union. Equifax also stores records in areas such as auto and home insurance, checking services, risk management, physician screening services, claims review, a health claims clearinghouse, and even Osborn Laboratories, a service which checks out potential customers (Garfinkel 1995). In 1995, Equifax, in tandem with AT&T, announced their entry into the healthcare business. If successful, they will control the nation's largest networked medical database and collect a fee every time a patient sees a doctor.

Is it really plausible to believe that all of this electronic information can be protected from the "snoopers"? Is electronic security even probable? Although they are reluctant to admit to security problems, companies such as Citicorp, American Express, and TRW Information Systems & Services are struggling to find ways to protect their databases. TRW, which maintains credit records on nearly 180 million Americans, has spent $30 million just to update and secure its network. The most stringent corporate safeguards can't always protect against mishaps, hackers, and unscrupulous uses of information.

At present, the private sector can exchange patient information on computer databases with little regulation. Medical and mental health records are easily available to life and health insurance companies, employers screening job applicants, direct marketers, credit companies, private investigators, law enforcement agencies, forensic psychologists, and anyone who can find an "in" to the right computer. If the information can't be legally obtained, then a "customer" can call one of hundreds of hackers who advertise their services online and in hacker magazines.

Ironically, it doesn't always take the sharpened skills of a hacker to get confidential information. In March 1997, the U.S. Social Security System had an innovative idea. They decided to set up a Web page where individuals could go to get their own Personal Earnings and Benefit Estimate Statement (PEBES) on the Internet. To receive a statement by mail or e-mail, all they needed was to provide name, social security number, date, place of birth, and mother's maiden name—information that can be readily found in many places. There was a public uproar over the system, so one month later it was taken off-line. Individuals can still request their statements, but it will be sent by snail mail ("The social security administration and online privacy" 1997).

Information needs to be controlled by more sweeping reform. Technology and privacy groups are well aware of the hazards of electronic information management, and they publish in paper and online information that will inform people of their rights. There are several bills pending in state and federal governments to protect privacy. Most of the bills are weak or ineffectual.

EPIC (Electronic Privacy Information Center) considers medical record privacy one of their "hot" topics. They suggest nine essential ingredients for protection of patient records (Tuckfelt et al. 1997):

1. Federal legislation;
2. Complete patient access to their own records;
3. Criminal or civil fines for unauthorized access, disclosure, or use of records;
4. Strict limitations on third-party access;
5. Patient consent for inclusion in national databases (no psychiatric records are included in databases);
6. Research conducted only with patient consent;
7. Use of the most powerful electronic security measures;
8. Social Security numbers not used to identify patients; and
9. Federal law sets minimum standards; state law should provide additional protection.

Currently, many of these actions are not being taken.

Issues of privacy, confidentiality, and security are particularly important in telehealth. In their report, the Council on Competitiveness (1996) stated that the domestic commercial market for telemedicine will never materialize unless, among other legal and regulatory issues, concerns regarding privacy and confidentiality are resolved. Similarly, the Joint Working Group on Telemedicine (JWGT), in their report to the U.S. Congress stated that "lack of privacy and security standards do play an important role in the legal challenges facing telemedicine (e.g., malpractice) and have profound implications for the acceptance of telemedicine services. This is of particular concern in the use of telemedicine technologies for treating mental illness, substance abuse, and other conditions that carry a social stigma" (1997d, p. 1).

The JWGT (1997d) identifies three separate features concerning patient record privacy:

1. Information privacy refers to the right of a individual to control the information that relates directly to himself or herself;
2. Confidentiality is a "tool" that protects sensitive information, using specific controls such as limits on access and disclosure; and
3. Security refers to the safeguards built into a computer-based information system, including training, policies, and laws as well as technologies.

Most legal protection is governed by state law—which varies greatly across the country. Federal protection is even more limited—there is no right of privacy specifically guaranteed by the U.S. Constitution.

Privacy, confidentiality, and security issues are of great concern to today's healthcare system, which is increasingly maintained by computerized records. However, telehealth makes these issues far more complicated. The use of video imaging, audio, electronic clinical information, and patient data in a telehealth treatment has, essentially, a different nature than the more traditional healthcare encounters. Imagine a telehealth consultation taking place between New York and Brush Prairie, Washington. The test results, diagnosis, history, and prognosis would be videotaped. The patient would have serious privacy and confidentiality issues. In addition, the practitioner would be vulnerable to a kind of scrutiny unavailable in an office where, say, the treatment highlights would be recorded and not the exact words. If the practitioner made certain comments or suggestions, it would go on record. For example, the practitioner might suggest the use of vitamins or a change in lifestyle that, taken out of context, could be used against him or her in a malpractice case. Or the practitioner might mistakenly mention sensitive, confidential material that would then become preserved on videotape. Adding to the complexity, all of the people involved in the technological aspect of the communications, such as the engineers and sysops (system operators), would also be privy to the conversation. Last, but far from least, can telemedicine ever offer security from unwanted telehackers?

The JWGT (1997d) plans to further evaluate the privacy, confidentiality, and security issues in telehealth. They state three goals in this area:

1. Examine the outcome of pilot projects to determine whether they provide insight into privacy concerns or identify specific areas that must be investigated;
2. Establish a formal process of investigating privacy, confidentiality, and security issues in telehealth; and
3. Link with other Federal groups to find solutions to these problems.

These are all very noble intentions on the part of the JWGT. Notwithstanding, are there really any solutions? Or will our postmodern telehealth, similar to cyberspace, be an environment fraught with gaping holes that accompany the good?

What Can We Do?: A Call to Action
Marlene Maheu

Telehealth, for better or worse, is here to stay. In this "call to action," Marlene Maheu, who is deeply involved in online and telehealth issues, states the inevitable: the future is upon us. If we don't take control of telehealth now, then we will be left behind.

Joanna sits comfortably at her home computer and dials her modem to connect to her insurance company. Her video monitor shows a smiling intake coordinator, who listens to her complaint and assigns her a therapist within minutes. The therapist sits in front of a soothing mountain scene, a projected image serving as a backdrop to the virtual office. Joanna has a telehealth therapy session that includes a thorough assessment. She is walked through several online tools that help to assess her current symptoms, situation, and coping strategies.

The assessment tools are immediately scored, digitized, and interpreted for the therapist, and the test scores, along with their norms, are clearly displayed on the therapist's monitor alongside Joanna's image as they speak. A white board viewed by both parties is used for Joanna to write her assignments for the week. At the end of the interaction, Joanna's therapist determines which portions of the interaction will be saved to the electronic medical record and then sends it off to the national database.

Is this the future of psychotherapy? It's already happening. Before the turn of the century, it will happen with greatly increased frequency.

What? Where? Who's protecting confidentiality? What training will be required of the therapists? What fee will be charged? What will go into a centralized, electronic database?

Many of those questions have as yet to be answered in detail, but the vehicle for developing such answers is already constructed. Clients/patients are already being serviced by mental health professionals through telemedicine in over 30 pilot projects throughout the U.S. Laws are being enacted in many states to regulate the how, where, when, and why of such service delivery.

WHAT'S HAPPENING?

Our world is undergoing another revolution: the Information Revolution. Touted as being as broad-sweeping as the Industrial Revolution, the tools for immediate information transfer are being introduced to all major spheres of banking, business, and professional information exchange. Medical and banking records will soon be centralized in large computerized data banks and then made available to designated individuals, businesses, and government agencies. The health care and banking industries are being greatly assisted by our government. Our legislators are passing laws while allocating large sums of money to building the infrastructure to support these technical advances.

DEFINITIONS

Telemedicine is generally considered to be any form of communication between doctor and patient through electronic equipment from remote locations. It is most likely that the equipment we will be using will include a blend of several technologies, such as audio, video, and text-based interactions for meeting the specific needs of each client, hospital, and insurance system. For our specific purposes as mental health professionals, telemedicine will revolve around video conferencing. Such equipment enables both parties to view and communicate in real time.

Telemedicine is being replaced with the term *Telehealth* in much current legislation, because newer legislation is advocating for the inclusion of allied health professions. For our industry, "behavioral telehealth" is the term being suggested by David Nicholson, a former legislative aid and current Special Assistant to the Director of the APA's Practice Directorate.

Pilot telemedicine/telehealth projects exist in many states, are typically funded by the federal government, and already use telecommunications equipment for many types of psychiatric interventions. The Commonwealth of Massachusetts even recently passed a law allowing psychiatrists to order 5150s from remote locations using video conferencing.

These projects usually involve a hub hospital with satellite hospitals or clinics. The hub hospital typically is staffed with specialists 24 hours a day. The satellite locations are staffed by nurse practitioners or mental health counselors. When a specialist is needed, the professional in the satellite location initiates a video conference into the hub hospital and accesses the specialist, usually within minutes. Some of the newer behavioral telehealth projects are beginning to offer combinations of technologies: website information, telephone screening, video conferenced consultation and/or education, home health care, and even continued professional education. The possibilities of this new form of service delivery are just beginning to be discussed.

WHY SHOULD WE BE INVOLVED NOW?

The California Telemedicine Development Act of 1996 was signed into law in September of 1996 by the Governor. Before I give you details, you might be surprised to know that the proposal for this law was submitted in March of 1996 and passed every committee, including the powerful insurance committee, without a single oppositional vote. It was signed into law only eight months after its introduction. It mandates insurance payment for scenes like the introductory scenario and much more in telemedicine. The law took effect in July 1997. Do you know what your state is doing with regard to telemedicine or telehealth? For information, see the resource list below.

The California law defines and regulates the practice of telemedicine on a statewide level. Here are the main provisions:

1. The Telemedicine Development Act of 1996 restricts California telemedicine services to practitioners licensed in California. This means we cannot communicate electronically as primary care providers with clients/patients outside our state;
2. We can serve as consultants connected by telecommunications equipment to professionals in other states;
3. Perhaps even more importantly, insurance carriers (including HMOs and Medi-Cal) are mandated to reimburse providers for the delivery of telemedicine. The new law amends four major state codes to add telemedicine as a normal part of healthcare services; and
4. The California law stipulates that third party carriers cannot "require" face-to-face contact as a condition for reimbursement.

How will this last provision impact us? How will it impact our clients and patients? As employees of insurance companies, those of us who are on panels must be wondering about our own future powers to determine how we will interact with patients. What will it mean if we think a patient needs to be seen face-to-face rather than electronically but our employer, the insurance company, cannot mandate face-to-face treatment as a condition of reimbursement? Do we get to decide how we will meet with our patient?

THE EVOLUTION OF MENTAL HEALTH CARE INTO THE 21ST CENTURY

Healthcare is moving in ways we haven't even begun to contemplate. For example, over 40 states have ongoing "telemedicine" projects, including a number of urban based "Telepsychiatry" centers serving the needs of rural primary care physicians and their patients. Over twenty medical schools have established departments, graduate programs, and fellowships in "Medical Informatics." The American Medical Association recently recommended unrestricted licensure for all physicians who wish to practice telemedicine across state lines.

There is a fierce battle waging between states like California and the U.S. Government. States do not want to lose their individual power, but the very nature of telecommunication requires some federal management. A newly introduced federal bill, the "Comprehensive Telehealth Act of 1996," would create a Federal Telehealth Agency, facilitate telehealth services across state lines, and *require Medicare reimbursement* for telehealth services by 1998.

A number of pilot programs have already begun. The Department of Health and Human Services recently awarded $42 million to nineteen new *physician-run* telemedicine projects, and the Health Care Financing Administration launched a three-year test of telemedicine services at fifty-seven Medicare-certified facilities. The Department of Defense spent over $48

million last year in developing the infrastructure for
telemedicine delivery last year.

WHAT CAN WE DO TO BE
A PART OF THIS?

If you can see the inevitable change we must undergo as
a profession, here are a few places to start:

1. Accept the fact that Telehealth is an important service
   delivery tool. Our skills can remain the same, but can
   be repackaged not only to address current traditional
   specialty areas but to address those related to new technology and the change required; services delivered to
   more people, more easily, more economically.
2. Get online.
3. Get information about telemedicine and telehealth.
   Here's where you can get the facts:

   Telemedicine Report to Congress (1997)
   http://www.ntia.doc.gov/reports/telemed/index.htm

   Federal Telehealth Act (Proposed Bill)
   ftp://ftp.loc.gov/pub/thomas/c104/s2171.is.txt

   Cybertowers Telehealth Office
   http://cybertowers.com/ct/telehealth/ethical.html

   Professional e-mail Discussion List: Get online with
   e-mail and join Telehealth, a free e-mail list that discusses telehealth as an international phenomenon. To
   subscribe, send a message to:
   LISTSERV@MAELSTROM.STJOHNS.EDU and
   in the body of the message type:
   SUBSCRIBE TELEHEALTH yourfirst yourlastname so the message will look like
   SUBSCRIBE TELEHEALTH Chuck Wagon

4. Educate others. Let's learn to make telehealth work for us, not against us. Let's be proactive, not reactive. Help someone with the next step. Get them online, show them how to access the professional lists, subscribe them to Telehealth, and teach them about Netiquette so they will know the cultural norms online.

5. Get involved politically. Find ways of being part of the new system of healthcare delivery being built by our entire government. Lobby, write to your legislative representatives, and use the Internet to voice your political opinions about the formation of telehealth federally, in our state, and in our county.

6. Consider computerizing something in your specialty area. If you already have software/hardware developed and ready to market, give it a free listing at this site: **<http://cybertowers.com/cgibin/prof.cgi>** where other professionals can learn about it and network with you.

7. Consider starting a pilot project for telehealth in your clinic, hospital, or professional group. Begin using video conferencing tools to facilitate interactions with other professionals and, eventually, with patients. Let's take a proactive approach to telehealth and not simply become reactive to the decisions made by other professionals.

8. When developing pilot projects, use sound research design to collect data about your project.

9. Publish your results and/or speak about them at local, state, and national Psychological Association meetings. Let others benefit from your experiences so our profession can grow strong. We have the potential of providing the mental health world with research-based information. We all need to work together to define psychology's role in behavioral telehealth delivery as

well as to develop ethical and effective therapeutic use of this new and rapidly changing medium.

10. And, most importantly, we need solid, academic research into how these technologies work, what populations will be best served using these tools, which treatment modalities are best suited to these delivery systems, how medical records need to be kept secure and confidential, and which clinicians will be best suited to deliver services through these technologies. The important truth is that if we do not become active in shaping new technology for our professions, who will?

PART III
INTERNET RESOURCES
FOR CLINICIANS

List of Internet Addresses

ONLINE RESOURCES IN PSYCHOTECHNOLOGY

Computer-mediated communication

Deja News—The Source for Internet Newsgroups!
    http://www.dejanews.com/

Dictionary of Computer Acronyms and Jargon
    **http://www.reading.ac.uk/~suqstmbl/jargon/jargon.
    html**

Emporium's Chat Links . . . .
    http://www.yepa.com/empo/empo.html

IRC Related Documents
    http://urth.acsu.buffalo.edu/irc/WWW/ircdocs.html

KIDLINK: Global Networking for Youth 10-15
    http://www.kidlink.org/

MUD/MU* Document Library
    http://lucien.sims.berkeley.edu/moo.html

Net Lingo: The Internet Language Dictionary
    http://www.netlingo.com/

The Mud Connector
http://www.mudconnect.com/

Reference.com Search
http://www.Reference.com/

Welcome to the Undernet
http://www.undernet.org/

Welcome to Yahoo! Chat, DigitX
http://chat.yahoo.com/

General resources

Hopeless Romantics Opening Page
http://www.gci-net.com/~users/j/jonese

Internet Index Home Page
http://www.openmarket.com/intindex/

Internet Mental Health
http://www.mentalhealth.com/

Metanoia Guide to Internet Mental Health Services
http://www.metanoia.org/imhs/index.html

Pharmaceutical Information Network Home Page
http://pharminfo.com/

Psychology Organizations on the Web
http://www.wesleyan.edu/spn/psych.htm

Search Page for articles in Psychology and Social Science Journals
http://www.shef.ac.uk/~psysc/journals/jsearch.html

Social Work and Social Services Web Sites
http://www.gwbweb.wustl.edu/websites.html

SWAN—National Organizations
http://www.sc.edu/swan/national.html

Telehealth Office at Cybertowers Professional Center
http://telehealth.net/telehealth/

Telemedicine Related Activities
http://www.fda.gov/cdrh/telemed.html

The 'Lectric Law Library's Entrance
http://www.lectlaw.com

The Social Statistics Briefing Room
http://www.whitehouse.gov/fsbr/ssbr.html

U.S. National Information Infrastructure Virtual Library
http://nii.nist.gov/

WandP: Feminist Yellow Pages
http://www.echonyc.com/~women/yellowpages.html

Welcome To The White House
http://www.whitehouse.gov/WH/Welcome.html

Women in Computing Bibliography
**http://www.sacbee.com/news/projects/women/
wcbiblio.html**

Mental health for professionals and their patients

An Internet Surfboard For Kids And Teens, Kidsurf Online!
http://www.kidsurf.net/index.html

Child Welfare Home Page
http://www.childwelfare.com/

Internet Mental Health
http://www.mentalhealth.com/

Mental Health Net
http://www.cmhc.com/

NIMH Home Page
http://www.nimh.nih.gov/

PsychCentral—John Grohol's Page
http://www.grohol.com/

Psyjourn, Inc.
http://www.psyjourn.com

Psychscapes Worldwide
http://www.mental-health.com

Psych Toons (humor)
**http://www.cybertowers.com/selfhelp/psychtoons/
index.html**

The Federal Telemedicine Gateway
http://206.156.10.7/

The ShrinkTank BBS Web Site
http://www.shrinktank.com/testing.htm

Online journals and publications

CMC Magazine Index
http://www.december.com/cmc/mag/index.html

Journal of Computer-Mediated Communication
http://jcmc.huji.ac.il/

Self & Psychology Magazine
http://www.cybertowers.com/selfhelp/

The Electronic Newsstand
http://www.enews.com/

The Nando Times
http://www2.nando.net

The New York Times on the Web
http://www.nytimes.com/

Today on HotWired!
http://www.hotwired.com/frontdoor/

Welcome to Pathfinder! (Time Warner Publications)
http://pathfinder.com/

Welcome to Psychotherapy Finances Online
http://www.psyfin.com/

Wired Magazine-Menu
http://www.wired.com/wired/95/41/index1a.html

ZD Net
http://www5.zdnet.com/

Women and Performance
http://www.echonyc.com/~women/

Professional organizations

American Academy of Child and Adolescent Psychiatry Home
Page
http://www.aacap.org/web/aacap/

American Psychiatric Association Online
http://www.psych.org/

American Psychoanalytic Association
http://apsa.org/

American Psychological Association PsychNet
http://www.apa.org

California Coalition for Ethical Mental Health Care
http://www.pw1.netcom.com/~donmar/home.html

National Coalition of Mental Health Professionals and Consumers
http://www.execpc.com/~mastery/coalitionMain. html

Clinical Social Work Federation
http://www.cswf.org

NASW Online
http://www.socialworkers.org/main.htm

Psychotechnology sites

Contact Consortium
http://www.ccon.org

CyberTowers Professional Center (CT)
http://www.cybertowers.com/

Outside the Light-Cone
http://hyperreal.org/~mpesce/

Philosophy and Psychology of the Internet
http://lists.village.virginia.edu/~spoons/internet_
txt.html

Psychotechnology Online
http://www.psychotechnology.com/

Storm A. King—Resources for Researching the Psychology of
Virtual Communities
http://www.contentric.net/~Astorm/

The Cyborg Overview
http://www.stg.brown.edu/projects/hypertext/landow/
cpace/cyborg/cyborgov.html

The Psychology of Cyberspace
http://www1.rider.edu/~suler/psycyber/psycyber.html

Self-help and support groups resources

Emotional Support on the Internet
    http://www.cix.co.uk/~net-services/care

Mental Health Net—Self-help Questionnaires
    http://www.cmhc.com/guide/quizes.htm

Mental Health Net - Self-help Resources Index
    http://www.cmhc.com/selfhelp.htm

Support-Group.com
    http://support-group.com

Virtual Sisterhood
    http://www.igc.apc.org/vsister/

Specific disorders

Alcoholics Anonymous
    http://www.alcoholics-anonymous.org/

ANXIETY-PANIC internet resource - articles
    http://www.algy.com/anxiety/

Bipolar and other mood disorders: Pendulum Resources
    http://www.pendulum.org

Children and Adults with Attention Deficit Disorders
(CH.A.D.D.)
    http://chadd.org/

COLA—Center for Online Addiction
    http://netaddiction.com/

Cyber-Psych: Eating Disorders
    http://www.cyber-psych.com/eat.html

Death, Dying and Grief Resources: The WEBster
    http://www.cyberspy.com/%7Ewebster/death.html

Depression Central
http://www.psycom.net/depression.central.html

disABILITY Resources on the Internet
http://www.eskimo.com/~jlubin/disabled.htm

Futur.com (schizophrenia and other psychoses)
http://www.futur.com/

International Society for the Study of Dissociation
http://www.issd.org/

Mental Health Resources
http://gopher.bu.edu/COHIS/hsource/mh.htm

Obsessive Compulsive Disorders
http://www.cmhc.com/guide/ocd.htm

The Samaritans (Suicide)
http://www.samaritans.org.uk/

E-MAIL DISCUSSION GROUPS
Storm A. King

Netpsy

Internet Psychology, a forum for the discussion of the psychological and psychotherapeutic services delivered via all aspects of the Internet. This list is a forum for psychologists and mental health workers interested in discussing the interactions, problems, and disorders arising out of the use of the Internet as well as the treatments developing to treat existing and developing disorders via the Internet.

NetPsy is an open, unmoderated list, but it is NOT a support group and it is NOT a forum for anyone seeking psychological services over the Internet.

To subscribe to this list send
subscribe NetPsy (your first name, your last name)
to
listserv@maelstrom.stjohns.edu

owner & Co-Admin: Marlene M. Maheu, Ph.D.
drm@cts.com
Self-Help & Psychology Magazine
CST Professional Center

Co-Admin: Storm A. King astorm@concentric.net
Pacific Graduate School of Psychology

Netdynam

This is a list to examine the group dynamics of lists: perceptions of other participants; the dynamics of flame wars, power, and persuasion; what is effective communication and why.

All messages regarding NetDynam subscription should go to:
listserv@sjuvm.stjohns.edu
To subscribe to NetDynam
send
subscribe netdynam (your-first-name, your-last-name)
to
listserv@maelstrom.stjohns.edu

It is possible to subscribe to the list in index (table of contents) and digest (one mailing with all messages for the day). This can be accomplished by sending mail to listserv@sjuvm.stjohns.edu with the message: SET NETDYNAM INDEX or SET NETDYNAM DIGEST

Archives of NetDynam mail items are kept in weekly files. You may obtain a list of files in the archives by sending either of the commands: INDEX NETDYNAM or GET NETDYNAM FILELIST to the listserver.

Archived messages are accessible only by current subscribers, but subscription to NetDynam is public (unrestricted).

More information on listserver operation and commands can be obtained with the message: GET LISTSERV REFCARD

Psychology of the Internet research e-mail forum

The topics that are appropriate to this list are broadly defined, but can include such things as:

- How to conduct psychological research via the Internet;
- Theory behind virtual support groups;
- Online psychotherapy;
- Internet Addiction Disorder; and
- Psychology of various online phenomenon, such as flame wars and relationships.

To subscribe to this mailing list, send a one-line e-mail
(leaving the subject blank) to:
listproc@cmhcsys.com
In your e-mail, please include the line:
subscribe research Your-name
(replacing "Your-name" with your real name).

The Interpersonal Computing and
Technology List (IPCT-L)

This is an international forum for pedagogical issues important to higher education involving teaching with technology, connectivity, and networking. Computing and other technology that can be used to promote learning is discussed. Topics may involve teaching and training; collaboration; the development of partnerships among learners, faculty or teachers, and other interested persons in the educational community; research that reflect these interests; and the fostering of collegial relationships.

To subscribe to IPCT-L send
subscribe IPCT-L (Your-First-Name, Your-Last-Name)
to
LISTSERV@LISTSERV.GEORGETOWN.EDU

Selfhelp

This list discusses issues and topics that commonly occur among the leaders of mutual self-help support groups online today. These leaders may be forum leaders, mailing list owners, or people who are the "glue" that hold together discussion on newsgroups or other discussion forums. The topics that are appropriate to this list are broadly defined, but can include such things as:

- How to build group cohesiveness;
- How to build group membership and contributions;
- How to handle an emergency or crisis online, such as a member's threat to commit suicide; and
- How to handle various online phenomenon, such as flame wars, relationships that form within the group, and so forth.

To subscribe to SELFHELP, send the following command to
LISTPROC@cmhcsys.com
in the BODY of e-mail:
SUBSCRIBE SELFHELP yourfirstname yourlastname
For example: SUBSCRIBE SELFHELP Jane Smith
Owner: John M. Grohol Psy.D. grohol@coil.com

SPECIAL CLINICAL SITES
FOR PROFESSIONALS

Journal of Computer Mediated Communication (M. McLaughlin and S. Rafaeli)
   http://jcmc.huji.ac.il

Clinical Social Work Federation (Dean Allman)
http://www.cswf.org

Colorado State Society For Clinical Social Work (Dean Allman)
http://www.cswf.org/states/colorado/colorado.html

Cybertowers (Marlene Maheu)
http://www.cybertowers.com/

Mental Health Net (John Grohol)
http://www.cmhc.com/

Psychotechnology Online (Jeri Fink)
http://www.psychotechnology.com

Resources for Researching the Psychology of Virtual Communities (Storm King)
http://rdz.stjohns.edu/~storm/

ShrinkTank (Rob Bischoff)
http://www.shrinktank.com/index.shtml

Glossaries

GLOSSARY OF NETSPEAK

AOL

abbreviation for America Online.

ASCII

American Standard Code for Information Exchange—a standard system of encoding letters, numbers, and symbols used in all computers.

Asynchronous

Communication that is not occurring at the same time.

avatar

An online graphic chosen or designed by a user to represent him or herself.

bandwidth

The capacity to carry information. For example, "broad bandwidth" refers to transmissions that will allow large amounts of information to move swiftly from one point to another.

BBS

Bulletin Board System. The BBSs were originally the backbone of internet communications providing space for messages, conferencing, and e-mail. Users must dial directly into the BBS machine, unlike online services that access the Internet.

bookmark

A standard feature of Web browsers. Users record the Web page and its address in a special file so it can be easily accessed at a later date.

bot

A small internet software program that works like a robot. For example, there are cancelbots that automatically delete certain messages from UseNet groups. Used to combat spammers; annoybots that bug chat rooms to give "speeches" for inappropriate language; and chatterbots that are programmed to answer questions.

chat

Online areas where people can talk "live," in real time, by typing messages onto a screen that appears on all of the participants' computers.

cyberspace

Anywhere a computer can go. The term was coined by William Gibson in his novel *Neuromancer* and it refers to the non-physical space where computer mediated communication takes place.

domain

The part of an internet address that comes after the @ and describes the type of organization. Some common domains are .com (commercial), .edu (educational), and .gov (government). For example, the address to the White House is **http:// www.whitehouse.gov**—with the .gov indicating the domain as government.

download

The process of taking a file from another computer and loading it (down) onto your computer.

e-mail

Electronic mail usually sent to a private mailbox or e-mail list.

emoticons

Graphical messages constructed from keyboard characters to convey a special feeling. Also known as smileys. The most common looks like the following : -) Turn your head sideways to see the "smiley."

encryption

The process that transforms electronic messages into codes so they cannot be read or intercepted by unwanted third parties.

flame war

When flaming gets out of control and there is all-out text warfare.

flaming

Nasty, obscene, insulting, and hurtful messages usually in response to a public statement on an e-mail, UseNet, or Web forum.

gopher

One of the predecessors of the World Wide Web. Gopher sites offered text-based menus linked to files open to the public on the internet. They are still available, but most prefer the "prettier" and easier-to-navigate World Wide Web.

hacker

Traditionally, a hacker is the individual who is so enamored with computers that he or she will go to all extremes to get information—even if it means breaking into computers. "Hacker" used to be a compliment, but now it refers to those techno whizzes who break into computers for the sole purpose of causing electronic chaos.

hit

This is an attempt to create a measurement that describes how often a particular site is visited. One "hit" is equivalent to one access. In other words, if a user accesses the White House, it is calculated as a "hit." However, if that same user clicks on to one of the options, like the White House tour that links to another page on the site, that is also registered as a "hit." Obviously, the number of hits can be very misleading.

homepage

Home page is used interchangeably with "Website." It is also used to refer to those millions of "personal pages" that are designed to introduce the surfer to the Web author—including things such as favorite music, favorite links, family photos, and anything of individual interest. Home page is also used to indicate the "top" or "main page" of the Website.

HTML

Hyper Text Markup Language is a quasi-programming language consisting of standardized tags that instruct a Web browser how to display certain documents.

HTTP

These are the letters that appear at the beginning of every Web address. They stand for Hyper Text Transfer Protocol or the protocol used by the Web browser and Web server to communicate.

hypertext

This is one of the "magical" qualities of the Web. It is specially underlined text that, when you click on it, automatically links you to the location chosen by the Web author.

Internet

A computer network is formed when two or more computers are linked. The Internet links networks. In other words, it is a huge, constantly expanding network of networks.

Internet Relay Chat (IRC)

The IRC is the Internet's chat area. It is particularly popular with college kids who can access it through the free connections provided by their schools.

Internet Service Provider (ISP)

The ISP is the local company that connects your computer to the Internet. They charge by either flat rate or hourly rate fees.

intranet

An internet-type system that is run in-house, usually in large companies. Intranets are becoming increasingly popular.

link

A Web address buried in a Web page that will automatically bring you to that site when you click on it. Links are generally clearly identified on websites.

list

An e-mail list.

list server

An automated program that manages mailing lists.

Listserv

A specific list server.

lurker

An electronic voyeur. Lurkers hang out on lists, newsgroups, chats, and other Web forums but do not actively participate in the group. Most people begin as lurkers and then de-lurk and take part in the discussion. Others remain permanent lurkers.

MOO

MUD object-oriented.

MORF

Male or female? It is an acronym to determine gender in cyberspace.

MUD

Multi-user Dungeon or Dimension. MUDs are text-based virtual reality environments that are the legacy of the old Dungeon & Dragons culture.

multimedia

This is the "in" media. Essentially, multimedia represents the combination of at least two different types of media in one place—such as text and graphics, or graphics and sound. These days, most of us think of multimedia as the whole production—sight, sound, and text—in some very broad bandwidth.

'net

Short for Internet.

netiquette

This is the online version of Miss Manners—the etiquette of cyberspace.

netizen

A citizen of the Internet—or anyone who goes online more than once.

newbie

An online greenhorn—someone who is new to the Internet.

newsgroup

A general term used to describe a public online message forum. Newsgroups topics are as diverse as human beings.

offline

The opposite of online or being linked or connected to other computers or networks in cyberspace.

online

Linked or connected to other computers or networks in cyberspace.

phreaks

Hackers who play with phone systems.

reboot

When you shut down the computer and start it up all over again. This is an extension of "boot," which means to start up the computer.

screen name

The name a user chooses to identify himself or herself on a certain online service. Most netizens have a collection of screen names.

search engine

Online programs, usually free, that provide searching and navigating services to users.

snail mail

United States Postal Service. The "snail" describes its pace compared to e-mail.

social engineering

A hacker's term, particularly favored by one of the most notorious, Kevin Mitnick. It refers to reaching a solution through a human, rather than a computer, interface. It involves using those somewhat maligned human interpersonal skills to gain access to information.

spam

Messages that are repeated over and over again in newsgroups, lists, and Web forums. Electronic junk mail.

Spoof

A message that does not originate from the claimed source. It's a form of electronic theft of identity.

sysop

System operator. One of the people who run the show. Depending on the site, the sysop might be a glorified moderator or the person in charge of the whole production.

thread

When public messages and their responses are grouped together in a sequence and comprise a specific topic or discussion.

upload

The opposite of download—taking a file on your computer and sending it out (or up) to someone else's computer.

URL

Uniform Resource Locator. The technical term for an internet address. It is standardized so internet software can read it. A URL, for example, is **http://www.whitehouse.gov**

UseNet

A public message forum that consists of thousands of different newsgroups.

Virtual Reality

A non-physical actuality that exists only through the mediation of a computer. It is often used to specifically describe the simulation of physical constructs in computer-generated environments.

Web

Short for World Wide Web

Web browser

Software that enables users to access sites on the World Wide Web through the URL (Uniform Resource Locator) or Web address.

webmaster

The individual responsible for the technical and content needs of a Website.

webpage

An individual document on the Web. Many Web pages make up a Web site.

Web server

Web server is a technical term that refers to the Internet

computer that hosts a website. A Web server can host many separate and independent websites.

Web site

A location on the Web that consists of one or more Web pages that are conceptually related to one another.

World Wide Web

The global system that links text, graphics, sound, and video in cyberspace through Web pages and Web sites.

GLOSSARY OF ONLINE ACRONYMS

TLAs and abbreviations are AUP on the net. FWIW, this is PANS. But if you don't know the stuff, someone might be ROTFL or LOL and you won't have any idea what's going on. IMHO, the best solution is to RTFM.

AFAIK	As far as I know
AFK	Away from keyboard
AKA	Also known as
AUP	Acceptable use policy
BAK	Back at keyboard
BBIAB	Be back in a bit
BBIAF	Be back in a few
BBL	Be back later
BBS	Bulletin board system
BCNU	Be seein' you
BFD	Big f***ing deal
BFN	Bye for now
BRB	Be right back
BTSOOM	Beats the s*** out of me
BTW	By the way
CUL8R	See you later
DH	Darling husband

DW	Darling wife
FAQ	Frequently asked question
FOAF	Friend of a friend
FU	F***ed up
FUBAR	Fouled up beyond all repair
FUD	(Spreading) fear, uncertainty, and disinformation
FUD	Fear, uncertainty, and doubt
FWIW	For what it's worth
FYA	For your amusement
FYI	For your information
G,D&R	Grinning, ducking & rolling (on the floor)
GIWIST	Gee, I wish I'd said that
GMTA	Great minds think alike
GR & D	Grinning running and ducking
GTRM	Going to read mail
GUI	Graphical User Interface
^5	High five
HIR	Him or her
IAC	In any case
IAE	In any event
IM	Instant message
IMHO	In my humble opinion
IMNSHO	In my not-so-humble opinion
IMO	In my opinion
IOW	In other words
IRC	Internet relay chat
IRT	In real time
JAM	Just a minute
JK	Just kidding
LOL	Laughing out loud
LTNS	Long time no see
MHOTY	My hat's off to you

MOO	MUD Object-oriented
MORF	Male or female?
MOTD	Message of the day
MOTOS	Member of the opposite sex
MUD	Multi-User Dungeon or Dimension
MUSH	Multi-User Shared Hallucination
NFG	No freakin' good
NFW	No f***ing way
NRN	No reply necessary
OIC	Oh I see
OnO	Over and out
OTOH	On the other hand
PANS	Pretty amazing new stuff
PMFJI	Pardon me for jumping in
PMJI	Pardon my jumping in
POV	Point of view
RL	real life
ROTFL	Rolling on the floor laughing
RSN	Real soon now
RTFM	Read the freakin' manual
SITD	Still in the dark
SO	Significant other
SorG	Straight or gay?
TIA	Thanks in advance
TIC	Tongue in cheek
TFN	TaTa for now
TLA	Three letter acronym
TPTB	The powers that be
TTYL	Talk to you later
TXS	Thanks
TYVM	Thank you very much
UnPC	unPolitically Correct
WAG	Wild ass guess

WB	Welcome back
WEG	Wicked evil grin
WTF	What the fudge
WTG	Way to go!
WWW	World Wide Web
WYSIWYG	What you see is what you get
YSR	Yeah, sure, right

GLOSSARY OF ONLINE EMOTICONS AND OTHER ELECTRONIC GRAFFITI

:) or	
:-) or	smile, happy face
:^)	
:*	kiss
:D	laughing
;)	wink
: (	frown
:/	yeah, right (skepticism)
:{)	smiley with mustache
8-)	smiley with sunglasses
::-)	four-eyes
B-)	cool smiley with shades
:-X	my lips are sealed
:-O	surprise
#:-(	bad haircut
:~(	crying smiley
:-t	cross smiley
:-&	tongue-tied smiley
:-c	bummed out smiley
:>|	smiley with a big nose
[:-)	smiley with headphones
:-Q	smoking smiley

(:)-)   scuba-diving smiley
:-)8   smiley with a bowtie
*<{:-)   Santa Claus smiley
>:-<   angry smiley
#-]   trashed smiley
<:)   clowning smiley
+<:-)   religious smiley
0:-)   angel
};->   devil
:-p   sticking tongue out
:-9   licking lips
:<>   yawn

Information SuperHighway Graffitti

(((((hugs))))) or {{{{name}}}} hugs
O.O eyes wide open

@>-'--,---------   long-stemmed rose
< ---------------   arrow (highlights)
<G>   Grin
<VBG>   Very big grin
<F>   Frown
<VBF>   Very big frown

Mr. Ascii does the Macarena

o	o	o	o	o	o	<o>	<o
^|\	^|^	v|^	v|v	/|v	|X|	|	|\
/\	>\	/<	>\	/<	>\	/<	>\

o>	o	o	o	o	o	o	o
\	x	</	<|>	</>	<\>	<)>	^|\
/<	>\	/<	>\	/<	>\	>>	/\

On the Internet, no one knows you're a dog

```
  | \
 /, ` . - """"""""""""""""")))))))
 /, *-)_ ) )-\ ____ ( )
@'---/ (_/        \_)
```

GLOSSARY OF SMILEYS WITH AN ATTITUDE

(-:	Left-hand Smiley
8-o	Omigod
:->	Sarcastic Smiley
:-@	Screaming Smiley
:-x	A big wet kiss
:-]	Smiley blockhead
>;->	A very lewd remark was just made
%-)	Smiley after staring at a screen for 15 hours
8:-)8<	Little girl Smiley
:-<	Walrus Smiley
:-?	Smiley smokes a pipe
:-{}	Smiley wears lipstick
:-!	Foot in mouth
=:-)	Smiley is a punk
:=)	Orangutan Smiley
@:-)	Smiley wears a turban
C=:-)	Chef Smiley
{:-)	Smiley wears a toupee
0-)	Message from Cyclops
:-3	Handlebar mustache Smiley
:-"	Whistling Smiley
p-(	Pirate Smiley
d:-)	Baseball Smiley
:-7	Smirking Smiley
8(:-)	Mickey Mouse

:-C	Real unhappy Smiley
:-W	Speak with forked tongue
$-)	Yuppie Smiley
:---)	You lie like Pinnochio
=:-(	Real punk never smiles
8<:-)	Smiley is a wizard
~:-P	Smiley with one single hair
|-(	Smiley lost his contact lenses

THE SIGNATURE MUSEUM: A GLOSSARY
OF INTERNET SIGNATURES
Menno Pieters

Signatures, or .sig, are identifying statements, information, quotes, aphorisms, or graphics that are composed by netizens and printed at the bottom of every message. In a few short words or designs, they tell a story about the sender. Whether in words or designs, signatures are created by using the letters and symbols on the keyboard.

Menno Pieters writes of his collection of signatures in *The Signature Museum*, "I do not think the signatures need comments, because they are some kind of comment themselves." The following signatures are selections from Pieters' extensive museum at **http://www.twi.tudelft.nl/~s652402/sigs/**. They have been used online by their authors.

Signature art

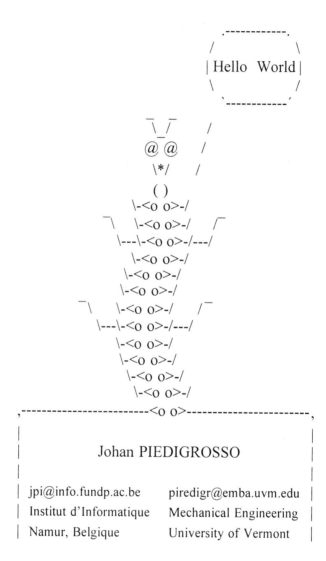

```
                              .------------.
                           /                 \
                          | Hello   World |
                           \                 /
                             `------------'

               _  _
               \ /        /
              @ @        /
               \*/      /
               ( )
               \-<o o>-/
         ¯\     \-<o o>-/      ┌¯
         \---\-<o o>-/---/
               \-<o o>-/
               \-<o o>-/
               \-<o o>-/
        ¯\      \-<o o>-/     /¯
         \---\-<o o>-/---/
               \-<o o>-/
               \-<o o>-/
               \-<o o>-/
               \-<o o>-/
,---------------------<o o>---------------------,
|                                               |
|               Johan PIEDIGROSSO               |
|                                               |
|   jpi@info.fundp.ac.be    piredigr@emba.uvm.edu  |
|   Institut d'Informatique  Mechanical Engineering |
|   Namur, Belgique          University of Vermont  |
```

```
       o O   / NON DIRMI DI NO        \
     `\|||/  | NON PRENDERMI IN GIRO |
     (o o)   \ _____/
  ooO_(_)_Ooo
```

```
             ,,,
            /'^'\
           ( o o )
-----------------------------oOOO--(_)--OOOo-------
```

Alexander Georg

EMail: alexander.georg@t-online.de

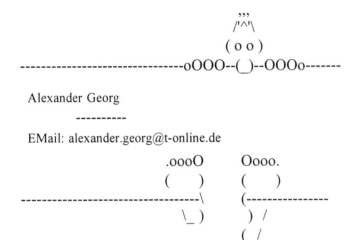

```
                    .oooO     Oooo.
                    (   )     (   )
-----------------------------\  (----------------
                     \_ )      ) /
                              (_/
```

```
             '''
           (O O)
     +----oOO--(_)---------+
     | menthols@hotmail.com |
     +-------------oOO------+
           |__|__|
           || ||
          ooO Ooo
```

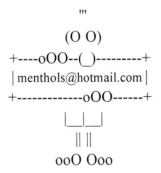

Jos Severens <jse@cuci.nl>

```
    A_A              A_A
   (o o)     Jos    (o o)
  /| /\_/\    &    /\_/\  |\
 ( ( / U \   his   / U \ ) )
  \ \/ ||||  Groens |||| \/ /
   \ \  ||||         ||||  / /
    \__()()          ()()__/
```

Dogs ain't so good with computers because
They can't stick their heads out of Windows 95

Signature text

Howard L. Bloom (USA)
howard@pc-man.com

The Bill of Rights—Void where prohibited by law

```
-----------------------------------------------------------------
| Joost Cassee          | Handle: apex                          |
| aka Merlin of Camelot | E-mail: cassee@ch.twi.tudelft.nl       |
| Student of Informatics| j.j.m.cassee@twi.tudelft.nl            |
|   TU Delft            |                                        |
| PGP key available on  | WWW: http://ch.twi.tudelft.nl/         |
|   request             |       ~cassee                          |
| --------------------------------------------------------------- |
|        Do not meddle in the affairs of wizards, for you         |
|             are crunchy and good with ketchup.                  |
-----------------------------------------------------------------
```

Packrat (USA)
I started out with nothing. I still have most of it left.

Anonymous
Life is what happens when you are busy elsewhere.

Reginald H. Gibbs" <rehagi@voyager.net>

There was peace everywhere. They had a war and nobody came.

Jay Fitzpatrick (U.S.A.)
JayFritz@caedm.et.byu.edu

Don't let studying get in the way of a good education.

Suggested Offline Reading List

NONFICTION BOOK LIST

Brockman, J. (1996). *Digerati: Encounters with the Cyber Elite.* San Francisco, CA: Hardwired.

Gergen, K. (1991). *The Saturated Self: Dilemmas of Identity in Contemporary Life.* New York: Basic Books.

Hafner, K., and Lyon, M. (1996). *Where Wizards Stay Up Late: The Origins of the Internet.* New York: Simon & Schuster.

Littman, J. (1996). *The Fugitive Game: The Inside Story of the Great Cyberchase.* New York: Little, Brown.

McLuhan, M. (1961). *Understanding Media: The Extensions of Man.* Cambridge, MA: MIT Press.

Reeves, B., and Nass, C. (1996). *The Media Equation: How People Treat Computers, Television, and New Media Like Real People and Places.* Stanford, CA: CSLI.

Rheingold, H. (1993). *The Virtual Community: Homesteading on the Electronic Frontier.* New York: HarperPerennial.

Slouka, M. (1995). *War of the Worlds: Cyberspace and the High-Tech Assault on Reality.* New York: Basic Books.

Turkle, S. (1995). *Life on the Screen: Identity in the Age of the Internet.* New York: Simon & Schuster.

FICTION BOOK LIST

Bantock, N. (1996). *The Venetian's Wife.* San Francisco: Chronicle.

Fletcher, S. T. (1996). *E-mail: A Love Story*. New York: Donald I. Fine.

Franklet, D. (1997). *Bad Memory*. New York: Pocket Books.

Gibson, W. (1984). *Neuromancer*. New York: Ace.

Greenberg, M. H., and Segriff, L., eds. (1996). *FutureNet*. New York: Daw.

Lovejoy, W. H. (1996). *Back\slash*. New York: Pinnacle.

Offit, A. (1994). *Virtual Love*. New York: Simon & Schuster.

Stephenson, N. (1993). *Snow Crash*. New York: Bantam.

Wilson, F. P., and Costello, M. J. (1996). *Mirage*. New York: Warner.

Logging Off: Tomorrow's Psychotechnology

The screen flickers and then it is dark. A faint glow lingers for a few seconds as if the machine is fighting for its digital life. And then it is quiet. The window has closed.

Logging on at the beginning of this book plunged you into an exciting, strange, and sometimes disturbing exploration into the psychology of cyberspace. Logging off is not a conclusion. The adventure has only just begun.

Technology continues to alter the way we communicate. The near future promises changes as dramatic as though in the near past. Douglas Engelbart, the "father of the Internet," predicted that before we reach the mid twenty-first century, we will hold as much computing power in our hands as we have today in a city or, possibly, in the whole world. In technological terms, that's a fairly safe bet.

Perhaps the largest influence on the Internet—voice and video communication—won't be in our hands—or even on our planet. Cyberspace will be moving to outer space as communications companies launch satellites into earth orbit in lieu of laying millions of miles of terrestrial cable.

In *U.S. News and World Report*, Michael Armstrong, the CEO of Hughes Electronics—the company who owns DirecTV (satellite television)—referred to the process as upgrading the

information superhighway to "information skyway: a wireless
expressway using satellites and space as the medium for delivering data, voice, and video to users around the globe" (Egan
1997, p. 54). The plan, while technologically complex, is conceptually simple. Launch a complete network of communications satellites at different orbital levels so there will be no place
on earth, from city to Third World village to remote
mountaintop, where you can't pick up a device of your choice
and . . . just plain talk.

Does it seem farfetched? In 1995, twenty commercial satellites were launched. In 1997, the number leaped to seventy-
six. In 1998, the number hovers at nearly one hundred and
twenty-one. Within the next decade, it is estimated that eighteen hundred satellites will be launched—three-fourths of them
for commercial use (Cook 1997).

With those numbers, one can't help but feel a twinge of
planetary claustrophobia. What about all that space garbage?
Is it going to fall or will we need the equivalent of orbital sani-
tation trucks regularly perusing our information skyway? Some
thirty-five laboratories across the U.S. are already studying the
problem of orbital debris. According to research engineer Andy
Piekutowski from the University of Dayton Research Institute,
who tests this in his earth laboratory, a tiny piece of plastic
approximating the speed of the space shuttle (15,560 miles per
hour) can make a crater in a steel plate. In a like manner, a
marble-sized fragment hitting a spacecraft in orbit would rup-
ture it ("Researcher tests impact of 'Space Junk' " 1996). What
does that mean to us back here in our clinical offices on Mother
Earth? While most of this garbage won't be touching down on
terrestrial soil, will the accumulation block our view? Will we
be living in a satellite shadow much like the grayness after a
massive volcanic eruption has spewed its ash? Will psychotherapy be increasingly a virtual process?

Iridium, a company owned by *Motorola*, promises that there will be a lot more satellites circling our globe. The company boasts that the new millennium will enable the entire world to have direct communications. This is impressive, considering that before *Iridium* more than half of the world's population did not even have telephone access. *Iridium* is not the only company investing billions of dollars in the technology— there is also *Global Star*, *Orbcom*, and, perhaps the most ambitious, *Teledisc*. *Teledisc*, a plan conceived by Bill Gates and Craig McCaw, calls itself the "Internet in the sky." *They* are boasting that in the very near future we will have broadband, multimedia satellite connections (i.e., video conferencing) that will zoom into cyberspace nearly one thousand times faster than today's basic internet dial-up connection (Cook 1997).

Like it or not, cyberspace is here to stay. And like it or not, the psychology of a species emerging from disembodied communications is also here to stay. As Dr. Maheu suggested in her "call to action" on telehealth, we can't stop it—so let's participate. We can help direct the future toward benefiting— not harming—humankind.

Obviously—and thankfully—no one yet controls the electronic environment. We pay a price for that unmitigated freedom: along with the well-intentioned come the abusers, the hate-mongers, and the criminals. But we also face a more serious danger. The Internet is an exciting, stimulating adjunct to our lives. It does not have to be a substitute for social relationships, but a complement. There must be a balance between actuality and virtuality.

Charles Wang, Chairman and CEO of Computer Associates International, the world's third largest software company, shared a parenting suggestion in a speech on information technology at the United Nations. He told the audience that he permits his four-year-old daughter to use the computer only one or two hours a week.

"Which is better for our children, playing soccer on a computer or going outside and playing soccer with other children?" Wang asked (Friedman 1997, p. A4).

Wang made an important statement regarding the role of computers in human life. One of the essential assumptions in psychotechnology is the existence of a basic, immutable human need for embodied socialization. Children need to learn how to socialize face-to-face before they can appropriately adapt to life in cyberspace. Putting them on the computer when they are very young, for long periods of time, disembodies children too early in their development. This does not mean that children should be denied computers or the campaign to wire American public schools should be abruptly stopped. Quite the opposite. Children need to interact face-to-face with their peers while educationally and intellectually having the opportunity to reach into the enormous depths of human knowledge through the Internet. This can be encouraged through an electronic curriculum.

The richness and diversity of information online can take young students beyond the walls of their classrooms into environments, ideas, and lives previously unreachable. For example, students already roam the world with The Jason Project, an educational program that sponsors scientific expeditions to places like the Galapagos Islands and Yellowstone Park while enabling students to participate in live interactive programs ("The Jason Project" 1996).

Perhaps one day the role of professor will change from its origins in the Latin *professus*, meaning to affirm openly, to something quite different. Maybe tomorrow's professors will act as learning facilitators, guiding students through the maze of human knowledge, highlighting pathways to thinking, analyzing, and understanding the nature of human life in a never-ending universe. Either way, each human being will continue to be faced with the task of learning, through psychosocial development, the art of living and communicating with others.

The cybernetic challenge to adults emulates the children. Mental health professionals can play an integral part in this New World, helping individuals, groups, and communities strike a balance between embodied and disembodied communication. Clearly, that is what psychotechnology is all about—utilizing psychology and technology to enhance our "human-ness," not to replace it with computer chips. Throughout this book, we have seen the many ways psychotherapists can use technology. We have also seen the effect of technology on individuals, groups, cultures, and the global community. It is only the beginning. The vast, uncharted frontier of cyberspace parallels the unknown regions of the human brain. Both offer an exciting, albeit precarious, exploration. One should never be sacrificed for the other. Together, they can enrich human life without losing things like the beauty of a pine forest, the sweetness of human touch, the dizzying experience of falling in love. Human senses were designed to work in a biological machine, not a cybernetic space. If they are not used they will atrophy along with the sensuality of the human physical experience. In contrast, cyberspace enables you to speak to someone on the other side of the planet as easily as your next-door neighbor. It offers you entry to the human noosphere without boundaries on time, place, or context. It tempts you with the seductive call of human technology, always changing, always striving to reach further and deeper—for better or worse.

Psychology and technology make quite a pair.

References

About Tripod (no date). *Tripod, Inc.* [Online], [http://www.tripod.com/tripod], accessed 10 June 1997.

Aguilar, R. (1996, January 3). Doc says kiddie net addicts common. *CNET news* [Online], 3 paragraphs, [http://www.cnet.com/], accessed 5 August 1996.

Ainsworth, W. (1997a, April 29–last updated). Directory of internet psychotherapists (1997, April 29–last updated). *Metanoia* and *Mental Health Net* [Online], 31 pp., [http://metanoia.org/imhs/direct1.htm], accessed 14 May 1997.

——— (1997b, April 29–last updated). Welcome to the metanoia guide. *Metanoia* and *Mental Health Net* [Online], 31 pp., [http://metanoia.org/imhs/intro.htm], accessed 3 May 1997.

——— (1997c, April 15–last updated). Terminology . . . is this "therapy"? *Metanoia* and *Mental Health Net* [Online], 6 paragraphs, [http://metanoia.org/imhs/isitx.htm], accessed 3 May 1997.

——— (1997d, April 15–last updated). Explanation: Intended interaction. *Metanoia* and *Mental Health Net* [Online], 17 paragraphs, [http://metanoia.org/imhs/type.htm], accessed 3 May 1997.

Allora, R. (1997). *Flatiron News* 3(2):49–50.

Alt.culture (No date). *Cybersex* [Online], [http://www.altculture.com/site/entries/cybersex.htm], accessed 3 March 1997.

American Heritage Dictionary of the English Language (3rd ed., Windows '95 version), [CD-ROM]. (1995). Available: Microsoft Bookshelf [1997, January 8].

American Psychiatric Association (1994). *DSM–IV* [CD-ROM], Available: American Psychiatric Association [1997, June 1].

American Psychological Association (1992). Ethical principles of psychologists and code of conduct. *American Psychologists* 47:1597–1611.

Ask Dr. Marla [Online]. (no date), [http://shoga.wwa.com/~docmarla], accessed 4 June 1997.

Atwood, J. D., and Chester, R. (1987). *Treatment techniques for Common Mental Disorders*. Northvale, NJ: Jason Aronson.

Auerbach, S. (no date). *Meditations of the metaphysics of home pages* [Homepage of Sarah Auerbach], [Online], [http://www.amherst.edu/~sbauerba/philo.html], accessed 8 February 1997.

Avalon (1996). The Cityports. *Avalon: The novice's guide* [Online], [http://www.avalon-rpg.com/intro/minman7.html], accessed 13 May 1998.

Baird, A. C. (1996–copyright). *Netaholics Modemheads* [Online], [http://members.gnn.com/acbaird/index.htm], accessed 23 December 1997.

Balch, D. C. (no date). *Telemedicine program: East Carolina University School of Medicine* [Online], [http://www.telemed.med.ecu.edu/r_folder/r_q&a.htm], accessed 7 May 1997.

Baumrucker, D. (no date). The do's & don'ts of online dating. *America Online* [Online Service]. Available: keyword: Love@aol [1997, March 3].

Becker, E. (1973). *The Denial of Death*. New York: Free Press.

Bloom, J. (1997, April 15). Online self-regulatory body & proposed NCDA Internet standards. *NetPsy* [Online]. Available e-mail: LISTSERV@MAELSTROM.STJOHNS.EDU [1997, April 15]. *Reference is obtained by searching the list's archive.

Brenner, C. (1974). *An Elementary Textbook of Psychoanalysis*. New York: Anchor.

Brockman, J. (1996). *Digerati: Encounters with the Cyber Elite*. San Francisco, CA: Hardwired.

Bruckman, A. (1994). *"Serious" uses of MUDs?* [Online], [http://www.oise.on.ca/~jnolan/muds/about_muds/asb/se], accessed 11 June 1997.

——— (no date). *Welcome to MOOSE Crossing!* [Online], 2 pp., [http://lcs.www.media.mit.edu/people/asb/moose-crossing], accessed 28 May 1997.

Bruckman, A. and Resnick, M. (1995). *The MediaMOO project: Constructionism and professional community* [Online], 13 pp., [http://asb.www.media.mit.edu/people/asb/convergence.htm], accessed 27 May 1997.

Buten, J. (1996). The first world wide Web personal home page survey. *The Personal Home Page Institute* [Online], 5 pp., [http://www.asc.upenn.edu/USR/sboten/survey1.htm], accessed 15 June 1997.

Calem, R. (1997, June 1). Online communities build net neighborhoods. *The New York Times CyberTimes* [Online], 47 paragraphs, [http://www.nytimes.com/library/cyber/week/060197 communities.htm], accessed 4 June 1997.

Cambridge Computer Lab (1995, October 1–last update). *The Cambridge coffee pot* [Online], [http://gensys.com/ccp.html], accessed 19 February 1997.

Caplan (1996, November 6). Impulsivity and e-mail [Discussion]. *Research and psychology* [Online]. Available e-mail: research @cmhcsys.com [1997, November 8].

Carlin, A., Hoffman, H., and Weghorst, S. (1997, May 1–last updated). Desensitization in virtual environments. *HITL: Therapeutic VR projects* [Online], 4 pp., [http://www.hitl.washington.edu/projects/therapeutic/exposure.html], accessed 8 October 1997.

Carlson, N. R. (1986). *Physiology of Behavior*, 3rd ed. Boston: Allyn & Bacon.

Chervokas, J., and Watson, T. (1997, May 2). Community: It takes an electronic village. *The New York Times CyberTimes* [Online], 24 paragraphs, [http://search.nytimes.com/search/daily], accessed 6 June 1997.

Cohen, E. (1997, January 17). Shrinks aplenty online, but are they credible? *The New York Times CyberTimes* [Online], 35 paragraphs, [http://search.nytimes.com/search/daily], accessed 5 May 1997.

CommerceNet/Nielsen Demographics Survey (1997). *Spring '97 release of the internet demographic study* [Online], [http: www.commerce.net/nielsen/index.htm], accessed 2 June 1997.

CommerceNet/Nielsen Internet Study (1995). *CommerceNet/Nielsen announce internet study results* [Online], [http:www. commerce.net/work/pilot/nielsen_96/exec.html], accessed 2 June 1996.

Cook, W. J. (1997). 1997: A new space odyssey. *U.S. News & World Report* 122(8):44–52.

Council on Competitiveness (1996, March 25–last updated). Chapter 2–Remote Care. *Highway to Health: Transforming U.S. Health Care in the Information Age* [Online], 20 pp., [http://nii.nist.gov/pubs/coc_hghwy_to_hlth/chp2.html], accessed 7 May 1997.

Credential check (1997, April 29–last updated). *Mental Health Net* and *Metanoia* [Online], 3pp., [http://www.cmhc.com/check/check.htm], accessed 14 May 1997.

CU-SeeMe (1997a, April). [Advertisement]. *Internet World* 8(4):13.
——— (1997b, May). [Advertisement]. *Internet World* 8(5):22.

CyberTowers Professional Center (1997) [Online], [http://www.cybertowers.com], accessed 9 February 1997.

Cyrano Server (1997–copyright). [Online service], [http://www.nando.net/toys/cyrano.html/], accessed 3 March 1997.

Davis, J. E. (1995, November 27). Telemedicine begins to make its case. *Fortune* [Online], 2 pp., [http://pathfinder.com], accessed 5 May 1997.

December, J. (1997, January). Notes on defining computer-mediated communication. *CMC Magazine* [Online], 11 pp., [http://www.december.com/cmc/mag/1997/jan/december.html], accessed 24 March 1997.

Diamond, D. (1997). In the zone. *Wired* 5.06, June, pp. 130–132.

Dibbell, J. (1993). *A rape in cyberspace or how an evil clown, a*

Haitian trickster spirit, two wizards, and a cast of dozens turned a database into a society [Online], [http://vesta.physics.ucla. edu/smolin/lambda/laws_and_history/VillageVoice.txt], accessed 24 November 1996.

DSM-IV (Windows version 3.62) [Computer software]. (1994, August). Available: Fusion Software [1997, February 4].

Dworetzky, J. P. (1985). *Psychology*. New York: West.

Egan, J. (1997). For satellite television, the limit is the sky. *U.S. News & World Report* 122(8):54–56.

Egger, O., and Rauterberg, M. (1996). *Internet behavior and addiction* [Online], [http://www.ifap.bepr.ethz.ch/~egger/ibq/ res.htm], accessed 1 June 1997.

ELIZA (No date). [Online], [http://www-ai.ijs.si/eliza/eliza.html], accessed 31 March 1997.

Engel, N. (1996). *Natalie Engel's chest of lust, longing and obsession* [Homepage of Natalie Engel], [Online], [http:// hampshire.edu/~dbtF93], accessed 12 February 1997.

Excite [Search engine] [Online]. (1995–1997–copyright). Excite, Inc., [http://www.excite.com], accessed 13 May 1997.

Feedback Research Services (1996, October 2). *Expanding telemedicine networks* [Online], 2 pp., [http://www.feed-bacl.com/p-rel-4.html#anchor2038129], accessed 7 May 1997.

Ferguson, T. (1996). A guided tour of self-help cyberspace. *Partnerships '96 Transcripts of Plenary Sessions and Selected Breakout Discussions* [Online], [http://odphp.osophs.dhhs.gov/ confrnce/partnr96/ferg.htm], accessed 28 May 1997.

Ferrell, K. (1997, February 6). NetCrime: Don't be a victim. *C/NET* [Online], 12 pp., [http://www.cnet.com/Content/Features/Dlife/ Crime/index.html], accessed 10 April 1997.

Ferris, P. (1997, January). What is CMC?: An overview of scholarly definitions. *CMC Magazine* [Online], 11 pp., [http:// www.december.com/cmc/mag/1997/jan/december.html], accessed 24 March 1997.

Flower, J. (1994). The other revolution in health care. *Wired*, 2.01, [Online], [http://www.wired.com/wired/2.01/features/ healthcare.html], accessed 14 May 1998.

Freud, S. (1923). The ego and the id. *Standard Edition* 19:3–68.

Friedman, J. (1997). Wang's warning: CA boss says parents must limit kids' computer time. *Newsday*, 57(289), June 18, p. A4.

Garfinkel, S. (1995). Separating Equifax from fiction, Parts 1 & 2. *Wired* [Online], [http://www.hotwired.com/wired/], accessed 22 May 1996.

Garton, L., Haythornthwaite, C., and Wellman, B. (1997, June). Studying online social networks. *Journal of Computer Mediated Communication* [Online] 3 (1), 31 pp., [http://www.ascusc. org/jcmc/vol3/issue1/garton.html], accessed 21 November 1997.

Geiser, F. (1996, November 7). Life story on e-mail [Discussion]. *Research and psychology* [Online]. Available e-mail: research @cmhcsys.com [1997, November 8].

Georgia, B. L. (1996a). *The Internet's best-kept secret* [Online], [http://www.zdnet.com/pccomp/features/fea1296/newsgrp/ welcome.html], accessed 25 April 1997.

———— (1996b). *The Internet's best-kept secret: Internet and Usenet* [Online], [http://www.zdnet.com/pccomp/features/fea1296/ newsgrp/ngiu.html], accessed 25 April 1997.

Gergen, K. (1991). *The Saturated Self: Dilemmas of Identity in Contemporary Life*. New York: Basic Books.

Gibson, W. (1984). *Neuromancer*. New York: Ace.

Gobbo, K., and Bolaski, J. (1997). Attention disorders on the internet. *Self-Help & Psychology* [Online], 3pp., [http://cyber towers.com/selfhelp/articles/internet/ipadd.htm], 3 June 1997.

Goldberg, I. (1995). *Internet addiction disorder* [Online], [http:// www.cog.brown.edu/brochure/people/duchon/humor/ internet.addiction.htm], accessed 28 May 1997.

———— (Psydoc@PsyCom.Net). (1997, May 27). *Internet addiction*. E-mail to Jeri Fink (onbase@ix.netcom.com).

Goode, J., and Johnson, M. (1991). *Putting out the flames: The etiquette and law of e-mail*. Online, pp. 61–65.

Grossan, B. (1997, March 12–last updated). Search engines: What they are, how they work, and practical suggestions for getting the most out of them. *webreference.com* [Online], [http:// webreference.com/conent/search], accessed 13 May 1997.

Guided tour (no date). *Tripod, Inc.* [Online], [http://www.tripod.com/tripod/tour], accessed 10 June 1997.

GVU (1996). *GVU's 6th WWW User Survey* [Online], [http://www.cc.gatech.edu/gvu/user_surveys/survey-10-1996], accessed 22 February 1997.

———— (1997). *GVU's 7th WWW User Survey* [Online], [http://www.gvu.gatech.edu/user__surveys/survey-1997-04], accessed 10 June 1997.

Hannon, K. (1996, May). Upset? Try cybertherapy. *U.S. News & World Report* 120(19):81–83.

Harris, S. (1997, April 7–last updated). *Emotional support on the internet* [Online], [http://www.compulink.co.uk/~net-services/care], accessed 28 May 1997.

Hart, B. (1995). Re-authoring the stories we work by: Situating the narrative approach in the presence of the family of therapists. *Australian and New Zealand Journal of Family Therapy* 16(4):181–189.

Herring, S. (1993). *Gender and democracy in computer-mediated communication* [Online], [http://dc.smu.edu/dc/classroom/Gender.txt], accessed 25 February 1997.

———— (1994). *Gender differences in computer-mediated communication: Bringing familiar baggage to the new frontier* [Online], [http://www.cpsr.org/cpsr/gender/herring.txt], accessed 25 February 1997.

Hines, M. H. (1994). Using the telephone in family therapy. *Journal of Marital and Family Therapy* 20(2):175–184.

History of telemedicine (1996, October 9–last updated). *Telemedicine Information Exchange* [Online], [http://tie.telemed.org/scripts/getpage.pl?client=text&page=history], accessed 4 May 1997.

———— (no date). Telemedicine program. *East Carolina University School of Medicine* [Online], 2pp., [http://www.telemed.med.ecu.edu/r_folder/r_hist.html], accessed 7 May 1997.

Hodges, L. F., and Rothbaum, B. O. (1995–last updated). Virtual reality for fear of heights: Researchers publish first controlled treatment study. *Georgia Tech Research News* [Online], 4pp., [http://www.gtri.gatech.edu/res-news/VIRTUAL.htm], accessed 8 October 1997.

Holland, N. N. (1996). The internet regression. *Psychology of Cyberspace* [Online], 14 pp., [http://www1.rider.edu/~suler/psycyber/holland.htm], accessed 3 March 1997.

Holmes, L. G. (1996–copyright). *Shareware Psychological Consultation* [Online], [http://www.netpsych.com/share/index.htm], accessed 21 May 1997.

Huang, M., and Alessi, N. E. (1996). The Internet and the future of psychiatry. *American Journal of Psychiatry* 153(7):861–869.

Infoseek [Search engine] [Online]. (1995–1997–copyright). Infoseek Corporation, [http://www.infoseek.com], accessed 13 May 1997.

IntelMed (1997, March 3). *IntelMed, The intelligent choice.* [Homepage of IntelMed], [Online], [http://www.devgroup.com/tele.html], accessed 5 May 1997.

Joint Working Group on Telemedicine (1997a, January 31). Executive Summary. *Telemedicine Report to Congress* [Online], 11 pp., [http:www.ntia.doc.gov/reports/telemed/execsum.htm], accessed 4 May 1997.

——— (1997b, January 31). Evaluation. *Telemedicine Report to Congress* [Online], 13 pp., [http:www.ntia.doc.gov/reports/telemed/evaluate.htm], accessed 4 May 1997.

——— (1997c, January 31). Introduction. *Telemedicine Report to Congress* [Online], 5 pp., [http:www.ntia.doc.gov/reports/telemed/intro.htm], accessed 4 May 1997.

——— (1997d, January 31). Privacy, security, and confidentiality in telemedicine. *Telemedicine Report to Congress* [Online], 5 pp., [http:www.ntia.doc.gov/reports/telemed/intro.htm], accessed 4 May 1997.

Jung, C. G. (1934). The concept of the collective Unconscious. *The archetypes and the collective unconscious.* (Collected works, Vol. 9) [Online], [http://www.geocities.com/Athens/158/collective.htm], accessed 22 January 1997.

Keith-Spiegal, P., and Koocher, G. (1985). *Ethics in Psychology: Professional Standards and Cases.* New York: McGraw-Hill.

Kidsurf Online [Online]. (1996–1997–copyright). Kid Surf, Inc., [http://www.kidsurf.net/index.html], accessed 4 June 1997.

Kim, T., and Biocca, F. (1997, September). Telepresence via television: Two dimensions of telepresence may have different connections to memory and persuasion. *Journal of Computer Mediated Communication* [Online], 3:2, 27 pp., [http://jcmc. huji.ac.il/vol3/issue2/kim.htm], accessed 4 September 1997.

King, S. (1995a). *The impersonal nature of interpersonal cyberspace relationships* [Online], [http://www.best.com/~storm/ impers.htm], accessed 16 September 1996.

——— (1995b). *Effects of mood states on social judgments in cyberspace: Self focused sad people as the source of flame wars* [Online], [http://www.coil.com/~grohol/storm1.htm], accessed 23 May 1997.

——— (1996a). Researching Internet communities: proposed ethical guidelines for the reporting of the results. *The Information Society* 12:119–127.

——— (1996b). Commentary on responses to the proposed guidelines. *The Information Society* 12:199–201.

——— (1997, April). *Ethics of online psychology*. Paper presented at the meeting of the California Psychological Association, San Jose, CA.

Kozma, T. (no date). *Cyberlore No. 2: The phenomenon of flaming* [Online], 2 pp., [http://www.pass.wayne.edu/ ~twk/flaming. htm], accessed 1 April 1997.

Leahey, T. H. (1987). *A History of Psychology: Main Currents in Psychological Thought.* Englewood Cliffs, NJ: Prentice-Hall.

Leonard, A. J. (1997). Search engines: Where to find anything on the Net. *C/NET* [Online], 8 paragraphs, [http//www.cnet.com/ Content/Reviews/Compare/Search], accessed 13 May 1997.

Lohr, S. (1996, May 6). Nintendo kids do Windows, but not for minimum wage. *The New York Times CyberTimes* [Online], 39 paragraphs, [http://search.nytimes.com/search/daily], accessed 4 June 1997.

——— (1997, March 17). Go ahead, be paranoid: Hackers are out to get you. *The New York Times CyberTimes* [Online], 41 paragraphs, [http://search.nytimes.com/search/daily], accessed 6 June 1997.

Lombard, M., and Ditton, T. (1997, September). At the heart of it all: the concept of telepresence. *Journal of Computer Mediated Communication* [Online], 39 pp., 3(2), [http://jcmc.huji.ac.il/vol3/issue2/lombard.htm], accessed 16 September 1997.

Love.net (1996, February 2). *WebReview* [Online], 41 paragraphs, [http://www.webreview.com/96/02/09/features/val/index.html], accessed 28 February 1997.

L-Soft InfoCenter [Homepage] [Online]. (1996, September 13–last updated), [http://www.lsoft.com/spamorama.html], accessed 3 April 1997.

Maheu, M. (1997–copyright). *CyberTowers Professional Center* [Online], [http://cybertowers.com/ct/index.html], accessed 28 May 1997.

———— (1997, April 22). Credentials online. *NetPsy* [Online]. Available e-mail: LISTSERV@MAELSTROM.STJOHNS. EDU [1997, April 23]. *Reference is obtained by searching the list's archive.

Mark's apology note generator [Online]. (1995, September), [http//net.indra.com/~karma/formletter.html], accessed 3 March 1997.

Marvin, L. (1994). Spoof, spam, lurk and lag: the aesthetics of text-based virtual realities. *Journal of Computer-mediated Communication* [Online], 1(2), 12 pp. Available: [11 February 1997].

Marx, L. (1997, January). Technology: The emergence of a hazardous concept. In A. Mack (Chair), *Technology and the rest of culture*. Symposium organized by the New School for Social Research, New York.

Maslow, A. H. (1954). *Motivation and Personality*. New York: Harper & Row.

McAllester, M. (1997a). Even the 'net has its elite inhabitants. *Newsday*, February 9, pp. A42.

———— (1997b). Predators prowl AOL for cybersuckers. *Newsday*, June 15, p. A47.

———— (1997c). NewsBytes. Bride 'nets $264,000. *Newsday*, May 25, p. A61.

McCafferty, D. (1996–copyright). *GoldenAge.Net*, [Online], [http:/

/elo.mediasrv.swt.edu/goldenage/script.htm], accessed 4 June 1997.

McKeon, D. (1997, February 26). Web can be a link to your shrink. *USA Today*, p. 4D.

MediaDome (1997). *C/NET* [Online service], 1 p., [http://www. mediadome.com/index.html], accessed 9 February 1997.

Moore, D. W. (1995). *The Emperor's Virtual Clothes.* Chapel Hill, NC: Algonquin Books of Chapel Hill.

Morningstar, C., and Farmer, R. (1990). *The lessons of Lucasfilm's habitat* [Online], [http://www.communities.com/paper/ lessons.htm], accessed 9 February 1997.

Mueller, S. H. (no date). What is spam? *Promote Responsible Net Commerce: Help Stamp Out Spam!* [Online], [http:// spam.abuse.net/spam/whatisspam.htm], accessed 3 April 1997.

Murray, P. (1997, January). A rose by any other name. *CMC Magazine* [Online], [http://www.december.com/cmc/mag/1997/jan/ murforms.html], accessed 24 March 1997.

Myers, B. (1997–copyright). Computer-related injuries. *Computer almanac: Interesting and useful numbers about computers* [Online], 21 pp., [http://www.cs.cmu.edu/afs/cs.cmu.edu/user/ bam/www/numbers.htm], accessed 13 May 1997.

Myers, L. (1995, September 14). FBI raids 120 homes in child pornography probe. *Detroit News* [Online], 20 paragraphs, [http:/ /detnews.com/menu/stories/16336.html], accessed 15 April 1997.

NASA's efforts (1997, February 20–last updated). History of telemedicine. *National Technology Transfer Center* [Online], [http://www.nttc.edu/telmed/contrib.html], accessed 6 May 1997.

North, M., and North, S. (1994, September 27). Relative effectiveness of virtual environment desensitization and imaginal desensitization in the treatment of aerophobia. *The Arachment Electronic Journal on Virtual Culture*, 2(4), 4 pp., [http:// www.monash.edu.au/journals/ejvc/north.v2n4], accessed 20 August 1997.

North, M., North S., and Coble, J. R. (1996–copyright). *Center for the Use of Virtual Reality Technology in the Treatment of Psy-*

chological Disorders [Online], [http://www.csswebs.com/alpha/
MaxNorth], accessed 20 August 1997.

Notable Research (1996, July 11–last updated). *Center for Online
Addiction* [Online], [http://www.pitt.edu/~ksy/], accessed 1
June 1997.

O'Connell, P. (1997, May 5). Defining a good homepage. *The Mining Company* [Online], 4 pp., [http://personal Web.miningco.
com/library/weekly/aa050597.htm], accessed 14 May 1997.

Olmsted, M. S., and Hare, A. P. (1978). *The Small Group.* New
York: Random House.

Online96 Senior's File [World Wide Web Site] [Online]. (1996-
copyright). Online Information Technology, [http://
www.online96.com/seniors], accessed 4 June 1997.

O'Reilly Research (1996, October 1). *Defining the internet opportunity* [Online], [http://www.ora.com/research], accessed 22
February 1997.

Ovid (1992). Metamorphoses. In *Literature of the Western World,*
ed. B. Wilkie and J. Hurt, Vol. 1, pp. 1168–1201. New York:
Macmillan. (Original work published circa 8 A.D.)

Parks, M., and Floyd, K. (1996, Winter). Making friends in
cyberspace. *Journal of Computer Mediated Communication*
[Online], 1(4), 17 pp., [http://jcmc.mscc.huji.ac.il/vol/issue4/
parks.html], accessed 28 October 1996.

Perry, M. (1996–copyright). What is Survey.Net? *Survey.net* [Online
public service network], [http://www.survey.net/sv-faq.htm],
accessed 31 May 1997.

——— (1997–copyright). Internet user survey #2 *Survey.net* [Online
public service network], [http://www.survey.net/inet2r.htm],
accessed 31 May 1997.

Pesce, M. (1994). Final amputation: Pathogenic ontology in
cyberspace. *Prologue to the 1994 edition in SPEED: A journal of technology and politics* [Online], 25 pp., [http://
www.hyperreal.com/~pesce/fa.html], accessed 15 September
1996.

——— (1995, November 30). *Connective, collective, corrective:
The future of VRML* [Online], [http://hyperreal.org/~mpesce/
vrworld.html], accessed 10 January 1997.

———— (1996, May 8). *Connective, collective, corrective: Lessons learned from VRML* [Online], [http://hyperreal.org/~mpesce/www5.html], accessed 14 January 1997.

Phillips, W. (1996, January). A comparison of online, e-mail, and in-person self-help groups using adult children of alcoholics as a model. *Independent Study Project of Rider University Psychology Department* [Online], 19 pp., [http://www1.rider.edu/~suler/psycyber/acoa.html], accessed 16 September 1996.

Pimentel, B. (1997, January 29). Woman who accused Oracle Chief guilty of perjury. *San Francisco Chronicle* [Online], 17 paragraphs, [http://www.sfgate.com/cgi-bin/chronicle/article.cgi?file=MN32281.DTL&directory= /chronicle/archive/1997/01/29], accessed 10 April 1997.

Pope, K. S., and Vetter, V. A. (1992). Ethical dilemmas encountered by members of the American Psychological Association: A national survey. *American Psychologist* 47(3):397–411.

Poster, M. (no date). *Postmodern virtualities* [Online], [http://www.hnet.uci.edu/mposter/writings/internet.html], accessed 9 November 1996.

Poulos, S. T. (1998). Literacy and the online professional. *Self Help & Psychology Magazine* [Online], [http://cybertowers.com/selfhelp].

Prilleltensky, I. (1997). Values, assumptions, and practices: accessing the moral implications of psychological discourse and action. *American Psychologist* 52(5):517–533.

Putnam, F. (1989). *Diagnosis and Treatment of Multiple Personality Disorder*. New York: Guilford.

Rafaeli, S., and Sudweeks, F. (1997, June). Networked interactivity. *Journal of Computer Mediated Communication* [Online], 2(4), 17 pp., [http://jcmc.mscc.huji.ac.il/vol2/issue4/rafaeli.sudweeks.html], accessed 19 March 1997.

Re: Internet addiction (1996, November 11). *Psychology & Research* [e-mail discussion list] [Online]. Available e-mail: research@cmhcsys.com [1996, November 12].

Reeves, B., and Nass, C. (1996). *The Media Equation: How People Treat Computers, Television, and New Media Like Real People and Places*. Stanford, CA: CSLI.

Reference.Com (1996b). *Reference.COM help overview: Usenet* [Online], 4pp., [http://www.reference.com/pn/help_1.0/ overview.html#mlist], accessed 4 April 1997.

Rheingold, H. (1993). *The Virtual Community: Homesteading on the Electronic Frontier*. New York: HarperPerennial.

Sampson, J. (1997a, March 11). Internet counselling. *NetPsy* [Online]. Available e-mail: LISTSERV@MAELSTROM. STJOHNS.EDU [1997, March 12]. *Reference is obtained by searching the list's archive.

——— (1997b). Counseling on the information highway: future possibilities and potential problems. *Journal of Counseling and Development* 75:203–211.

Savicki, V., Lingenfelter, D., and Kelley, M. (1996, December). Gender language style and group composition in internet discussion groups. *Journal of Computer-Mediated Communication*, [Online], 2(3), 12 pp., [http://jcmc.huji.ac.il/], accessed 1 March 1997.

Scheibe, K. E., and Erwin, M. (1979). The computer as alter. *Journal of Social Psychology* 108:103–109.

Schramm, M. G. (1997). No fine print–part one: The basics of a group contract. *Self-Help & Psychology Magazine* [Online], 3 pp., [http://cybertowers.com//selfhelp/ppc/group/grnfine1/ html], accessed 21 November 1997.

Schwartz, B. (1984). *Psychology of learning and behavior*, 2nd ed. New York: Norton.

Schwartz, J. (1997, March 30). Shouting porn! On a crowded net: Supreme Court Justices in search of a metaphor. *The Washington Post Technology Post* [Online], 22 paragraphs, [http:// washingtonpost.com/wp-srv/tech/analysis/decency/ decency.html], accessed 10 April 1997.

Scott, R. (1995–copyright). Interneters Anonymous. *Richard's Web Central* [Online], 3 pp., [http://www.itw.com/~rscott/ia.htm], accessed 1 June 1997.

Seabrook, J. (1994). My first flame. *The New Yorker*, June, pp. 70–79.

Sellu, D. (1996). Clinical encounters in cyberspace. *British Medical Journal* 312:49.

Sempsey III, J. (1995). *The psycho-social aspects of multi-user dimensions in cyberspace* [Online], [http://www.netaxs.com/~jamesiii/mud.htm], accessed 11 June 1997.

Seniors information page (1997). Welcome to our BEV-Seniors information page. *Blacksburg Electronic Village* [Online], [http://www.bev.net], accessed 5 June 1997.

Serino, J. (no date). Teens in cyberspace. *JMCTTouch* [Online], 2pp., [http://www.imcweb.com/IMM/Archives/IMMf2_05.htm], accessed 4 June 1997.

Shea, V. (1994). *Netiquette*. San Francisco, CA: Albion.

———— (no date). *Netiquette* [Online], [http://www.in.on.ca/tutorial/netiquette.htm], accessed 11 February 1997.

Shirky, C. (1995). *Voices from the Net*. Emeryville, CA: Ziff-Davis.

Shrink-Link (1996, June 28). [Online service], [http://www.westnet.com/shrink/], accessed 7 November 1997.

Siegal, D. J. (1996, March). Cognitive neuroscience encounters psychotherapy: Lessons from research on attachment and the development of emotion, memory and narrative. *Psychiatric Times* [Online], 7 pp., [http://www.mhsource.com/edu/psytimes/p960348.htm], accessed 7 December 1997.

Sigmund (No date). [Online psychotherapy service], [http://www.sigmund.com], accessed 27 May 1997.

Slouka, M. (1995). *War of the Worlds: Cyberspace and the High-Tech Assault on Reality*. New York: Basic Books.

Smith, C. B., and McLaughlin, M. L. (1997, March). Conduct control on UseNet. *Journal of Computer Mediated Communication* [Online], 2(4), 13 pp., [http://jcmc.mscc.huji.ac.il/vol2/issue4/smith.mclaughlin.html], accessed 25 April 1997.

Sproull, L., and Kiesler, S. (1995). Computers, networks and work. In *The Computer in the 21st Century. Scientific American: A Special Issue*, pp. 128–139.

Steiner, P. (1993). Cartoon. *The New Yorker*, July 5, p. 61.

Steuer, J. S. (1993). Defining virtual reality: dimensions determining telepresence. *Journal of Communication* 42(4):73–93.

Stevenson, R. L. (1987). *Dr. Jekyll and Mr. Hyde*. New York: Signet. (Original work published in 1886.)

Stewart, K. (1995). Narrative therapy. *Dulwich Centre* [Online],

3pp., [http://www.massey.ac.nz/~Alock/virtual/narrative.htm], accessed 7 December 1997.

Stokes, P. (1996, November 13). Six years for priest who broadcast abuse of boys to Internet paedophiles. *Electronic Telegraph* [Online], 25 paragraphs, [http://www.telegraph.co.uk:80/et?ac=000226604720238&rtmo=3321be47&pg=/et96/11/13/npaed13.html], accessed 8 March 1997.

Strangelove, M. (1994). Cyberspace and the changing landscape of the self. *The Geography of Consciousness* [Online], 3 pp., [http://www.clas.ufl.edu/anthro/cyberanthro/cybgeog.html], accessed 20 November 1996.

Suler, J. (1996a, May). Mom, dad, computer: Transference reactions to computers. *Psychology of cyberspace* [Online], 9 pp., [http://www1.rider.edu/~suler/psycyber/comptransf.html], accessed 16 September 1996.

——— (1996b). Cyberspace as dream world. *Psychology of cyberspace* [Online], [http://www1.rider.edu/~suler/psycyber/cybdream.html], accessed 16 September 1996.

——— (1996c). e-mail relationships. *Psychology of cyberspace* [Online], [http://www1.rider.edu/~suler/psycyber/emailrel.html], accessed 16 September 1996.

Support-Group.com [Online]. (1997, May 30–last updated). H.I. Incorporated, [http://support-group.com], accessed 30 May 1997.

Swett, H. A., and Holaday, L. (1996, November 7–last updated). Telemedicine at Yale. *Yale Telemedicine Center* [Online], [http://info.med.yale.edu/telmed], accessed 5 May 1997.

Telemedicine Information Exchange (1997). *What is telemedicine?* [Online], [http://tie.telemed.org/scripts/getpage.pl?client=text&pagewhatis], accessed 4 May 1997.

The Couch (1996). Cyberorganic Corporation [Online serial], [http://www.thecouch.com], accessed 27 May 1997.

The Internet Personals [Online service]. (No date), [http://.montagar.com/personals/ip-hints.html], accessed 3 March 1997.

The Jason Project (1996–copyright). *Jason Foundation for Education* [Online], [http://www.jason.org/JASON/HTML/backgrnd.htm], accessed 22 June 1997.

The Personal Home Page Institute (1996). *The first world wide Web personal home page survey* [Online], [http://www.asc.upenn. edu/usr/sbuten/survey1.htm], accessed 8 February 1997.

The Social Security Administration and online privacy (1997). *Electronic Privacy Information Center* [Online], [http://www. epic.org/privacy/databases/ssa], accessed 10 May 1997.

Thompson, S. (1996). *Internet connectivity: Addiction and dependency study* [Online], [http://personal.psu.edu/users/s/j/sjt112/ iads/], accessed 1 June 1997.

Toon, J. (1996, April 18). High-tech therapy: Virtual technology from Georgia Tech and Emory may help in reducing acrophobia. *Research Horizons* [Online], 3pp. Available: [http:// www.gtri.gatech.edu/rh-spr95/phobia.htm] 29 September 1997.

Toulmin, S. (1990). *Cosmopolis: The Hidden Agenda of Modernity*. New York: Free Press.

Truong, H. (1993). Gender issues in online communications [Online], 10 pp., [http://cpsr.org/cpsr/gender/bawit.cfp93], accessed 2 March 1997.

Tuckfelt, S., Fink, J., and Warren, M. (1997). *The Psychotherapists' Guide to Managed Care in the 21st Century: Surviving Big Brother and Providing Quality Mental Health Services*. Northvale, NJ: Jason Aronson.

Turkle, S. (1995). *Life on the Screen: Identity in the Age of the Internet*. New York: Simon & Schuster.

University of Belgrade Protest (1996, 1997) [Online], [http:// galeb.etf.bg.ac.yu/~protest96], accessed 9 February 1997.

Vander Zanden, J. W. (1993). *Sociology: The Core*, 3rd ed. New York: McGraw-Hill.

Verne (no date). *Verne's wild, wired, weird home page* [Homepage of Verne], [Online], [http://www.teleport.com/~verne], accessed 12 February 1997.

VR Body Project (1996–last updated). *Rationale of the system* [Online], 4pp., [http://www.ehto.be/ht_projects/vrepar/ eating.htm], accessed 8 August 1997.

Wallace, D. J. (1997, February 6). AOL reaches settlement with ad-spamming firm. *The New York Times CyberTimes* [Online], 19 paragraphs, [http://search.nytimes.com/search/daily], accessed 4 April 1997.

Wallis, D. (1997) Just click no. *The New Yorker* 72(42):28–29.

Walther, J. B. (1996). Computer-mediated communication: impersonal, interpersonal, and hyperpersonal interaction. *Communication Research* 23(1):3–43.

What is telemedicine? (1997, January 29–last updated). *Telemedicine Information Exchange* [Online], [http://tie.telemed.org/scripts/getpage.pl?client=text&page=whatis], accessed 4 May 1997.

WhoWhere? (1995–1997–copyright). *WhoWhere? Inc.* [Online], 2pp., [http://www.whowhere.com], accessed 13 May 1997.

Witham, D. (1997, April 9). Pedophiles active and elusive online. *San Jose Mercury News* [Online], 30 paragraphs, [http://www.sjmercury.com/news/nation/netsex0409.html], accessed 12 April 1997.

Witmer, D. (1997, June). Risky business: Why people feel safe in sexually explicit online communication. *Journal of Computer Mediated Communication* [Online], 2(4), 13 pp., [http://jcmc.mscc.huji.ac.il/vol2/issue4/witmer2.html], accessed 19 March 1997.

Yahoo! History (1996–copyright). *Yahoo information* [Online], 1 p., [http:www.yahoo.com/docs/pr/history.html], accessed 13 May 1997.

Yale Telemedicine Center (1996). *Telemedicine at Yale* [Online], 7pp., [http://info.med.yale.edu/telmed], accessed 5 May 1997.

Young, K. (1996a). Audio interview on internet addiction disorder. *Ann Online* [Online Audio Service], [http://audionet.com/shows/annonline/960731/interview.html], accessed 1 June 1997.

———— (1996b). *Internet addiction: The emergence of a new clinical disorder* [Online], 5 pp., [http://www.pitt.edu/~ksy/apa.htm], accessed 1 June 1996.

Index